John Warner Barber

Elements of general history

Embracing all the leading events in the world's history

John Warner Barber

Elements of general history
Embracing all the leading events in the world's history

ISBN/EAN: 9783337224486

Printed in Europe, USA, Canada, Australia, Japan

Cover: Foto ©ninafisch / pixelio.de

More available books at **www.hansebooks.com**

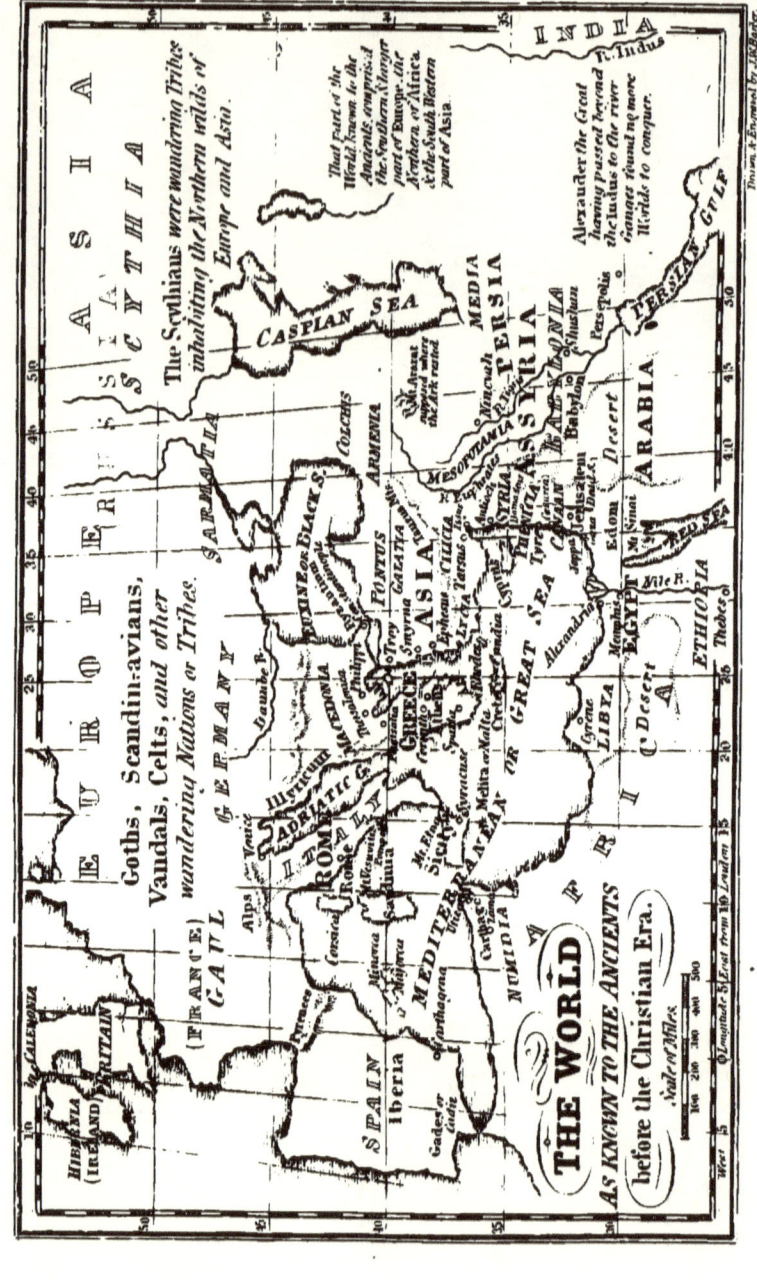

REVISED AND ENLARGED EDITION.

ELEMENTS

OF

GENERAL HISTORY;

EMBRACING ALL THE LEADING EVENTS

IN THE

WORLD'S HISTORY,

FROM THE EARLIEST PERIOD,

TO THE END OF THE

LATE CIVIL WAR IN THE UNITED STATES.

BY JOHN W. BARBER,
Author of several Historical Works.

NEW HAVEN, CONN.:
PUBLISHED BY HORACE C. PECK.
1866.

Entered according to Act of Congress, in the year 1865,
BY JOHN W. BARBER,
In the Clerk's Office of the District Court of Connecticut.

PREFACE.

THE study of Geography is now to a great extent introduced into our schools, but History, its counterpart, is to some extent neglected. The works on Geography now in use, give a description of every part of the known world; but most of those on History, comprise the United States only. The great events of the age in other countries, as well as in our own, affect the destiny of all. Geography and History being closely connected, each ought to be equally comprehensive.

History is a narrative of what has taken place on the earth among human beings, and is considered by many as "Philosophy teaching by example." It opens a vast field for study and contemplation; the rise and fall of empires, the connection of virtuous principles with public happiness, the causes which have degraded individuals and nations, are all subjects worthy of the close attention of beings destined for immortality.

Works on History have had their usefulness much impaired by the introduction of too many *names*, *dates* and *details* which give no valuable information. The multiplicity of these is apt to confuse the mind, and make the study itself dry and uninteresting. This evil the author has endeavored to avoid.

The plan adopted in this work is substantially that

used by Dr. Webster, the great American lexicographer, in his historical works for the use of schools. Every paragraph, or section, is prefixed with a title expressing its subject matter in *italic letters*. By this, at one glance, each subject is distinctly brought before the mind; an arrangement claimed to be *superior to any other*. Something of this kind has been in use ever since the art of printing was discovered, and its obvious utility must be acknowledged.

It has been generally supposed that the details of Universal History could not be introduced into one work with sufficient fullness without swelling it to a size which would prevent a wide circulation. This is believed to be a mistake. The author, in this work, which is of the size of the Geographies most in use, has given an epitome, or summary, of all the most prominent events in Ancient and Modern History. He has endeavored, by simplicity of language, to make every subject introduced, *clear, comprehensive, instructive* and *interesting*. It is believed that this work will be found well adapted to our Common and other Schools as a History, or as a Reading Book, and also useful to all who are desirous to obtain some knowledge of the World's History.

New Haven, Conn.   J. W. B.

CONTENTS.

ANCIENT HISTORY.

FIRST PERIOD, 2553 YEARS.

	Page.		Page.
Creation,	13	Egyptian Antiquities,	18
Fall of Man,	14	Founding of the Hebrew or	
The Deluge, or Flood,	14	Jewish nation	19
Division of the Earth among		Bondage of the Hebrews in	
the sons of Noah,	15	Egypt,	19
Building of Tower of Babel,	15	Account of the Phœnecians,	20
Assyria and Babylon,	15	Colonization of Greece,	20
Kingdom of Egypt,	16	Grecian States or Kingdoms,	21
Government and Laws,	16	Return of the Hebrews,	21
Embalming the Dead,	17	The Decalogue,	22
Religion of the Egyptians,	18		

SECOND PERIOD, 700 YEARS.

Siege of Troy,	23	Reign of Solomon,	28
Grecian Games,	24	Account of Homer, the Gre-	
Religion of the Greeks,	24	cian Poet,	29
Worship of the Gods,	25	Republic of Sparta,	29
Grecian Oracles,	26	Laws of Lycurgus,	30
Divination, or foretelling of		Republic of Athens,	30
Future Events,	27	Draco and Solon,	31
Court of Areopagus,	27	Founding of Carthage,	32
The Israelites,	28	Founding of Rome,	32

THIRD PERIOD, 430 YEARS.

Captivity of the Ten Tribes,	34	Defeat of the Persians,	42
Captivity of the Jews in		War of the Peloponnesus,	43
Babylon,	35	Defeat of the Athenians,	44
Conquest of Babylon,	35	War between Sparta and	
Persian Empire,	36	Thebes,	44
Religion of the Persians,	37	Epaminondas, the Theban	
Government and Laws,	38	General,	45
Implements of War,	38	Grecian Philosophy,	45
Method of attacking and de-		Socrates, the Philosopher,	46
fending places,	39	Death of Socrates,	46
War between the Greeks		Plato, the Philosopher,	47
and Persians,	39	Pythagoras,	48
Battle of Marathon,	40	Cynic Philosophers,	49
Ingratitude of the Athenians,	41	Of the Stoics,	49
Xerxes, the Persian,	41	Of the Epicureans,	50
Battle of Thermopylæ,	41	Of Aristotle and Pyrrho,	51

	Page.		Page.
Grecian Historians,	51	Rome,	61
Archimedes,	52	Romar. Kings,	61
Grecian Architecture,	53	Death of Lucretia,	62
Grecian Sculpture, &c.	54	Roman Republic,	63
Demosthenes, the Orator,	55	Judgment of Brutus,	63
Philip, of Macedon,	56	Cincinnatus, the Dictator,	64
Alexander the Great,	57	The Decemvirs,	64
Battle of the Granicus,	57	Military Tribunes,	65
Battle of Issus,	58	Censors,	65
Siege of Tyre,	58	Invasion of Rome,	66
Final Conquest of Persia,	59	Rome taken and burnt,	66
Conquest of India,	59	Expulsion of the Gauls,	67
Death of Alexander,	60	Character of the Romans,	67

FOURTH PERIOD, 323 YEARS.

	Page.		Page.
Successors of Alexander,	69	Death of Pompey,	85
Conquest of Italy by the Romans,	70	Cesar's Expedition into Egypt,	85
		Death of Cato,	86
First Punic or Carthaginian War,	70	Triumphs of Cesar,	87
		Cesar's Administration and Improvements,	87
Regulus, the Roman Patriot,	71		
Second Punic War,	71	Conspiracy against Cesar,	88
Passage of the Alps by Hannibal,	72	Assassination of Cesar,	88
		Speech of Antony,	89
Victories of Hannibal,	73	Second Triumvirate,	89
Ending of the Second Punic War,	73	Death of Brutus and Cassius,	90
		Antony and Cleopatra,	90
Third Punic War,	74	Death of Antony and Cleopatra,	91
Destruction of Carthage,	75	Reign of Octavius, or Augustus Cesar,	91
Corruption of the Roman Commonwealth,	75	Character and Education of the Romans,	92
The Gracchi,	76		
War of Jugurtha,	77	Industry of the illustrious Romans,	92
Social and Civil Wars,	77		
Caius Marius,	78	Their Religion,	93
Return of Marius to Rome,	78	Government,	93
Sylla, the Dictator,	79	Roman Senators,	94
Catiline's Conspiracy,	80	Other Roman Magistrates,	95
Discovery of Catiline's Plot,	80	Roman Citizens, &c.	95
Julius Cesar and the First Triumvirate,	81	Arts and Sciences,	96
		Roman Poets, Historians, &c.,	96
Invasion of Britain by Cesar,	81	Cicero, the Roman Orator,	97
Rivalship between Pompey and Cesar,	82	Domestic Life and Manners,	98
		Diet, and Luxurious Habits,	99
Cesar passing the Rubicon,	83	Public Amusements,	99
Cesar's pursuit of Pompey,	83	Military Affairs,	100
Battle of Pharsalia,	84	Military Triumphs,	101

'MODERN HISTORY.

FIRST PERIOD, 306 YEARS.

	Page.		Page.
Coming of Jesus Christ,	. 103	Christian Martyrs, . . .	. 109
State of the Roman Empire,	104	Christian Fathers, . . .	. 110
Conquest of Britain, .	. 104	Trajan, the Emperor, .	. 111
Caligula and Nero, .	. 105	Successors of Trajan, .	. 111
Invasion of Judea, . .	. 106	Partition of the Empire,	. 112
Siege of Jerusalem, .	. 106	Constantine, the first Christian Emperor, . . .	. 112
Dispersion of the Jews,	. 107		
Spread of Christianity, .	. 108	Government of the Emperors,	113
Persecution of Christians,	. 108		

SECOND PERIOD, 263 YEARS.

Reign of Constantine, .	. 114	Extinction of the Western Roman Empire, . .	. 121
Corruption of Christianity,	. 115		
Removal of the Seat of the Empire from Rome to Constantinople, . .	. 115	Reign of Theodoric the Great,	122
		Eastern Roman Empire,	. 123
		Belisarius, ...	. 123
Julian, the Apostate,	. 116	Conquest of Italy by the Lombards, . . .	. 123
Attempt to rebuild the Temple at Jerusalem,	. 116		
Barbarians, . . .	. 117	State of the World on the Extinction of the Western or Roman Empire, .	. 124
The Goths, . . .	. 117		
Religion of the Goths, or Scandinavians, . .	. 118	Of Spain, . .	. 125
		Of Britain, . . .	. 125
Vandals, . . .	. 118	Of England, . . .	. 126
Ancient Germans, . .	. 119	Saxon Conquest of England,	126
Druidical Religion, .	. 119	Introduction of Christianity into Britain, . . .	. 127
Poetry and Learning, .	. 120		
Sacking of Rome by Alaric,	. 120	Of France, ...	. 127
Ravages of Attila, the Hun,	. 121	Of the Arabs, or Saracens,	. 128

THIRD PERIOD, 231 YEARS.

Of Mahomet, . . .	. 129	Conquest of Spain by the Saracens, or Moors, .	. 134
Of the Koran, . .	. 130		
Mahometan Paradise, .	. 130	Christian Kingdoms in Spain,	135
Flight of Mahomet, .	. 131	Defeat of the Saracens, by Charles Martel, . .	. 135
Propagation of Mahometanism,	132		
Death of Mahomet, .	. 133	State of the Eastern Empire,	136
Successors of Mahomet,	. 133	Arabian Literature, .	. 136
Mahometan, or Saracen Empire, ...	. 134	Arts and Sciences, .	. 137
		Attack on Constantinople,	. 138

CONTENTS.

	Page.		Page.
Greek Fire,	138	Decline of the Feudal System,	140
Feudal System,	138	Bishop of Rome,	140
Of the Barons, or Lords,	139	Temporal power of Popes,	141
Of the Serfs, or Villeins,	139	Charlemagne,	141

FOURTH PERIOD, 295 YEARS.

	Page.		Page.
Reign of Charlemagne,	142	Baronial Castles, &c.,	149
Danish invasion of England,	143	Dark Ages,	149
Alfred the Great,	143	Collection of Relics,	150
Success of Alfred,	144	Monastic Institutions,	150
Character of Alfred,	145	Progress of the Monastic System,	151
Conquest of England by the Danes,	145	Corruption of the Monastic System,	152
Canute and his Successors,	146	Increase of Papal Power,	152
Norman Conquest,	146	Of the Clergy,	153
Battle of Hastings,	146	State of Learning,	153
William the Conqueror,	147	Trials by Ordeal,	154
State of the Arts, &c. at the Norman Conquest,	148	Trial by Combat,	154
Norman Nobles, or Barons,	148	Peter the Hermit,	155

FIFTH PERIOD, 200 YEARS.

	Page.		Page.
First Crusade,	156	Effects of Chivalry,	165
March of the Crusaders,	157	Henry II., of England,	166
March of the main body of the Crusaders,	157	Murder of Becket,	166
		Magna Charta,	167
Taking of Jerusalem,	158	Of the Inquisition,	168
Second Crusade,	159	Establishment of the Inquisition,	168
Third Crusade,	159	Scriptural Plays,	169
Fourth Crusade,	160	Genghis Khan,	169
Chivalry, or Knighthood,	161	End of the Saracen Empire,	170
Education of Knights,	161	Empire of the Assassins,	171
Of the Esquires,	162	Method of making Assassins,	171
Of the Knights,	162	End of the Crusades,	172
Character, &c. of the Knights,	163	Effects of the Crusades,	173
Of Tournaments,	164		
Orders of Knighthood,	164		

SIXTH PERIOD, 222 YEARS.

	Page.		Page.
Conquest of Wales,	174	Insurrection of Wat Tyler,	177
War between the English and Scots,	175	War between the houses of York and Lancaster,	177
Swiss Republics,	175	Wars between England and France,	178
William Tell,	175		
Wickliffe, the English Reformer,	176	Joan of Arc, the Maid of Orleans,	179

	Page.		Page.
Founding of the Turkish Empire,	. 179	Moorish Kingdom of Grenada,	183
		Conquest of Grenada,	. 184
Of Tamerlane,	. 180	Portuguese Discoveries,	. 184
Taking of Constantinople by the Turks,	. 180	Of Columbus,	. 185
		Columbus' application for Assistance,	. 186
Invention of the Mariner's Compass,	. 181	First Voyage and Discovery of Columbus,	. 186
Gunpowder, Firearms,	. 182		
Art of Printing,	. 183		

SEVENTH PERIOD, 115 YEARS.

Columbus' Return from his first Voyage,	. 188	Reformation by Luther,	. 196
		Progress of the Reformation,	197
Fate of Columbus,	. 189	Overthrow of the Papal power in England,	. 198
Of Vespucius, Cabot, and other Discoverers,	. 189	Reformation in Scotland,	. 199
Invasion of Mexico,	. 191	Of the Jesuits,	. 200
Advance of Cortez to the City of Mexico,	. 191	Progress of the Jesuits,	. 200
		Massacre of St. Bartholomew's,	. 201
Death of Montezuma,	. 192		
Conquest of Mexico,	. 193	Reign of Queen Mary,	. 202
Invasion of Peru,	. 194	Queen Elizabeth's Reign,	. 202
Conquest of Peru,	. 194	Spanish Armada,	. 203
Civilization of the Mexicans and Peruvians,	. 195	Gunpowder Plot,	. 203
		French Settlements in North America,	. 204
Religion of the Mexicans,	. 195		
Religious State of Christendom,	. 196	First English Settlement,	. 205

EIGHTH PERIOD, 168 YEARS.

Of the Virginia Settlers,	. 206	Salem Witchcraft,	. 215
Pocahontas, the Indian Princess,	. 207	Account of the Bucaneers,	. 216
		Sovereigns of the House of Stuart,	. 216
Indian Massacre in Virginia,	. 207		
Of the Native Indians,	. 208	Tyranny of Charles I.,	. 217
Manners, Customs, &c., of the Indians,	. 209	War between Charles and the Parliament,	. 218
Of the Puritans,	. 209	Execution of Charles I.,	. 218
Persecution of the Puritans,	. 210	Oliver Cromwell,	. 219
Plymouth Settlers,	. 210	The Commonwealth,	. 220
Sufferings of the Plymouth Colonists,	. 211	Character of Cromwell,	. 220
		Of Russia,	. 220
Dutch Settlements,	. 212	Peter the Great,	. 220
Destruction of the Pequots,	. 212	Of Sweden and its Sovereigns,	221
King Philip's War,	. 213	Of Prussia and the two Fredericks,	. 222
William Penn,	. 214		

CONTENTS.

	Page.
Of Holland,	223
Of Germany,	223
French and Indian Wars,	224
King William's and Queen Anne's Wars,	225
Indian War in Carolina,	225
Capture of Louisburg,	226
Braddock's Defeat,	227
Progress of the War,	227
Capture of Quebec,	228
Causes of the American Revolution,	229
Stamp Act,	229
Destruction of Tea at Boston,	230

NINTH PERIOD.

	Page.
Continental Congress,	231
Skirmish at Lexington,	232
Battle of Bunker's Hill,	233
Arnold's March through the Wilderness,	234
Assault on Quebec, and death of Gen. Montgomery,	234
Declaration of Independence,	235
Battle on Long Island,	236
Death of Capt. Hale,	236
Retreat of Washington, and Battle of Trenton,	237
Expedition of Gen. Burgoyne,	238
Treason of Arnold,	239
Sufferings of the American Army,	239
Arrival of the French Troops,	240
War in the Southern States,	240
Capture of Cornwallis,	241
Conclusion of the War,	241
Disbanding of the Army,	242
Confederation of the States,	242
Organization of the Federal Government,	243
Causes of the French Revolution,	244
Of the National Assembly,	244
Progress of the Revolution,	245
Trial and Execution of Louis XVI.,	246
Triumph of Infidelity,	247
Of the Directory and Napoleon Bonaparte,	247
Bonaparte the First Consul and Emperor,	248
Battle of Austerlitz,	249
Other victories of Napoleon,	249
Napoleon's Campaign in Russia,	250
Defeat of Napoleon by the Allies,	251
Napoleon's Return from Elba,	251
Battle of Waterloo,	252
War between the United States and Tripoli,	252
War between the United States and Great Britain,	253
Progress of the War in 1812,	253
The War in 1813,	254
The War in 1814,	255
Battle of New Orleans,	256
Revolution in Spanish America,	257
Of Hayti,	258
Of Toussaint L'Ouverture,	259
Progress of the Revolution in Hayti,	259
Of Brazil and Portugal,	260
Revolution in Greece,	261
Massacre at Scio,	262
Progress of the War,	262
Battle of Navarino,	263
French Revolution of 1830,	264
Progress of the Revolution,	264
Accession of Louis Philippe to the Throne,	266
Revolution in Belgium,	266
Revolution in Poland,	267
Progress of the Revolution,	267
Of India,	268
British East India Company,	269
Of China,	269
BIOGRAPHICAL SKETCHES,	271

CONTENTS.

RECENT EVENTS.

	Page.
Condition of France in 1847,	271
French Revolution of 1848,	271
Louis Napoleon, President and Emperor,	272
The Roman Republic,	272
Hungarian Revolution,	273
Subjugation of the Hungarians,	273
Origin of the Crimean War,	274
Allied movements against Russia,	275
Battles of the Crimea,	275
Capture of the Malakhoff and Fall of Sebastopol,	276
Of Texas,	276
War with Mexico,	277
Operations of Gen. Scott,	278
Capture of Mexico,	279
War in British India,	279
Progress of the war in India,	280
Causes of the Secession War,	281
Commencement of the War,	282
Uprising of the People,	282
Battle of Bull Run,	283
Capture of Hilton Head, South Carolina,	283
Capture of Forts Henry and Donelson,	284
The Merrimac and Monitor,	285
Burnside's Expedition,	286
Battle of Shiloh, or Pittsburg Landing,	286
Capture of New Orleans,	287
Gen. McClellan—Mititary Operations, &c.,	288
Battle of Antietam,	289
Proclamation of Emancipation,	289
Battle of Gettysburg,	290
Capture of Vicksburg,	291
Operations near Chattanooga, Tenn.,	291
Sherman's March through Georgia,	292
Capture of Fort Fisher,	293
Capture of Richmond,	294
Surrender of Lee's Army,	295
Assassination of President Lincoln,	295
BIOGRAPHICAL SKETCHES,	297

[ADVERTISEMENT.]

Since the first edition of the Universal History was published, the author has prepared a Chart, or Compend, entitled "*Pictorial History of the World*," on an entirely original plan. It is printed on a double medium sheet, and gives, at one view, an outline of the World's history. The pictorial part consists of twenty-seven separate cuts or engravings, the first of which is emblematic of Chaos and the Creation of Light, as described in the first chapter of Genesis: the second, the *Antediluvian* period, from the creation of Adam and Eve, to the Flood. The four cuts next in order are illustrative of the four great Monarchies of the World: the ASSYRIAN, the PERSIAN, the GRECIAN and the ROMAN. The *nineteen* cuts following, represent the prominent events in each of the nineteen centuries in the Christian era. The last engraving is descriptive of the *Millennium*, or the reign of the Messiah for a thousand years. Isa. xi., Rev. xx.

This sheet, or chart, will, it is believed, be found very useful in giving a scholar, or general reader, a clear and comprehensive view of the prominent events in the history of the world, as to the time, and order, in which they occurred. This chart is mounted on rollers, and is not only appropriate for a school room, but also for other places. It is furnished *gratis* for every ten copies purchased of the Elements of General History, and at a reduced price for those who purchase a single copy.

ANCIENT HISTORY.

PERIOD I.

FROM THE CREATION TO THE DEATH OF MOSES.

(2553 YEARS.)

Map, showing where the Earth was first peopled.

SECTION 1. *Of History.* History is a relation of past events. It is usually divided into *sacred* and *profane*, *ancient* and *modern*. Sacred history is that which is contained in the Old and New Testaments; profane is that which is found in other historical records of past ages Ancient history extends from the creation to the birth of Christ; modern, from the birth of Christ to the present time.

2. *Creation.* The only true account we have of the

QUESTIONS. *Section 1.* What is history? How is history divided? What is sacred history? What is profane history? How far does ancient history extend? How far modern?

creation of the world, and of man, is given by Moses in the book of Genesis. According to the Hebrew computation, man was created 4004 years before the coming of Christ. Our first parents were placed in the garden of Eden, in a state of innocence and happiness. This place, also called Paradise, is supposed to have been situated somewhere about the head waters of the Euphrates, a river in Asia.

3. *Fall of Man.* Our first parents, *Adam* and *Eve*, being tempted or persuaded by the devil, fell from their state of happiness, by disobeying their Creator. Having departed from duty, man lost the favor of God, and was driven out of Paradise. Sin, thus introduced into the world, is the origin of the miseries of mankind. Cain, the first-born of Adam and Eve, murdered his brother, Abel; and before the flood, we are informed that the wickedness of man was great, and the earth was filled with violence.

4. *The Deluge or Flood.* After mankind had multiplied in the earth, they became so extremely wicked, that their Maker determined to destroy the whole race by a flood, except Noah and his family. Noah, being warned of God, prepared an ark, or vessel, which was more than 480 feet in length, 81 in breadth, and 41 in height, and was most wisely formed to answer the purpose for which it was designed. In 1656 years from the creation, the fountains of the deep were broken up, the flood covered the earth, and every creature without the ark perished. Noah and his companions continued

---

2. Where do we find an authentic account of the creation? By whom given? How long before Christ, was man created? Where were our first parents placed? Where is it supposed that Paradise was situated?

3. How did our first parents fall from a state of happiness? What followed their departure from duty? What is the origin of the miseries of mankind? What of Cain? What of man before the flood?

4. Why were mankind destroyed by a flood? How was Noah saved? Describe the ark. How long did the ark float, and where did it rest? Is there proof of the deluge? Any traditions respecting it?

in the ark one year and ten days. The ark floated on the water 150 days, and on the falling of the waters, rested on Mount Ararat. The scripture account of the deluge is proved to be true, by the appearance of the earth in many places; and traditions respecting this great event have been handed down among many nations.

5. *Division of the Earth among the sons of Noah.* Noah had three sons, *Shem, Ham* and *Japheth*, from whom the earth was re-peopled after the flood. Shem and his posterity went forth into Eastern and Southern Asia: of this family are the Chaldeans, Syrians, and Arabians. The descendants of Ham peopled Egypt, and other parts of Africa. From Japheth descended the inhabitants of Northern Asia, and all the nations of Europe.

6. *Building of the Tower of Babel.* About one hundred years after the deluge, the descendants of Noah collected themselves on the plain of Shinar, for the purpose of building a city, and a tower of very great height, that they might acquire renown, and prevent their dispersion. God, however, having determined to form mankind into different nations, prevented their design by confounding their language, so that they were compelled to abandon their project, and disperse themselves abroad in the earth. The city which they attempted to build, was called Babel, or *Confusion.*

7. *Assyria and Babylon.* The name of Assyria appears to have been derived from *Ashur*, the son of Shem, who is supposed to have founded Nineveh, the chief city of Assyria. Nimrod, a grandson of Ham, is said to have founded Babylon, the capital of Babylonia,

---

5. What were the names of the sons of Noah? Where did Shem go, and who were his posterity? By whom was Egypt and other parts of Africa peopled? Who are the descendants of Japheth?

6. When did men begin to build the tower of Babel? Where, and for what purpose, did they build? How was the building prevented?

7. From whom was the name Assyria derived? Who founded Nineveh? Who founded Babylon? What is said of

about 150 years after the deluge. He is supposed to be the same with Belus, who was afterwards worshiped as a god. Nineveh and Babylon were perhaps the most magnificent cities in the world. It is stated that Semiramis, a queen of Babylon, employed two millions of men in enlarging and adorning this city. It appears that Babylonia and Assyria formed but one empire. Babylon was at first the capital, then Nineveh, then Babylon, till the conquest of the empire by Cyrus.

8. *Kingdom of Egypt.* The Mosaic writings represent Egypt, about 450 years after the flood, as a well regulated kingdom. The great fertility of the soil on the banks of the Nile, it is supposed, caused Egypt to become populous and civilized at an early period. Accordingly Egypt was the seat of arts and learning while Greece and Italy were in a barbarous state. It claims the honor of inventing the art of writing, and has been styled "the cradle of the sciences." *Menes,* or *Misraim,* the son of Ham, is supposed to have been the first monarch of the Egyptians, about 160 years after the deluge.

9. *Government and Laws.* The government of Egypt was a hereditary monarchy.* The king had the chief regulation of all matters relating to the worship of the gods, and the priests were considered as his deputies, and filled all the offices of state. In order to prevent the evils of borrowing, the borrower had to pledge the embalmed body of his father, and it was regarded impious and infamous not to redeem it; and if he died with-

---

Nimrod? What of Nineveh and Babylon? What of Semiramis? What of Babylon and Assyria?

8. How do the Mosaic writings represent Egypt? What is supposed to be the cause of its early settlement? What is said of Egypt? What invention does i claim the honor of? Who is supposed to have been the first monarch?

9. What was the form of the government of Egypt? What did the king regulate? How were the evils of borrowing prevented? After persons died, what was done respecting their conduct?

---

* A government descending from father to son, or other relative

out having performed this duty, he was deprived of the customary funeral honors. All persons, immediately after death, had their conduct examined; even kings were not excepted. If they had been virtuous, their bodies were embalmed, and laid in the tomb with various marks of honor: if their lives had been vicious, or if they had died in debt, they were left unburied, and supposed to have been deprived of future happiness.

Egyptian Mummies placed at a Feast.

10. *Embalming the Dead.* The ancient Egyptians embalmed the bodies of their relatives with the greatest care. These bodies, now called *mummies*, embalmed more than 3000 years ago, and perhaps before Moses was born, are now found in Egypt in good preservation. The body is filled with drugs and spices, closely wrapped over with many folds of linen, and inclosed in a coffin, the lid of which is covered with paintings and hieroglyphics, relating, it is supposed, to the character of the deceased. Many of these coffins are found in tombs cut into solid rocks. Many of the Egyptians kept the bodies of their ancestors in their houses, preserved in

---

10. What are mummies? How old are they supposed to be? In what state are they found? What did the Egyptians do with the embalmed bodies of their ancestors?

2*

such perfection, that they had very much the appearance of life. On feast-days, and on other occasions, the dead bodies of their friends were brought out, and placed at the table, among the living.

11. *Religion of the Egyptians.* Though the Egyptians were advanced in civilization, yet they were low and degraded in their religious opinions. Their two principal gods were *Osiris* and *Isis*, which are supposed to be the sun and the moon. Besides these, they worshiped the ox, the dog, the cat, the crocodile, the ibis, or stork, &c. If any person killed one of these animals, he was punished with death. In one instance, a city of Egypt being besieged, the invaders placed in front of their army a large number of dogs, cats, and other animals held sacred by the Egyptians, who, not daring to injure their deities, suffered their enemies to come into their city without opposition. The bull *Apis* had a splendid temple erected to him: great honors were paid him while living, and still greater after his death. The golden calf, set up by the Israelites near Mount Sinai, appears to have been an imitation of the god Apis.

12. *Egyptian Antiquities.* Egypt abounds with the monuments and remains of antiquity. The pyramids, one of which is 500 feet high, are the most astonishing monuments of human labor. It is supposed, and not without reason, that the Israelites, during their slavery in Egypt, were employed in making these enormous piles. The remains of the artificial lake *Mœris*, the *catacombs*, those vast places for the burial of the dead, have been the wonder of ancient and modern times. The ruins of Thebes, a city in Upper Egypt, supposed to have been

---

11. What is said of the religion of the Egyptians? The names of the principal gods? What other objects did they worship? Relate the manner in which one of their cities was taken. What is said of the bull *Apis*? What of the golden calf of the Israelites?

12. Of what height is one of the pyramids of Egypt? What people are supposed to have been employed in making them? What is said of the catacombs? Where is Thebes? What is said of its ruins? Of its history?

laid in desolation more than 3000 years ago, is viewed with astonishment. Almost the whole extent of eight miles, along the river Nile, is covered with magnificent portals, obelisks, covered with sculpture, forests of columns, and long avenues of statues of a gigantic size. One of its temples is a mile and a half in circumference. Its history is recorded only by uncertain tradition and poetry, which might be suspected fabulous, did not such mighty witnesses to their truth remain.

13. *Founding of the Hebrew or Jewish nation.* About 417 years after the flood, mankind appear to have lost, in a great measure, the knowledge and worship of the true God. Abraham, a descendant of Shem, was born in Chaldea, and in the midst of an idolatrous people, retained the knowledge of the true religion. By the divine direction, he removed into Canaan, which was appointed to be the residence of his posterity. To Abraham, God committed the true religion, and formed of his family a peculiar people, to whom his will was revealed, and from whom the Messiah, or Saviour, was to proceed. Jacob, the grandson of Abraham, had twelve sons, who were the heads of the twelve tribes of Israel.

14. *Bondage of the Hebrews in Egypt.* Joseph, one of the twelve sons of Jacob, or Israel, having displeased his brethren, was sold by them to a company of merchants, who took him into Egypt. Here, after various trials and changes, he became, (under Pharaoh) lord over Egypt. There being a sore famine in the land of Canaan, Joseph invited his father and brethren into the land of Egypt, where they increased rapidly in numbers. After the death of Joseph, the Israelites had become so numerous and powerful, that they began to be an object of fear to the Egyptians. In order to prevent their pros-

---

13. What was the state of mankind after the flood? Who was Abraham? Where born? What is said of him? Where did he remove? What is said of his family? What of Jacob and his sons?

14 Who was Joseph? What is said of him? How came the Israelites into Egypt? What is said of the Israelites after the death of Joseph? What did the Egyptians do to preven their increase? Did they succeed?

perity and increase, task-masters were set over them, who made their lives miserable with hard bondage, and all their male children were ordered to be destroyed at their birth. It is stated by Moses, the sacred historian, that the more they were afflicted, the more they multiplied and grew.

15. *Of the Phœnicians.* The Phœnicians were among the earliest civilized nations in the world. They are called *Canaanites* in the scriptures, from their living in the land of Canaan. Inhabiting a sterile country, on the borders of the Mediterranean sea, they turned their attention to commerce, and were a commercial people in the time of Abraham. Tyre and Sidon, their principal cities, were the most ancient of any we read of in history, and were, in early ages, the greatest seats of commerce in the world. The Phœnicians colonized various places bordering on the Mediterranean sea, and its islands, at an early period. They are said to have invented glass, purple, and coinage. The invention of letters has also been ascribed to them, as well as to the Egyptians; and *Cadmus*, a Phœnician, is said to have first carried letters into Greece.

16. *Colonization of Greece.* Civilization appears to have been introduced into Greece by a colony of Phœnicians, who founded the kingdom of *Argos*, 490 years from the deluge, and 1857 before the Christian era. Greece was called, by the natives, *Hellas*, and the inhabitants, *Hellenes*. They were extremely barbarous, and they wandered in the woods, without law or government, having but little intercourse with each other. It is said they were ignorant of the use of fire, lived on acorns, berries, and raw flesh, and clothed themselves

---

15. What were the Phœnicians called in the scriptures? Why were they a commercial people? What is said of Tyre and Sidon? Where did the Phœnicians have colonies? What are they said to have invented? What is said of Cadmus?

16. By whom was civilization introduced into Greece? At what time was the kingdom of Argos founded? What was Greece called by the natives? What is said of the ancient inhabitants? On what did they live, and how were they clothed? When were Athens, Sparta, and Thebes, founded?

with the skins of wild beasts. *Athens, Sparta,* and *Thebes,* were founded about 800 years after the deluge, and fifteen centuries before Christ.

17. *Grecian States or Kingdoms.* The most celebrated states or republics of Greece were, Athens Sparta, and Thebes: the two leading states were *Athens* and *Sparta.* Athens, the capital of Attica, was founded by a colony from Egypt. It was the most celebrated city in Greece, being distinguished as the seat of learning and the arts. It was also celebrated for its commerce, wealth, and magnificence, and was the birth-place of many illustrious men. The Spartans became distinguished for military valor and discipline, their singular laws and institutions making them a nation of soldiers. Thebes was founded by Cadmus, the Phœnician. Very little is known respecting its early history; but in after times, it rose from obscurity, and became celebrated, while Athens and Sparta were in a state of decline.

18. *Return of the Hebrews to Canaan.* The Hebrews or Israelites, having remained in Egypt 215 years, were, by the direction of God. assembled under Moses, their leader, and commanded to leave the country. By a miracle they passed through the Red sea, and the Egyptian army, in pursuing them, were all drowned. Although God continually performed miracles before the Israelites, to supply their wants, yet they murmured and rebelled against him. For this, the nation was compelled to wander *forty years* between Egypt and Canaan, and the rebellious generation died in the wilderness.

17. What were the most celebrated states of Greece? Which was the most celebrated city in Greece? What is said of Athens? For what were the Spartans distinguished? What is said of Thebes?

18. How long did the Hebrews remain in Egypt? In what manner did they leave Egypt? Why were they compelled to wander in the wilderness? How long? Where did the Israelites receive the divine law? From whom did they receive it? What was the supposed number of the Israelites at this time? In what manner did this multitude pass through the wilderness? What became of Moses? Who was his successor?

While at Mount Sinai, the Israelites received the divine law, and their national institutions from God himself, by the hand of Moses. At this time, it is supposed, they were *three millions* in number. This vast multitude were formed into a regular body, and the utmost order was observed in their marches and encampments. Moses, having arrived in sight of Canaan, died on Mount Nebo, and Joshua, his successor, conducted the people into the promised land.

19. *The Decalogue, or Ten Commandments.* The ten commandments given to Moses on Mount Sinai, are the most ancient code of laws now in existence. It is a complete summary of all the duties which mankind owe to God and each other; it enforces the observance of these duties by the powerful motives of gratitude, hope and fear. By it, man is directed to adore and love the true God, the Author of all good; it commands him to reverence his holy name, and to observe stated times for his worship. Four of these commands, 1, *Thou shalt not kill;* 2, *Thou shalt not commit adultery;* 3. *Thou shalt not steal;* 4. *Thou shalt not bear false witness*, have formed the basis of all criminal law in all civilized nations. The concluding commandment is directed against selfishness, the principal source of all crime.

---

19. What is said respecting the Decalogue or ten commandments? What four of them form the basis of criminal law? What is said respecting the tenth?

PERIOD II.

FROM THE DEATH OF MOSES TO THE FOUNDING OF ROME

(700 YEARS.)

Map showing places mentioned in Period II.

20. *The Siege of Troy.* The account of the Trojan war is derived principally from the *Iliad*, a poem by Homer, the great poet of antiquity. Although there is much which is fabulous in the poem, yet the main facts are believed to be correctly stated. The war originated in the following manner: *Helen*, the most beautiful woman of her age, ran away from her husband, the king of Sparta, with Paris, the son of the king of Troy, who came to Sparta on a visit. The Greeks united under *Agamemnon, Achilles,* and others, and sent a fleet of 1,200 open vessels, which conveyed an army of 100,000 men to the Trojan coast, to avenge the outrage. The

---

20. From what is the history of the Trojan war derived? How did the war originate? Who were the Greek and Trojan commanders? How long was Troy besieged? How taken?

Trojans, commanded by *Hector, Eneas,* and others, sustained a siege of ten years, when the city was entered by storm, or stratagem, and burnt to the ground. The poets relate that the Greeks made a large wooden horse, which they secretly filled with armed men; the Trojans having taken possession, they drew it in triumph into the city. In the night the Greeks came out, opened the gates to their companions, who rushed in and made themselves masters of the city.

21. *Grecian Games.* The Greeks had four solemn games, called the *Olympic,* the *Pythian,* the *Nemean,* and the *Isthmian.* They consisted of contests of skill in wrestling, boxing, running, leaping, and such exercises. There were also horse and chariot races; contentions of skill between poets, musicians, orators, philosophers, and artists. These games had a great political effect in promoting national union, in extending the love of glory, and training the youth to martial exercises. They cherished at once a spirit of heroism and superstition, which led to great and hazardous enterprises. The *Olympic* games were instituted 1222 years before Christ, by Hercules. They were not, however, regularly celebrated till 775 years before the Christian era. From this period the *Olympiads* constitute an epoch in profane history, to which all important events are referred.

22. *Religion of the Greeks.* The Greeks, and afterwards the Romans, worshiped great numbers of gods and demi-gods, which they divided into a number of classes. The celestial deities were Jupiter, Apollo, Mars, Mercury, Bacchus, Vulcan, Juno, Minerva, Venus, Diana, Ceres, and Vesta. *Jupiter* was considered

---

21. What were the solemn games of the Greeks called? What did they consist of? What effect did these games have? When were the Olympic games instituted? At what time were they regularly celebrated? What is said of them?

22. What did the Greeks and Romans worship? Who were their celestial deities? What is said of Jupiter? Apollo? Mars? Mercury? Bacchus? Vulcan? Minerva? Venus? What is said of Neptune? The Syrens? Cupid? The Nine Muses? What of deities of a lower order?

the father of gods and men; *Apollo*, the God of music and poetry; *Mars*, of war; *Mercury*, represented with winged feet, was the messenger of the gods; *Bacchus* was the god of wine; *Vulcan* was patron of those who worked in metals, and is represented as forging thunderbolts for Jupiter; *Minerva* was the goddess of wisdom; *Venus*, of love and beauty. These divinities were supposed to possess the passions and infirmities of mankind; and even Jupiter, their supreme god, was represented as having recourse to the most unworthy artifices to gratify the basest passions.

Among the deities of a lower order, was *Neptune*, who reigned over the sea; the *Syrens*, who were said to have the faces of women, and the lower part of their bodies like fish, and by their melodious voices allured mariners to destruction. *Cupid* was the god of love; the *Nine Muses*, who presided over the liberal arts; they also had infernal deities, and gods, and goddesses, of the woods, streams, winds, &c. Besides their own they often adopted the gods of other nations.

23. *Worship of the Gods.* The worship of the Grecian divinities was conducted by priests dressed in costly robes, who offered sacrifices of animals, fruits, perfumes, and sometimes human victims. These sacrifices were sometimes accompanied with prayers, music, and dancing. Various degrees of worship were offered to the gods, and the souls of departed heroes. The temples dedicated to the gods, were very numerous and splendid. Their festivals were observed with every circumstance of pomp and splendor, to charm the eye, and please the imagination. The temples were attended by the idle and vicious, and the most disgraceful licentiousness was often allowed. Their philosophers appear to have been in doubt respecting a future state of existence; their poets, however, inculcated a belief in *Tartarus*, or Hell, and in *Elysium*, or Paradise.

---

23. How was the Grecian worship conducted? What is said of their festivals? Their temples? Their philosophers? What belief did their poets inculcate?

Priestess of the Delphic Oracle.

24. *Grecian Oracles.* The oracles were certain temples, where it is said future events were made known to those who sought to know the will of the gods, by means of priests and priestesses, who were supposed to be inspired by their deities with the power of foretelling what was to come. They obtained such credit among the Greeks, that nothing of importance was undertaken without first consulting the gods. There were several hundred of these oracles in different parts of Greece, but the most celebrated were those of Apollo, at *Delphi*, and *Delos*, and the oracle of Jupiter, at *Dodona*. The *Delphic oracle* was on Mount Parnassus, the supposed residence of the god Apollo. Here the priestess called *Pythia*, being placed over a fissure from which proceeded a sulphurous vapor, began to foam at the mouth, tore her hair and flesh, and the incoherent words uttered during her frenzy, were put in verse, and delivered as he answer of the oracle. At Dodona, the priestess oretold future events by observing attentively the mur-

---

24. What were the oracles? Where were the most celebrated oracles? What is said of the priestess, or *Pythia*? Of the priestess at Dodona? What kind of answers did the oracles give?

mur of the sacred oaks, the voice of falling water, &c. The answers by these oracles were generally given in such obscure language, that they would admit of different interpretations.

25. *Divination, or foretelling of future events.* The Greeks also endeavored to obtain a knowledge of future events by *dreams*, and by observing *omens*. They were very superstitious in this respect; almost every accident, or appearance of nature, was believed to be an omen of good or evil. For the purpose of obtaining *prophetic dreams*, they fasted, clothed themselves in white, and underwent various ceremonies. In the *sacrifices*, when the beast was dragged by force to the altar when it kicked, or bellowed, or was long in dying, it was ominous of evil; if otherwise, the gods were deemed propitious. The entrails of beasts were examined in order to gain a knowledge of the future; the Grecian *augurs*, clothed in white, with a crown of gold upon their heads, observed the flight of birds for the same purpose. *Toads* were accounted lucky omens; *serpents*, unlucky; a *hare*, in time of war, signified defeat and flight. *Comets* and *eclipses* portended evil, and caused much alarm.

26. *The Court of Areopagus.* This far-famed court of justice was held in Athens, on *Mars' Hill*, and so upright and impartial were its decisions, that they were considered as standards of wisdom and humanity. The *Areopagites*, or judges, were guardians of education and manners, and took cognizance of crimes, abuses, and matters relating to religion and government. They always heard causes, and passed sentences in the night, or in the dark, so that they might not be led to favor either party on account of their outward appearance.

---

25. How did the Greeks seek a knowledge of future events? What is said of prophetic dreams? Of sacrifices? What of augurs? Lucky and unlucky omens?
26. What is said of the court of the Areopagus? Of the Areopagites? When did they hear causes? Why in the dark? Why was not oratory or fine speaking allowed? What was done when the votes of the judges were equally divided?

No oratory, or fine speaking, was allowed, lest it should corrupt their judgment, and in this august tribunal nothing was attended to but *truth* alone. If the votes were equally divided, Minerva, the goddess of wisdom, was supposed to add her vote or suffrage, and always to incline on the side of mercy.

27. *The Israelites.* After the death of Moses and Joshua, the Israelites were under the direction of leaders called *Judges*, during the space of about 350 years. The people, dissatisfied with the immediate government of God, desired a king, in order to be like the nations around them. About 1100 years before Christ, *Saul* was appointed their sovereign. He was a warlike prince, but was finally, with his three sons, killed on Mount Gilboa. He was succeeded by *David*, who was distinguished for his skill in war, music, and poetry. He restored the purity of the Hebrew worship, conquered the enemies of his country, and commenced building *Jerusalem*, which afterwards was the royal residence. He made an alliance with Hiram, king of Tyre, the capital of Phœnicia, then a powerful and wealthy kingdom, and collected materials for building the magnificent temple of Solomon.

28. *The Reign of Solomon.* When Solomon succeeded to the throne of his father, David, the Israelitish nation had arrived to its height of splendor and power. The dedication of *Solomon's Temple*, at Jerusalem, took place *one thousand and four years* before Christ. The building of this structure was completed in seven years. An immense amount of gold was used in its construction, and it was probably the most superb and costly edifice the world ever saw. The reign of Solomon was attended with peace, prosperity, and abundance; but to-

---

27. After the death of Moses and Joshua, who were the leaders of the Israelites? Why did they desire a king? What is said of Saul? Who was his successor? What is said of David? With whom did he make an alliance?

28. Who succeeded David? What is said of Solomon's Temple? What is said of the reign of Solomon? What of the ten tribes? What tribes formed the kingdom of Judah

wards the close of his life he became luxurious and effeminate, and by the sin of idolatry brought dishonor and distress upon the nation. About thirty years after the dedication of the temple, *ten* tribes of the Israelites revolted from Rehoboam, the son of Solomon, and formed a separate kingdom, which was called the *Kingdom of Israel;* the tribes of Judah and Benjamin continued their allegiance to Rehoboam, and formed the *Kingdom of Judah.*

29 *Homer, the Grecian Poet.* Homer, the great poet of antiquity, is supposed to have lived in Greece about the time of Solomon. He is supposed to have been a wandering minstrel, and in that capacity composed in detached parts these sublime stories, which in 367 years afterwards were collected into two poems, the *Iliad,* which is a description of the Trojan war, and the *Odyssey,* in which is described the return of Ulysses from the siege of Troy. These poems, which have been the admiration of all succeeding ages, are distinguished for their minute description of ancient manners, their fire, sublimity, and eloquence, which hardly have been equalled by any succeeding poet. The ancients had such a veneration of Homer, that they raised temples and statues to his memory, and even offered sacrifices and worshiped him as a god.

30. *Republic of Sparta.* Lacedemon, or Sparta, a weak and distracted state, arose to great power and distinction among the Grecian states, by the introduction of the institutions of *Lycurgus.* This *lawgiver* gave most of his attention to the regulation of manners; one of the leading principles which governed his system, was that " Luxury is the bane of society." His regulations appear to have had no other end than to form a nation of soldiers. All the servile offices were performed by the *Helots,* or slaves, whom they treated with se-

---

29. At what time is Homer supposed to have lived? What is said of him? What is said of the *Iliad* and *Odyssey*? For what are these poems distinguished?

30. How did Sparta become powerful? What was one of the leading principles of his system? What appeared to be

verity, and often killed for sport. Lycurgus having bound his countrymen by an oath to observe his laws till he returned, he left Sparta, it is said, with the intention of never returning, and in order to give sanction and durability to his laws, he starved himself to death The Spartans observed his laws for 500 years, during which time they continued a powerful people.

31. *Laws of Lycurgus.* Lycurgus made an equal division of land among the people, and to prevent their becoming rich by commerce, he destroyed the value of gold and silver, and ordered all money to be made of iron. This *iron money* was of no value in any other state, and even by the Spartans themselves, it was despised. It was ordained that all the citizens should eat at the public tables, where the food was of the plainest kind, and the conversation grave and instructive. Every man was obliged to send his provisions to the common stock once a month. The Spartan children were considered as belonging to the state, and at the age of seven years were taken from their parents and put into classes for a public education. They were taught the duties of religion, obedience to the laws, respect for parents, contempt of danger and hardship, and above all, the love of glory and of their country. Although there was much which is worthy of praise, yet there were some evils in their institutions. The Spartan women were taught to be bold and immodest; the youth were taught to subdue the feelings of kindness and humanity, and in some instances theft was allowed.

32. *Republic of Athens.* Athens was at the first governed by kings. A war having been waged against Athens, it was declared by an oracle, that the nation whose king was first killed in battle, should be victorious. *Codrus*, disguising himself, went into the camp

---

the object of his regulations? What is said of the *Helots*, or slaves? What became of Lycurgus? How long did the Spartans observe his laws?

31. How did Lycurgus prevent the people from becoming rich? Where did the citizens take their food? What is said of their children? What were they taught? What were some of the evils of the Spartan institutions?

of the enemy and sacrificed his life for the good of his country. The Athenians were the conquerors; and to honor the memory of Codrus, they decreed that no man was fit to reign after him, and therefore changed the government by appointing nine persons as magistrates, who were styled *Archons.* This took place 1070 years before Christ. The manners of the Athenians formed strong contrast to those of the Spartans. In Athens the arts were highly esteemed; in Sparta they were despised. In Athens peace was the natural state of the republic, while war seemed to be the great business of life with the Spartans. The Athenian was luxurious, and the Spartan frugal; they were, however, equally jealous of their liberty, and equally brave in war.

33. *Draco and Solon.* These celebrated lawgivers of Athens, Draco and Solon, flourished about *six hundred* years before the Christian era. *Draco* prepared the first written code of laws which the Athenians possessed. His laws, on account of their severity, are said to have been *written in blood.* By them idleness was punished with as much severity as murder, and death was the penalty of both. Such was the inhumanity of these laws, that it prevented their being fully executed. *Solon,* one of the "seven wise men of Greece," in one of his first acts repealed the laws of Draco. The general character of his laws was mild, equitable, and adapted to the prevailing habits of the people. The father who did not teach his son a trade, could not claim any support from him in his old age. It was forbidden to use ill language in public. The proposer of a law, which was found on experience to be impolitic, was liable to punishment. Those persons who on questions

---

32. How was Athens first governed? What is said of Codrus? How was the government changed? What was the difference between the Athenians and Spartans?

33. Who were the lawgivers of Athens? At what time did they flourish? What is said of the laws of Draco? Who was Solon? What was the general character of his laws? Mention some of them. What was done to those who would not declare their sentiments?

of importance to the country, refused to declare their sentiments till they could see which was the strongest party, were declared infamous, condemned to banishment, and their property confiscated.

34. *Founding of Carthage.* Carthage, in Africa, is said to have been founded upwards of 869 years before the Christian era, and about 100 before the building of Rome. It existed more than seven hundred years. It is said to have been founded by *Dido*, a princess, with a colony from Tyre. The government at first was monarchical, but became afterwards republican, and it retained, in a great measure, the laws and manners of the parent state. Commerce was the principal business of the Carthaginians; and by means of their wealth they hired foreign troops, conquered various places lying on the borders of the Mediterranean sea, and established colonies. Their history was not much known till their war with the Romans; they are generally represented as avaricious, and as wanting in integrity and honor. During the period of the Carthaginian, or *Punic wars*, Carthage, with a population of 700,000, became one of the most splendid cities in the world. It had under its dominion 300 smaller cities, in various places bordering on the Mediterranean.

35. *Founding of Rome by Romulus.* The early history of the Romans, like that of other ancient nations, is mixed with fable. The most authentic account we have, is, that Rome was founded by Romulus, 752 years before the Christian era. The city took its name from its founder, and it appears to have been first peopled by runaway slaves and criminals. Romulus being king, made his new city an asylum for fugitive slaves, and by a stratagem at a public festival, his subjects seized and carried off the *Sabine women* for wives. For about 250 years Rome was governed by kings; afterwards the form of government became republican. The Romans

---

34. When was Carthage founded? By whom? What is said of its government? What was their principal business? How is their character generally represented? What is said of Carthage during the *Punic* wars?

were generally at variance with the tribes around them, and generally settled their disputes by battles, in which they were most always victorious. The citizens of Rome were divided into two classes, the *Patricians*, who were the nobility, or higher classes, and the *Plebeians*, or common people. Between these two orders many broils and dissentions occurred.

---

35. What is said of the early history of Rome? By whom founded, and at what time? How was it first peopled? What is said of the Sabine women? How were the citizens of Rome divided? Who were the Patricians? Who were Plebeians?

PERIOD III.

FROM THE FOUNDING OF ROME TO THE DEATH OF ALEXANDER

(430 YEARS.)

36. *Captivity of the Ten Tribes.* The ten tribes of Israel existed in a separate kingdom for about 250 years, which was called the *kingdom of Israel*, of which Samaria was the capital, their kings were idolaters, and the nation were sunk in wickedness. In 721 years before Christ, *Shalmanezer*, king of Nineveh, besieged Samaria, and after a siege of three years, the city was surrendered, and the people carried captives into the mountainous regions of the interior of Asia. From this period they ceased to exist as an independent nation, and we have no authentic history respecting their fate. It

---

36. What kingdom did the ten tribes form? How long did it exist? What was the capital? What is said of their kings and nations? By whom were they carried into captivity, and where? What is said of their fate as a nation? In the time of our Saviour, who were called Samaritans?

is supposed by some, that they are still existing as a distinct people somewhere in Asia. Some few people belonging to the tribes remained in Canaan, and were intermixed with strangers, and from that mixture sprung the motley race, who, in the time of our Saviour, were called *Samaritans*, and held in contempt by the Jews.

37. *Captivity of the Jews in Babylon.* About a century after the captivity of the ten tribes, *Nebuchadnezzar*, king of Babylon, took Jerusalem by storm,* after a siege of twelve months. The city, with the temple built by Solomon, was leveled with the dust, 588 years before the coming of Christ. *Zedekiah*, the Jewish king, after the murder of his children in his presence, had his eyes put out, and then carried captive to Babylon. All the principal persons and the skillful artists of every kind, and the sacred treasures of the temple, were likewise taken away, and the country laid waste. The Jews, according to the prophecy of *Daniel*, one of the captives, remained in captivity just *seventy years*, and were restored to their country by *Cyrus*, the conqueror of Babylon, who permitted them to rebuild their city and its temple. The scripture narrative in the Old Testament, ends about 100 years after this period.

38. *Conquest of Babylon by Cyrus.* This celebrated city, one of the wonders of the world, was taken by Cyrus, the Persian, 538 years before Christ, and by this event the Babylonian or Assyrian Empire was ended. Cyrus having defeated *Belshazzar*, the king of Babylon, he retreated to his capital, which the Persians immediately besieged. The city was fortified in such a manner, that it seemed impossible to take possession. It was, however, taken by a stratagem : a channel was

---

37. When did Nebuchadnezzar take Jerusalem? What is said of the siege and temple? What of Zedekiah? How long did the Jews remain in captivity? By whom were they restored? At what period does the scripture narrative end?

38. By whom was Babylon taken? In what manner? What is said of Belshazzar? What remarkable appearance? What is said of Isaiah? What of his predictions?

---

* A violent attempt in going over walls or through gates.

dug to turn the course of the river Euphrates, which passed through the city. A great festival was to be celebrated in the city, in which the Babylonians were accustomed to pass the whole night in drinking and debauchery. Cyrus, on this night, opened the channel to receive the water of the Euphrates, which soon became dry, and marched his troops in the bed of the river into the city. Belshazzar and his nobles, while reveling with wine, drank from the sacred vessels taken from the temple of Jerusalem, were suddenly arrested by the appearance of a hand-writing on the wall, warning Belshazzar of the destruction of his kingdom. The troops of Cyrus finding the gates open on the banks of the river, entered the city almost without resistance, and slew Belshazzar and his attendants.

Isaiah, the sacred prophet, many ages before its final accomplishment, foretold its utter desolation, in the following words: "And Babylon, the glory of kingdoms, the beauty of the Chaldees' excellency, shall be as when God overthrew Sodom and Gomorrah. It shall never be inhabited, neither shall it be dwelt in from generation to generation." So completely has this prediction been fulfilled, that it has been a matter of dispute where the city stood.

39. *Persian Empire.* There is but little known respecting the early history of the Persians. They rose into notice and power by the conquest of Cyrus, who is celebrated both in profane and sacred history. Cyrus was the son of a Persian nobleman, and married the daughter of the king of the *Medes*, and by this means Persia and Media became one kingdom. He conquered the *Lydians*, made himself master of *Sardis*, their capital, and took prisoner their king *Crœsus*, so celebrated for his vast riches. He conquered Babylon and subjected the greatest part of Asia Minor, and made himself master of Syria and Arabia. Cyrus was a great

---

39. What is said of the early history of the Persians? What is said of Cyrus? Of Persia and Media? Relate the conquests of Cyrus. How long did the Persian Empire continue? How was it ended?

and virtuous king ; he spent the last part of his life in regulating his vast conquests, being beloved not only by his own natural subjects, but those of the conquered nations. The Persian Empire continued for two hundred years, when it was ended by the conquests of Alexander the Great.

Persians Worshiping the Sun.

40. *Religion of the Persians.* The religion of the ancient Persians was of great antiquity. *Zoroaster* was the founder of the sect of the *Magi*, in the eastern world, and particularly in Persia. This set adored the sun, and paid great veneration to fire; hence they were called fire worshipers. The keeping of the *sacred fire* was entrusted to the Magi, and it was always carried before their kings in all their marches, with the greatest respect, and it would have been deemed the greatest misfortune, had it been suffered to go out. In their tenets, they believed there were two principles in existence, one the cause of all good, the other the cause of all evil, and that there is a perpetual struggle between them, which will last to the end of the world. The priests of the Magi were deeply skilled in astronomy, and all the learning of the age in which they lived. They were so much superior in knowledge to the rest of mankind, that they were thought by the vulgar to be inspired by supernatural powers. Hence in after ages, those who

---

40. Who was Zoroaster ? What is said of the Magi ? What was their belief ? What is said of the priests of the Magi ? What of Magic and Magicians ?

4

performed any act which seemed to be beyond human power, were said to have used *Magic*, and were called *Magicians.*

41. *Government and Laws.* The government of Persia was an absolute monarchy; the will of the monarch was law, and his person held sacred. He always appeared with great pomp and dignity: having at some periods a body-guard of 13,000 men, besides another guard of 10,000 horsemen, styled *the Immortals*, their number being always the same. The king, like the rest of the eastern monarchs, styled himself " *The King of Kings.*" The laws of Persia were mild and just, and the utmost purity was observed in the administration of justice. The ancient Persians bestowed great attention to the education of youth. Children at the age of five years were put under the care of the *Magi* for the improvement of their minds, and were at the same time trained to every manly exercise. Before they were corrupted and weakened by the luxury of later times, the Persians were temperate, brave, simple, and virtuous in their manners.

42. *Implements of War.* The ordinary arms of the Persian and other eastern nations, were a *scimitar*, a short curved sword, a dagger which hung in a belt on the right side; a *javelin*, a short spear pointed with iron, five and a half feet in length. Spears, or *lances, shields, bows, arrows,* and *slings*, were used. They covered the most exposed parts of their bodies, and also their horses, with an *armor* of brass. They often used *chariots* armed with sythes: these had only two wheels, with sythes three feet long, placed horizontally into both ends of the axletree; other sythes were also placed under the same axletree, with their edges turned to the ground, that they might cut in pieces men and horses, over which

---

41. What was the government of Persia? What is said of the Persian monarch? What of his guard? What of the laws of Persia? Of the education of children? Of the Persian manners?

42. What were the ordinary arms of the eastern nations? What was a scimitar? A javelin? What is said of their armor? Of their chariots? How drawn and occupied?

they passed. The chariots were generally drawn by four horses abreast, and were occupied by two distinguished warriors. When an opportunity occurred, they drove furiously into the ranks of the enemy, and did horrid execution.

43. *Method of attacking and defending places.* The first course taken in besieging a place, was to blockade it, by building a wall around it. This was to prevent succors or provisions being brought in. In this manner they waited till the besieged were reduced by famine; and we read of some instances where cities were besieged for more than ten years. This being very tedious, the walls of places were sometimes *scaled*, by means of ladders. In order to prevent this, the walls were often built very high, and towers were built at intervals in the walls still higher, so that the ladders of the besiegers might not be able to reach the summit. Another method of attack was, to build a wooden *movable tower*, still higher than the walls, which was moved against them. On the top of these movable towers, a body of soldiers was placed, who, with their darts and arrows, cleared the walls of the city of its defenders, and thus effected an entrance. The ancients also used the *battering-ram*, a vast beam of timber, with a strong head of brass or iron at one end, which was pushed with the utmost force against the walls.

44. *War between the Greeks and Persians.* The conquest of the Grecian states seems to have been a favorite object with the Persians from the time of Cyrus. Their growing power and independent spirit were wounding to the pride of the monarchs of Asia. Greece was at this time composed of a number of small and independent states, jealous of each other, and often engaged in quarrels and hostilities: Athens and Sparta, however, had obtained a pre-eminence. The invasion of the Persians

---

43. What was the first course in besieging a place? How long were cities sometimes besieged? How did they prevent the scaling of walls? What is said of movable towers? O˙ the battering-ram?

44. What was a favorite object with the Persians? How

had the effect of uniting them in one common effort for the preservation of their liberties, and thus, by awakening a national spirit, laid the foundation of their future greatness. *Darius*, the *Persian* king, sent heralds into Greece, and demanded of all the states, " *earth* and *water*," the usual token of submission to his government. Many of the cities and islands submitted; but Athens and Sparta, instead of offering up " earth and water," threw the heralds, one into a well, the other into a ditch, and contemptuously bade them take earth and water from thence.

45. *Battle of Marathon.* The Persian army, having approached Athens, encamped on the *plains of Marathon*, about ten miles from the city, which they summoned to surrender. The Athenians, 10,000 heroes, under *Miltiades*, fired with patriotism, marched on to Marathon, to oppose *ten* times their number in the Persian host. The strength of the Persians consisted much in its cavalry: Miltiades, therefore, drew up his little army on a narrow plain, where the cavalry could not act to advantage. The Persian commander, although aware of the skillful disposition of the Greeks, was too confident of the superiority of his numbers, to delay the battle. The signal for action being given, the Athenians advanced running, and at once engaged the enemy in close fight. The battle was fierce and obstinate; but Grecian valor prevailed, and the whole Persian army retreated in disorder to their ships. The loss of the Persians was more than six thousand men, while the Greeks lost but two hundred. This was one of the most important battles ever fought in ancient times, and on its event seemed to depend the liberty of Greece, and the progress of the refinement of mankind. It took place 490 years before the Christian era.

---

was Greece at this period? What was the effect of the Persian invasion? What is said of Darius? How were the Persian heralds treated by Athens and Sparta?

45. How many Athenians engaged in the battle of Marathon? How many Persians? Describe the order of the battle. What was the loss of the Persians? The Greeks?

46. *Ingratitude of the Athenians.* Miltiades, by this victory, rose to the highest popularity in the republic, and was sent with a fleet to expel the Persians from the Grecian islands. He laid siege to *Paros,* but being dangerously wounded, in attempting to enter the town, raised the siege, and was obliged to return to Athens. On the accusation of one of the citizens, he was tried for treason. Though he was absolved from the capital charge, yet he was condemned to pay a fine of fifty talents. Being unable to pay this fine, he was thrown into prison, where he died of the wounds received in the service of his ungrateful country. Even his body was not allowed to be buried, until his son *Cimon,* who was very young, had procured the money and paid the fine.

47. *Xerxes, the Persian.* Xerxes, the young monarch, having succeeded to the throne of Persia, was eager to subdue Greece, and avenge the defeat of his father. Having spent four years in preparation, he collected the greatest army the world ever saw. The whole number of fighting men in the army and fleet, exceeded *two millions;* and, including the camp followers, the sutlers, slaves, and women, the whole number is said to have exceeded *five millions.* The fleet consisted of 1200 ships of war, and 3000 ships of burthen. It is related that Xerxes, having taken a station on an eminence, in order to gratify his vanity, by viewing the vast assemblage which he had collected,—the earth covered with his troops, the sea with his vessels,—is said to have shed tears, on the reflection that, in the space of one hundred years, not one of the vast multitude before him would be found alive.

48. *Battle of Thermopylæ.* Landing in Thessaly, Xerxes marched without opposition, till he came to *Thermopylæ,* a narrow pass defended by *Leonidas,* king of Sparta, whom he commanded to deliver up his arms.

---

46. What is said of Miltiades? How was he treated after his return from the siege of Paros?
47. What is said of Xerxes? How many fighting men did he have? And how many followers? What is related of Xerxes, on viewing his vast army?

Leonidas, with the Spartan Band, at Thermopylæ.

With Spartan brevity, Leonidas replied, "*Come and take them.*" For two days, the Persians in vain strove to force their way. At length, an unguarded track was discovered; the defence of the pass was of no avail. Leonidas, foreseeing certain destruction, commanded all to retire, except three hundred of his countrymen. His motive was, to show the Persians what sort of people they had to encounter, and to acquire immortal fame, in obedience to a law of his country, which forbade its soldiers to flee from an enemy. They all fell, to a man, after having made dreadful havoc of the enemy. A monument was erected on the spot, bearing this noble inscription: "*Go, stranger, tell it at Lacedemon, that we died here in obedience to her laws.*"

49. *Defeat of the Persians.* From Thermopylæ the Persians came down upon Attica. The inhabitants of Athens, after conveying their women and children to the islands for security, betook themselves to their fleet, and abandoned the city, which was pillaged and burnt by the Persians. The fleet of the Greeks, consisting

---

48. Who was Leonidas? What was his reply to Xerxes? What did Leonidas do, when he foresaw his destruction? What was the inscription on the monument of the Spartans

of 380 sail, was attacked by the Persian fleet, consisting of 1200 ships, in the straits of *Salamis*. Xerxes, from an eminence on the coast, saw the destruction of his fleet, and determined to return, with all possible speed, to Asia. Leaving Mardonius, with 300,000 chosen men, to prosecute the war, he retreated towards the Hellespont, which he crossed in a small fishing-boat, with scarcely a remnant of his followers with him, they having died of famine, fatigue, and pestilence. Mardonius was totally defeated at *Platæa*, 479 years before Christ. From this time, the ambitious schemes of Xerxes were at an end, and he himself was soon after murdered.

50. *War of the Peloponnesus*. This civil war among the Greeks commenced about 430 years before the Christian era, and continued for twenty-seven years. It is called the *Peloponnesian* war, from the peninsula of that name, (now Morea,) in which the southern Grecian states were situated. It was partly caused by Athens, who wished to rule the rest of Greece, and partly from the jealousy of Sparta and the other Grecian states, who bore with impatience the supremacy of Athens. All the Greeks partook in this destructive quarrel, and arranged themselves on the side of Sparta or of Athens. The Spartans were generally the most powerful on the land, the Athenians on the sea. Sparta menaced Athens with all her forces, ravaged the country, and blockaded the inhabitants within their walls. Athens avenged herself by landing her forces at various places, and by laying waste the country of her enemies, compelling them to fly to the defense of their own habitations. Although this contest took place at an era distinguished for refinement, philosophy, and the cultiva-

---

49. How were the Persians defeated? What did Xerxes do, after the defeat of his fleet?

50. At what time did the Peloponnesian war commence, and how long did it continue? How did it originate? Who were the most powerful on land? Who on the sea? What is said of this contest?

tion of the arts, yet it was carried on with the utmost party rage and savage ferocity.

51. *Defeat of the Athenians.* Lysander, one of the ablest of the Spartan commanders, having utterly defeated the Athenian fleet, reduced Athens to great distress. The city was blockaded by land and sea, and the Athenians, to avoid total destruction, agreed to demolish their port and all their fortifications. They also agreed to limit their fleet to twelve ships, and in future undertake no military enterprise, except under the command of the Spartans. By these means Lacedemon, or Sparta, became the leading power in Greece. Lysander, after the reduction of Athens, abolished the popular government, and in its place, thirty magistrates were appointed, whose power was absolute. The magistrates, from their acts of cruelty, were called the "*thirty tyrants.*" In the space of eight months 1500 citizens were sacrificed to their avarice, or vengeance, and many fled from their country. At length a band of patriots attacked, vanquished, and expelled these usurpers, and once more established a democratic form of government.

52. *War between Sparta and Thebes.* While Athens and Sparta were visibly declining, the Theban republic rose from obscurity. Sparta was jealous of its rising greatness: a war between the two states ensued. The two armies met at *Leuctra;* the Spartan forces, consisting of 25,000 men, were defeated by the Thebans, who had only 6,400, but were commanded by *Epaminondas,* the greatest soldier of his time. In the battle, the Spartan king, and 4,000 of his men, were killed; the Theban loss was but 300. The Spartans had never before received so severe a wound as this battle. The victorious Thebans now overran the territories of Sparta, and carried fire and sword to the very suburbs of the

---

51. Who defeated the Athenians? What did the Athenians do? What was done after Athens was reduced? What is said of the magistrates?

52. By whom were the Spartans defeated? State the number and losses of each army. What is said of the Spartan territories?

capital. This country had not been ravaged by a hostile army for 600 years; and the boast of the inhabitants, "*that never had the women of Sparta beheld the smoke of an enemy's camp,*" was now done away.

53. *Epaminondas, the Theban General.* Epaminondas is considered as one of the greatest characters of Greece; he was distinguished for patriotism, learning, military talents, and private virtues. When he returned to Thebes, after his victory at Leuctra, he was seized as a traitor, for having violated a law of his country, which prohibited any citizen retaining the supreme command for more than one month. In answer to this he said, that he would submit to the law of his country, but he wished to have it inscribed on his tomb, "*that he suffered death for saving his country from ruin.*" This reproach was felt, he was pardoned, and again invested with the sovereign command. After a variety of conflicts, the combined forces of Sparta and Athens met the Theban army at *Mantinœa*. A severe battle ensued, in which the Thebans gained a complete victory. Epaminondas, however, was killed in this battle. He had raised his country to the highest eminence in military renown, but its power and splendor perished with him, 363 years before the Christian era. The battle of Mantinœa was followed by a peace between all the Grecian states, which established their independence.

54. *Grecian Philosophy.* Philosophy among the Greeks was said to be, the love and the pursuit of knowledge, or wisdom, and comprehended two distinct branches, namely, the study of nature, which elevates and enobles the soul, and the study of morals, which inspires us with virtue, and leads us to happiness. After the time of Homer, the increasing relish for poetic composition gave rise to a set of men called *Rhapsodists,* who used to recite the compositions of the older poets, on public occasions, and make comments on their merits

---

53. What is said of Epaminondas? Why was he seized as a traitor? What was done with him? What did he do for his country? What effect did his death have?

and doctrines. Some of them established schools, and were dignified with the titles of *Sophists*, or teachers of wisdom. Hence originated various schools, or systems of philosophy, many of which were but little else than a picture of the folly and caprice of the human mind. Some of the philosophers believed in the immortality of the soul, and in the rewards and punishments of a future life, while by others it was supposed that the soul perished with the body.

55. *Socrates, the Philosopher.* Socrates, the wisest, the most virtuous, and the most celebrated philosopher of antiquity, was born at Athens, 470 years before Christ. He was fond of labor, inured to hardships, and was calm and serene in the midst of dangers and calamities. He bore injuries with patience, which virtue he had sufficient opportunities to practice towards his wife *Xantippe*, a woman of the most whimsical and provoking temper. His principal employment was the instruction of youth ; he kept, however, no fixed public school, but took every opportunity to deliver his lectures, which were given in the most enticing and agreeable manner. He was attended with a number of illustrious pupils, whom he instructed by his exemplary life, as well as by his doctrines. He spoke with freedom on various subjects, religious as well as civil. This independence of spirit, and superiority of mind over the rest of his countrymen, created him many enemies. Socrates taught the belief of a *first cause*, whose beneficence is equal to his power, the Creator and Ruler of the universe. He also taught the immortality of the soul, and a state of future rewards and punishments.

56. *Death of Socrates.* Socrates was accused by his enemies of corrupting the Athenian youth, of making innovations in the religion of the Greeks, and of ridiculing

---

54. What was philosophy among the Greeks said to be? What did it comprehend? What is said of the Rhapsodists? The Sophists? What is said of the systems of philosophy, and the philosophers?

55. Who was Socrates, and where was he born, and at what time? What is said of him? What did he teach?

ANCIENT HISTORY. 47

Socrates about to drink the Hemlock poison.

the gods. He was summoned before the council of five hundred, and by a majority of three, was condemned to death by drinking hemlock. In his defense he spoke with great animation, and the whole of his discourse was full of simplicity and noble grandeur. The hour appointed for drinking the hemlock having come, they brought him the cup, which he received without any emotion, and then addressed a prayer to heaven; he then drank off the poison with the utmost tranquillity. Observing his friends weeping, he reproved them with the greatest mildness, for, says he, " I have always heard that it is our duty calmly to resign our breath, giving thanks to God." After walking about a little while, feeling the poison begin to work, he lay down on his couch, and in a few moments expired, at the age of 70 years. After his death the Athenians lamented his fate, and considered the misfortunes which afterwards befell the republic, as a punishment for the injustice of putting him to death.

57. *Plato, the Philosopher.* Plato, a celebrated philos-

---

56. Of what was Socrates accused? What was done wi h him? Relate the manner of his death. What did he say to his friends?

opher of Athens, was at the age of twenty introduced to Socrates, and during eight years continued to be his pupil. After the death of Socrates, Plato visited Egypt, Persia, and other places, for the purpose of improving himself in the various branches of knowledge. On his return, he gave public lectures in the public grove called the *Academy*, which was adorned with temples, statues, &c., and his disciples were called the *Academic* sect. He was attended by crowds of noble and illustrious pupils, and for forty years labored in teaching the sublimest precepts, and composing those dialogues which have been the admiration of every age. His writings were so celebrated, and his opinions so respected, that he was called *divine*. Plato had the most sublime ideas of the Supreme Being; he taught, that amid all the changes and afflictions of life, man was an object of his regard, and that his soul was immortal. His philosophy and ideas were remarkably refined; hence those sentiments and affections which are highly refined, pure, and spiritual, are called *Platonic*. Plato died in the 81st year of his age, 348 years before Christ.

58. *Pythagoras.* This philosopher, the founder of the Italian, or *Pythagorean* sect, was born at Samos, it is supposed about 550 years before the Christian era. Pythagoras introduced into the western world a doctrine which it was supposed he obtained somewhere in the East, during his travels, namely, that of the *transmigration of souls*; which taught, that when men died, their souls passed into, and animated other bodies. If, for example, a man was wicked, his soul animated the body of some unclean animal, and passed through a progress of misery, proportioned to his crimes in this life. His disciples lived in common, strictly abstained from eating flesh, and held music in high estimation, as a corrector of the passions. Pythagoras was also distinguished for his discoveries in geometry, astronomy, and mathematics. His system of the universe, in which he

---

57. Who was Plato? Where did he give lectures? What were his disciples called? What did he teach?

placed the sun in the center, and all the planets moving about it, was deemed a wild fancy, till it was proved to be true by the discoveries of modern times.

59. *Cynic Philosophers.* Antisthenes, a disciple of Socrates, founded the sect of the *Cynics*, so celebrated for the austerity of its maxims, and audacity of its followers. Virtue, in their opinion, consisted in a great measure in renouncing all the conveniences of life. They clothed themselves in rags, slept and eat in the streets, condemned knowledge as useless, and indulged themselves in censuring all the rest of mankind. *Diogenes* was also a philosopher of this sect. When he came to Athens, Antisthenes at first refused to admit him into his house, and even struck him with a stick. Diogenes calmly said, "Strike, but never shall you find a stick hard enough to remove me from your presence, whilst there is any thing to be gained from your conversation and acquaintance." Such firmness recommended him to Antisthenes, and he became his most devoted pupil. Diogenes walked about with a tub or cask on his head, which served him as a house, and a place of repose. Such singularity, joined to the greatest contempt for riches, gained him great reputation, and Alexander the Great condescended to visit him in his tub. He asked Diogenes if there was any thing in which he could gratify or oblige him? "*Get out of my sunshine,*" was the only answer from the philosopher.

60. *Of the Stoics.* The sect of the *Stoics* was founded by Zeno, a native of Cyprus, who died 264 years before Christ, at the age of 98. His followers derived their name from a portico at Athens, where Zeno gave his lectures. The Stoics believed that all

---

58. Who was Pythagoras? Where born, and at what time? What doctrine did he introduce? What is said of his disciples? In what discoveries was he distinguished? What is said of his system of the universe?

59. Who was the founder of the Cynics? What were their opinions and manners? What is said of Diogenes? What did he say to Alexander the Great?

60. By whom was the sect of Stoics founded? From what

nature, and God himself, the soul of the universe, was regulated by fixed and unalterable laws; that every thing took place by unavoidable necessity, or fate. Their chief aim seems to have been, to render themselves insensible to the miseries incident to human life. For this purpose they labored to convince themselves that "every thing that happens, is for the best." "One part of valuable knowledge," said Zeno, "is to be ignorant of what we ought not to know." A perfect Stoic did not regard even pain as an evil. Their philosophy was calculated to render them devoid of passion and frailty; and it must be allowed, that some of the greatest and most virtuous men of antiquity embraced the principles of the Stoic philosophers.

61. *Of the Epicureans.* This sect was founded by *Epicurus*, who was born near Athens, about 200 years before Christ. He gave proofs of his great genius at an early age. After having improved his mind by traveling in many countries, and hearing the lectures of the wise men of the age, he established himself at Athens, at that time the common resort of philosophers of every sect. By the sweetness and gravity of his manners, and by his social virtues, he soon attracted followers. He taught them, that the happiness of mankind consisted in *pleasure;* not such as arises from sensual gratifications and vice, but from the enjoyments of the mind, and the practice of virtue. Epicurus, however, held that the Deity was indifferent to the actions of men. His doctrines were rapidly spread over the world, and as the great majority of mankind, practically at least, appear to consider the gratification of the senses as the greatest pleasure, in preference to the practice of virtue, the morals of the people were undermined and destroyed. So addicted were those who professed to be his followers, to gluttony, intemperance, &c., that to this day

---

was their name derived? What was their belief? What is said of the Stoics and their philosophy?

61. By whom were the Epicureans founded? What is said of Epicurus? What did he teach? What is said of his doctrines?

those who indulge their appetites in like manner, are called *Epicures.*

62 *Of Aristotle and Pyrrho.* Aristotle was a native of Macedonia. He went to Athens and spent twenty years under the instructions of Plato, and afterwards opened a school for himself. He was a number of years instructor to Alexander the Great. The writings of Aristotle treat of almost every branch of knowledge known in his time: moral and natural philosophy, metaphysics, grammar, criticism, and politics, all occupied his attention. His philosophy had great influence over the minds of men during sixteen centuries. *Pyrrho* was a *sceptic* philosopher in Greece, who flourished about 300 years before Christ. The *Sceptics* held that universal doubt is the only true wisdom; and in their opinion, there was no material difference between virtue and vice. Tranquillity of mind they considered as the state of the greatest happiness, and this was to be obtained by indifference to all creeds and opinions. When Pyrrho was at sea, during a storm, and destruction seemed inevitable, he appeared calm and unconcerned, and pointing to a pig at the time quietly feeding, he told the crew, who were lost in lamentations, " this is a true model of a wise man."

63. *Grecian Historians.* Herodotus, the first authentic historian among the Greeks, was born in Asia Minor, about 484 years before the Christian era. In his travels he made himself acquainted with the history of other countries; he arranged the materials which he had collected into the history which is still preserved. He recited to the people, at the Olympic games, the history he had composed; it was received with such applause, that the name of the Nine Muses was given to the nine books into which it was divided, and procured for its author the title of " father of history."

Thucydides, a few years younger than Herodotus,

---

62. What is said of Aristotle? How long did his philosophy have influence? Who was Pyrrho? What is said of the Sceptics? Relate an anecdote of Pyrrho.

wrote with great ability the history of the first twenty-one years of the Peloponnesian, or civil war of Greece. He was a commander in this war for seven or eight years, examined every thing, collected materials, and made accurate memorandums of every transaction. Having lived in exile a number of years, he had sufficient leisure to execute his purpose. His history is distinguished for the fire of his descriptions, the conciseness, and at the same time, the strong and energetic manner of his narratives. Demosthenes, the celebrated orator, so much admired the history of Thucydides, that he transcribed it eight times, and could almost repeat it by heart.

Xenophon was celebrated as a general, historian, and philosopher; he was born about 450 years before Christ, and was a disciple of Socrates. He accompanied Cyrus the younger, in his attempt to dethrone his brother from the Persian throne. Cyrus was killed, and Xenophon, with 10,000 Greeks, was left in the midst of a victorious enemy, without money and provisions, 600 leagues from home. Xenophon, by his courage and masterly military skill, succeeded in guiding his countrymen, in their celebrated *retreat*, to their homes in safety, an interesting account of which he has given. His writings are distinguished for simplicity and elegance.

Plutarch was a native of Boetia, in Greece; he died about 120 years after the Christian era. His lives of illustrious men are the most valuable literary works of the ancients, describing the private character and manners of celebrated persons, whose actions are recorded by historians.

64. *Of Archimedes.* This celebrated geometrician of Syracuse, flourished about 250 years before Christ. He is distinguished for the ingenious machines which he invented for the defense of Syracuse, when that city

---

63. Who was Herodotus? Where did he recite his history? How was it received? What is said of Thucydides? For what is his history distinguished! Who was Xenophon? What did he do? Who was Plutarch? What is said of his writings?

was besieged by Marcellus, the Roman consul. Some of these machines were so constructed, that he hoisted many of the Roman ships into the air, and then let them fall with such violence into the water, that they were broken and sunk : by his burning glasses he set others on fire. He also constructed engines, which threw stones of an enormous size. He is said to have declared, that if he could find a place out of the earth on which to place a lever, " he could move the world." Syracuse was taken after a siege of three years. The Roman general gave strict orders to his soldiers not to hurt Archimedes. A private soldier, who did not know him, found him deeply engaged in solving a mathematical problem. Being commanded by the soldier to go with him to Marcellus, Archimedes very quietly begged of him to wait for a few moments, till he could finish his problem : but the soldier mistaking his request for a refusal to obey him, killed him on the spot.

65. *Grecian Architecture.* After the defeat of Xerxes, the active spirit of the Athenians wishing for an object to distinguish itself, was signally displayed in works of taste in the fine arts. In these, the Greeks surpassed every nation ; and the monuments which remain are models of imitation, and the standard of excellence among the most polished nations in modern times. The golden age of the arts in Greece endured about a century, after the death of Alexander the Great. The Greeks were the founders of that system of architecture which is universally allowed to be the most perfect. It consisted of three distinct orders, the *Doric*, the *Ionic*, and *Corinthian.*

The *Doric* order has a masculine grandeur, and a superior air of strength to both the others. It is therefore best adapted to works of great magnitude, and of a sublime character. Of this order is the temple of Theseus,

---

64. Who was Archimedes, and when did he flourish ? For what was he distinguished ? Relate what is said he declared. What was the manner of his death ?

65. What is said of the Grecian fine arts ? Mention the three distinct orders of architecture. **Describe the Doric, the**

5*

at Athens, built ten years after the battle of Marathon, and is at this day almost entire.

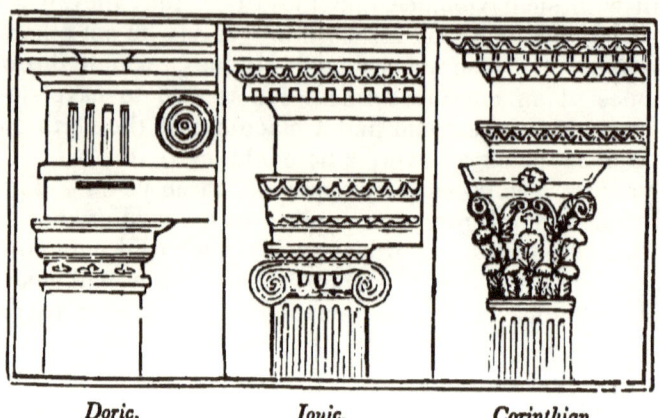

Doric.   Ionic.   Corinthian.

The *Ionic* order is light and elegant, and distinguished for simplicity, which is essential to true beauty. Of this order were the temple of Apollo, at Miletus, and the temple of Diana, at Ephesus.

The *Corinthian* marks an age of luxury and magnificence, where pomp and splendor had become the ruling passion, but had not yet extinguished the taste for the sublime and beautiful. It attempts, therefore, an union of all these qualities. [The *Tuscan* and the *Composite* orders are of Italian origin, but they show that the Greeks had in the three original orders exhausted all the principles of grandeur and beauty.]

66. *Grecian Sculpture, &c.* Sculpture was brought by the Greeks to great perfection. The remains of their sculpture are, to this day, the most perfect models of the art; and modern artists have no means of attaining to excellence so certain, as the study of these

Ionic, and the Corinthian. What is said of the Tuscan and Composite orders?

66. What is said of the Grecian sculpture? What was the cause of their excelling in this art? What is said of their painting? Their music?

ANCIENT HISTORY. 55

master-pieces. The Grecians had the advantage of the moderns in this respect: they had an opportunity of seeing the human figure in its most perfect shape, in their frequent gymnastic exercises, &c.; and their manner of clothing did not disfigure the human form. Another great cause of their excellence in sculpture was, their attempts to represent the numerous gods and goddesses which they worshiped. In the art of *painting*, the Greeks appear to have been inferior to the artists of modern times. The *music* of the ancients, also appears to have been greatly inferior to that of the moderns.

67. *Demosthenes the Orator.* Demosthenes, one of the most celebrated orators that ever lived, was born at Athens, 381 years before the Christian era. At the age of 17, he gave proofs of his eloquence and abilities; but his rising talents were impeded by weak lungs and a

Demosthenes, declaiming by the sea-shore.

difficulty of pronunciation; and on his first attempt to speak in public, he was hissed by his hearers. He, however, overcame all obstacles, by close application. To correct the stammering of his voice, he spoke with pebbles in his mouth. That his pronunciation might be

---

67. Who was Demosthenes? What is said of his first attempt to speak in public? By what means did he cure his

loud, and full of emphasis, he frequently ran up the steepest and most uneven walks. In order to accustom himself to the noise and tumult of a public assembly, he declaimed on the sea-shore, when the waves were uncommonly agitated. That he might devote himself closely to his studies without interruption, he retired to a cave, and shaved half his head, to prevent himself from appearing in public. His abilities as an orator raised him to the head of the government at Athens, and his eloquence carried all before him, and was more dreaded by his enemies than the fleets and armies of Athens. Demosthenes, however, was charged with having received a bribe from the enemy, for which he was banished, but was afterwards recalled. When the generals of Alexander approached Athens, he fled; and to prevent himself from falling into their hands, he took poison.

68. *Philip of Macedon.* The Grecians, after their civil wars, lost in a great measure their simple manners, and the spirit of patriotism. In this situation, Philip of Macedon, by the artifices which he used, and by his military talents, brought the whole of Greece under his dominion. *Demosthenes,* the Athenian orator, endeavored to arouse his countrymen to make a vigorous effort for their liberties. But the event was unsuccessful. The battle of *Cheronæ,* fought 338 years before Christ, decided the fate of Greece, and subjected all her states to the control of the king of Macedon. It was not, however, the policy of Philip to treat them as a conquered people. He allowed them to retain their separate and independent governments, while he controlled and directed all national measures. In a general council of the states, Philip was chosen commander-in-chief of all the forces of Greece. He now formed a project for the conquest of the Persians, whose invasions of Greece, under Xerxes

---

defects in speaking? How did he accustom himself to speak, during noise and tumult? What did he do to apply himself to study?

68. How did Philip of Macedon bring the Greeks into subjection? What was his policy towards them? What project did he form, and what became of him?

and Darius, he resolved to punish n the eve of this enterprise, he was assassinated, a. .e marriage of his daughter, by one of his captains.

69. *Alexander the Great.* Alexander, (afterwards surnamed the *Great,*) the son of Philip, succeeded to the throne at the age of 20 years. He was educated by Aristotle, for whom he ever afterwards had the highest respect, and under such a master, made a most rapid progress in learning. He possessed a generous and heroic disposition, distinguished talents, and unbounded ambition. He very early became the most expert horseman in his father's court, and was the only person who dared to back the famous war-horse *Bucephalus,* sent as a present to Philip, which was so fiery and highmettled, that no one could break him. Philip seeing Alexander on this ungovernable horse, cried out in rapture, " Seek, my son, another kingdom; Macedonia is not worthy to contain you!" The Thebans having risen in rebellion, Alexander defeated them with great slaughter, destroyed their city, and sold 30,000 of the inhabitants for slaves. He then assembled the deputies of the Grecian states at Corinth, who solemnly elected him to be commander-in-chief of the Greeks against Persia.

70. *Battle of the Granicus.* Alexander, having assembled an army of 30,000 foot and 5000 horse, with the sum of 70 talents, and provisions only for a month, crossed the Hellespont. *Darius,* king of Persia, resolving to crush at once the young hero, met him at the river Granicus, with 100,000 foot and 10,000 horse. Alexander, eager to engage the enemy, plunged into the river, and was followed by his troops, and gaining the opposite banks, attacked the astonished Persians, and put to flight their whole army. The Persians lost in this engagement 20,000 foot and 2500 horse: the

---

59. Who was Alexander? What is said of him? Of his war-horse? How was he elected commander?

70. State the number of Alexander's army, and that of Darius. What were their losses? What did Alexander do, after his first victory?

loss of Alexander was only about 200 men, among whom were 25 horsemen of the royal guard, to whose memory he ordered statues to be erected. Drawing from his first success a presage of continued victory, he sent home his fleet; thus showing his army that they must conquer Asia, or perish in the attempt.

71. *Battle of Issus.* Alexander, having for some time continued his march without resistance, was at length attacked by the Persian army under Darius, in a narrow valley of Cilicia, near the town of *Issus*. The Persian host amounted to 400,000 men; but their situation was such, that only a small part of their force could come into action, and they were defeated with great slaughter, their loss being 110,000, while the Greeks lost only 450 men. The mother and two daughters of Darius fell into the hands of the conqueror. The real greatness and heroism of Alexander, now in the bloom of youth, unmarried, and a conqueror, shone forth in the greatest luster. He would not trust himself in the presence of the queen of Darius, who was a woman of great beauty. Far from attempting to derive any ungenerous advantage from his victory, he treated his illustrious captives with the greatest kindness and respect. In consequence of the battle of Issus, the whole of Syria submitted to Alexander. Damascus, where Darius had deposited his treasures, was surrendered by the governor, and the whole of Phœnicia, with the exception of Tyre.

72. *Siege of Tyre.* Alexander now directed his course towards Tyre, and demanded admittance into it, in order to offer a sacrifice to the Tyrian Hercules. Being refused, he immediately besieged the city. New Tyre, which was situated on an island opposite the old city, seemed to be unconquerable without a fleet. Alexander, with immense labor, attempted to join the island to the continent by a causeway. The Sidonians, and some other people, whom he had treated with gentle

---

71. What is said of the battle of Issus? What of the mother, daughters, and queen of Darius?

ness, at last found ships for carrying on the enterprise. He then hastened the siege, and all sorts of warlike instruments were employed by both parties. The place was finally taken by storm, after a siege of eight months. About 8,000 of the inhabitants were put to death, and 30,000 sold into slavery. Having taken Gaza, Alexander passed into Egypt, which readily submitted to his authority, and while here, he founded the city of Alexandria, at the mouth of the Nile.

73. *Final conquest of Persia.* Returning from Egypt, Alexander went into Assyria, where he was met by Darius, at *Arbela*, at the head of 700,000 men. Darius offered Alexander, as terms of peace, ten thousand talents, his daughter in marriage, and the whole country from the Euphrates to the Hellespont. These terms being rejected, Alexander informed Darius that he had no occasion for his money, and as for the provinces he named, he had already conquered them, and that he was ready for another battle, which would probably decide who should remain the conqueror, and that "the world could no more admit two masters than two suns." A battle took place, in which the Persians were defeated, with the loss of 300,000 men. Darius escaped, and fled from province to province, until he was at last murdered by one of his own officers. Thus ended the Persian empire, which submitted to the conqueror 330 years before the Christian era, after having existed two hundred and six years from the time of Cyrus the Great.

74. *Conquest of India.* After the conquest of Persia, Alexander projected the conquest of India, fully persuaded that the gods had decreed him the sovereignty of the whole habitable globe. Finding his troops incumbered with baggage, by which his march was retarded, he gave orders to set fire to it, and began by burning his

---

72. How did Alexander conquer Tyre? By whom was he assisted? What did he do, after the conquest of Tyre, and what city did he found?

73. What did Darius offer Alexander, as terms of peace? What was Alexander's reply? What became of Darius? What is said of the Persian empire?

own. He penetrated into India, where *Porus*, a powerful monarch, opposing his further progress, was defeated and taken prisoner. He penetrated to the Ganges, and would have advanced to the eastern ocean, had the spirit of his army kept pace with his ambition. But his soldiers, seeing no end to their toils, refused to proceed any farther eastward. He therefore returned to the Indus, and caused his army to sail down that river to the ocean: here he sent his fleet to the Persian Gulf, under Nearchus, and with the main body of his army, marched across the desert of Persepolis.

75. *Death of Alexander.* "Finding no more worlds to conquer," Alexander abandoned himself to every excess of luxury and debauchery. It is related, that, through the instigation of *Thais*, a woman of low character, while he

Alexander and Thais burn Persepolis.

was in a drunken frolic, he fired the city of *Persepolis* This place was the ancient capital of Persia, the ruins of

---

74. What did Alexander do, after the conquest of Persia? How far did he penetrate? What prevented his proceeding farther eastward?

75. After Alexander had conquered the world, what did he do? Why did he burn Persepolis? What is farther said of Alexander? What caused his death?

ANCIENT HISTORY. 61

which astonish the traveler to this day, by their grandeur and magnificence. The arrogance of Alexander was now increased, and the ardor of his passions, heightened by continual intemperance, broke out into acts of outrageous cruelty; and while in the heat of passion, he killed Clitus, his best friend. At this period of his life, he appears to have been swollen by flattery and enervated by vice, and to have acted the part of a tyrant. While at Babylon, at an entertainment which he gave to one of his officers, he drank to such excess, that it brought on a fever. Finding that there was no hope of recovery, he delivered his ring to Perdiccas. On being asked to whom he left the empire, he replied, "To the most worthy." Perdiccas having asked him how soon he desired they should pay divine honors to his memory, he answered, "When ye shall be happy." These were his last words.

76. *Of Rome.* Rome, the last of the four great empires of antiquity, becomes, after the conquest of Greece, the leading object of attention. It rose gradually from small beginnings to almost universal empire. The duration of the Roman power, or that of its history, embraces a period of about *twelve centuries,*—from the foundation of Rome to the destruction of the empire, after the Christian era. This great interval may be divided into three grand and distinct epochs, or periods, namely: 1. Rome under *The Kings;* 2. *The Republic;* 3. *The Emperors.*

77. *Roman Kings.* The early history of the Romans, like that of other ancient nations, is mixed with fable. It appears, however, that they were governed by kings for 244 years; and during the reign of the kings, and the early part of the republic, the Roman territories extended only about fifteen or twenty miles around the capital. Of *Romulus,* the first king, some account has been given.

---

76. What is said of Rome? What was the duration of the Roman power? Into what periods may this time be divided?
77. What is said of the early history of the Romans? How long were they governed by kings? Who was the first

Numa Pompilius, a Sabine, was elected second king of Rome. He is represented as a virtuous prince, who cherished the arts of peace, obedience to the laws, and a respect for religion.

Tullus Hostilius, the third king, was of a warlike disposition. His reign is memorable for the romantic story of the *Horatii*, three brothers, who fought for *Rome*, and the *Curiatti*, also three brothers, who fought for *Alba*. One of the Horatii survived, all the rest being slain, and by this contest the Romans became masters of Alba.

Ancus Martius, the fourth king, conquered the Latins, and built the port of Ortia, at the mouth of the Tiber.

Tarquin, the *Elder*, was elected the fifth king of Rome, which he embellished with various works of utility.

Servius Tullus succeeded Tarquin. He created the Roman aristocracy, established the census, in which the number of citizens, their dwellings, number of children, and amount of property, were ascertained.

Tarquin, surnamed the *Proud*, the last king, began his reign by putting to death the chief senators; and by his tyranny and cruelty disgusted all classes of his subjects, and was expelled the throne.

78. *Death of Lucretia.* Sextus, a son of Tarquin the Proud, having entered the house of *Collatinus*, under the mask of friendship, did violence to his wife, *Lucretia*, a noble Roman lady, distinguished for her beauty and domestic virtues. The unhappy Lucretia immediately sent for her husband and father, revealed to them the indignity she had received, conjured them to avenge her wrong, and stabbed herself with a dagger she had concealed about her clothes. Her husband and friends were filled with grief, rage, and despair. Brutus, a relative, and a reputed fool, seizing the bloody dagger, and lifting it towards heaven, exclaimed; "Be

---

king! What was the reign of Tullus Hostilius memorable for! What is said of Servius Tullus? Who was the last king, and what did he do?

78. Who did violence to Lucretia? What did she do? What is said of Brutus? What was done with Tarquin?

witnesses, ye gods, that from this moment I proclaim myself the avenger of the chaste Lucretia's cause. Henceforth, my life shall be employed in opposition to tyranny, and for the freedom and happiness of my country." The body of Lucretia was carried to the public square, the vengeance of the people was aroused, the senate banished Tarquin and his family forever from the Roman state, and the kingly government was abolished, 509 years before the Christian era.

79. *Roman Republic.* The regal or kingly government being abolished, a republican form of government was established. The supreme power belonged to the senate and people; and it was agreed to commit the supreme authority to two *consuls*, who were to be chosen annually from the patrician families. These consuls had the disposal of the public money, the power of assembling the people, raising armies, naming all the officers, and the right of making peace and war. In fact, their power scarcely differed from that of the kings, except their authority was limited to a year. The first consuls were, *Collatinus*, the husband of Lucretia, and Brutus, her avenger.

80. *Judgment of Brutus.* The new form of government was brought to the brink of ruin, almost at the moment of its formation. Tarquin found means to organize a conspiracy among the young nobility of Rome, whose object was to replace him on the throne. This plot was discovered, and the brave and patriotic Brutus had the mortification and unhappiness to discover, that his two sons were ringleaders in this conspiracy. His office was such, that he was compelled to sit in judgment upon them; and while, in this deeply interesting scene, all the spectators were in tears, he condemned them to be beheaded in his presence. The most powerful feelings

---

79. What was the form of government in Rome, after that of kings? To whom was committed the supreme authority? What power did the consuls have?

80. Who conspired against the new government, and who were ringleaders in the plot? What did Brutus do, and what is said of him?

of natural affection were overruled by a sense of his duty as an impartial judge. "He ceased to be a father," says an ancient author, "that he might execute the duties of a consul, and chose to live childless, rather than neglect the public punishment of a crime."

81. *Cincinnatus, the Dictator.* Ten years after the commencement of the Roman republic, Largius was appointed the first *dictator.* This magistrate was chosen only in times of difficulty and danger, when quick and decisive measures were necessary, and could continue in power no longer than six months. The dictator was clothed with power to *dictate*, that is, to direct what should be done, and his power was absolute. About 50 years from the expulsion of Tarquin, the Romans, being in great and immediate danger from an invasion, a solemn deputation was sent to *Cincinnatus*, to invest him with the sovereign power of dictator. They found him laboring on his farm, consisting only of a few acres, which he cultivated with his own hands for the support of his family. He left the plough with regret, and repaired to the field of battle, where he vanquished the enemy, returned to Rome with the spoils, resigned his office, which he held but sixteen days, and though a poor man, would receive no compensation for his important services. At the age of 80 years, he was again called from his farm to the office of dictator, which he held for twenty-one days, during which time he again vanquished the enemy.

82. *The Decemvirs.* The Romans had hitherto possessed no body of written laws. The arbitrary proceedings of their kings and consuls were frequently the subject of complaint, and the citizens became desirous of having a fixed code of laws, for the security of their rights. Three commissioners were therefore sent to Greece in order to procure the laws of *Solon*, and such others as were deemed useful in forming a suitable code. Upon the return of the commissioners, ten of the princi-

---

81. What is said of the dictator? How long could he continue in power? What is said of Cincinnatus?

pal senators, called *decemvirs*, were appointed to frame a body of laws, and put them in force for one year. This was the origin of the celebrated statutes called the "*Laws of the twelve tables.*" The decemvirs were invested with absolute power; each decemvir, by turn, presided for a day. They governed so well for the first year, that they obtained a new appointment, but they soon became tyrannical.

Appius Claudius, one of the decemvirs, having made a base attempt to obtain possession of *Virginia*, a beautiful maiden, her father, Viginius, in order to prevent the dishonor of his daughter, plunged a dagger into her breast. Brandishing the bloody weapon, he exclaimed, "By this blood, Appius, I devote thy head to the infernal gods," and running wildly through the city roused the people to vengeance. Appius soon after killed himself in prison; the other decemvirs were exiled, and the decemvirate having continued three years, was abolished, and the consular government restored.

83. *Military Tribune Censors.* The common people of Rome, or Plebeians, were prohibited intermarrying with the Patricians, or higher class, who held the higher offices of state. If this restraint could be removed, the plebeians and patricians would be placed on an equality. After a long struggle, the distinctions were done away, and it was agreed on both sides, that instead of consuls, *six military tribunes*, with the power of consuls, should be chosen, three plebeians and three patricians. This measure satisfied the people for a time; the consuls, however, were soon restored. The disorders of the republic had interrupted the regular enumeration of the citizens. Two officers were appointed, under the title of *censors*, whose duty it was to make a *census* every five

---

82. Why did the Romans wish for a fixed code of laws? What was done for this purpose? What is said of the decemvirs? What is related of Virginius? How long did the decemvirate continue?

83. What is said of the Plebeians and Patricians? What of the military tribunes? What was the duty of the censors? How did the senate raise an army when wanted?

years, inspect the morals and regulate the duties of the citizens—an office of great dignity and importance. To do away the frequent necessity of the *dictatorship*, as the people many times refused to enrol themselves in the army when wanted, the senate gave regular pay to the troops. In order to raise money, a moderate tax was laid upon the citizens, in proportion to their wealth. By this means the government found soldiers at command ; the army was under its control ; the enterprises of the republic were more extensive, its successes more important, and from this period the Roman system of war assumed a new aspect.

84. *Invasion of Rome by the Gauls.* Veii, a powerful city, 12 miles from Rome, and its proud rival, was taken after a siege of ten years, by *Camillus*. This event was succeeded by a war with the *Gauls*, one of the barbarous nations inhabiting France, then called *Gaul*. These men are represented as exceedingly bold, fierce, of great size and strength, and terrible in war. A numerous body of these men had two centuries before crossed the Alps, and settled themselves in the northern parts of Italy, and were a terror to all the country. Under the command of *Brennus*, their king, they laid siege to *Clusium*, the inhabitants of which implored the assistance of the Romans. The senate sent ambassadors to Brennus, to demand of him what right he had to invade that city. He sternly replied, that the "rights of valiant men lie in their swords," and demanded, in return, what right the Romans had to the many cities they had conquered. The ambassadors having entered Clusium, assisted the inhabitants against Brennus, who was so incensed that he raised the siege, and marched directly against Rome ; and in a great battle, he defeated the Roman army with great slaughter.

85. *Rome taken and burnt by the Gauls.* Brennus, after his victory, marched into Rome without opposition, and going into the forum beheld the ancient senators

---

84. What is said of the city of Veii ? What of the Gauls ? What is said of Brennus ?

sitting in their order unmoved; the splendid habits, the gravity and venerable appearance of these old men, awed the enemy for a while into reverence, but at length they put them all to the sword, massacred all the inhabitants which remained in the city, which they burnt to ashes, and razed the walls to the ground. The Gauls next attacked the capitol; but they were repelled with great bravery. At length, having found a passage to the top of the *Tarpeian* rock, a body of Gauls attempted to gain the summit in the night, which they accomplished while the sentinel was asleep. At this moment, the cackling of some geese in the temple of Juno, awakened Marius Manlius, with his associates, who instantly threw the Gauls headlong down the precipice.

86. *Expulsion of the Gauls.* Brennus having grown weary of the siege of the citadel, proposed to the Romans, if they would pay him a thousand weight of gold he would draw off his army and give them no farther trouble. The gold was brought, but while it was weighing some of the Gauls attempted to kick the beam, to prevent a just weight; the Romans complained of the injustice, but Brennus immediately threw his sword into the balance, and gave them to understand their complaints would be useless. At this moment news was brought, that Camillus, the Roman general, was approaching with an army to the assistance of his countrymen. Having been informed of the deception and insolence of the Gauls, he ordered the gold to be carried back to the capitol, adding, that " Rome must be ransomed by steel, and not by gold." Upon this a battle ensued, in which the Gauls were entirely routed, and Camillus was honored as the second founder of Rome. These events took place about 385 years before the Christian era.

87. *Character of the Ancient Romans.* The Roman people, in these ancient times, exhibited a mixture of

---

85. What did Brennus do? How was the capitol saved?
86. On what terms did Brennus propose to leave them? What was done when the gold was brought? What is said of Camillus?

bravery, superstition, barbarity, discipline, enthusiasm, and wisdom. They were often engaged in war, and generally successful. Their small territory was ravaged, their city burnt by the Gauls, and many of their bravest men killed in battle ; yet they were not conquered, for they had resources left. These consisted of firm and determined spirits,—great souls, fearless of danger and death. To brave danger was to them the field of glory : their only alternative was death or victory. They enjoyed a victory, or endured a defeat, with moderation. They possessed independent and unconquerable minds, endued with invincible bravery and magnanimity. The effect of the invasion of the Gauls roused their martial spirit, and they became more warlike and formidable than ever.

---

87. What is said of the character of the Ancient Romans? What of their territory and resources ! What was the effect of the invasion ?

PERIOD IV.

FROM THE DEATH OF ALEXANDER TO THE CHRISTIAN ERA.

(323 YEARS.)

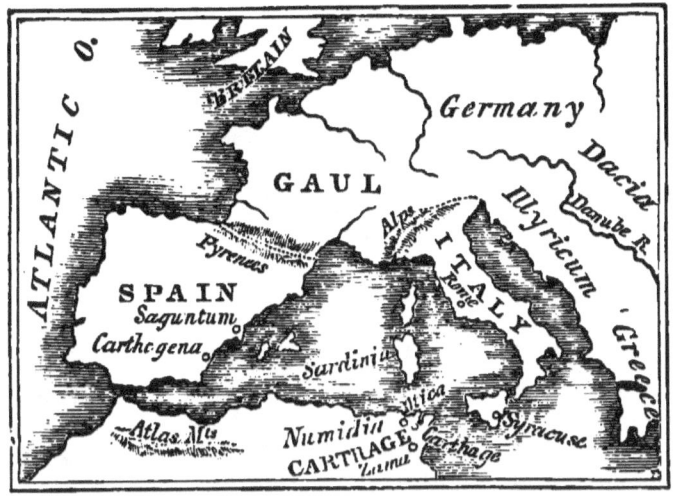

Map showing places mentioned in Period IV.

88. *Successors of Alexander.* Alexander, on his death-bed, having named no successor, his vast empire was soon rent in pieces by the greedy soldiers who had assisted him in acquiring universal dominion. The empire was divided among thirty-three of the principal officers. Hence arose a period of confusion, bloodshed, and crime, with a series of intrigues, fierce and bloody wars, which resulted in the total extirpation of Alexander's family, and a new partition of the empire into four monarchies; namely, that of *Egypt*, under *Ptolemy*; *Macedonia*, including *Greece*, under *Cassander*; *Thrace* with *Bithynia*, under *Lysimachus*; and *Syria*, &c., under *Seleucus*

---

88. To whom was Alexander's empire divided? Into what monarchies? Which were the most powerful?

The two most powerful kingdoms were Syria and Egypt Syria was governed by Seleucus and his descendants, and Egypt by the Ptolemies, till they were both brought under the dominion of the Romans, who, after Alexander, became masters of the world.

89. *Conquest of Italy by the Romans.* After the Romans had expelled the Gauls, they next turned their arms against the *Samnites*, a hardy race of mountaineers inhabiting a tract in the south part of Italy. This contest continued for fifty years; the Samnites fought with great valor and skill, but were finally subdued; and soon after all the states of Italy submitted to the Romans. In the course of the war the *Tarentines*, the allies of the Samnites, sought the aid of Pyrrhus, king of Epirus, in Greece, the greatest general of his age; he landed in Italy with 20,000 men, and a train of elephants, 280 years before Christ. Pyrrhus was at first successful, but afterwards defeated, and he returned to his own dominions.

90. *First Punic or Carthaginian War.* The first Punic war was undertaken by the Romans against Carthage, 264 years before Christ, and lasted 24 years. The two nations had viewed each other with jealousy for a long period, when Sicily, an island of the highest importance to the Carthaginians, as a commercial nation, became the seat of the first dissentions. From a private quarrel the war became general. The Romans gained a victory in Sicily, but as the Carthaginians were masters of the sea, it was of but little consequence. The Romans now earnestly devoted themselves to create a navy. A Carthaginian vessel being wrecked on their coast, it served as a model, and within two or three months they fitted out a fleet of 120 galleys, and put it under the command of the consul *Duillious*, who

---

89. What is said of the Samnites? Of the Tarentines? Of whom did they seek aid? What of Pyrrhus!
90. When was the first Punic War? How long did it last? What was the cause of the war? Who were masters of the sea? How did the Romans create a navy? How did Carthage obtain peace?

defeated the Carthaginian fleet, and took fifty of their vessels. The war continued to rage with various success, in Africa and Sicily, till Carthage, to obtain a peace, was compelled to abandon Sicily, and pay to the Romans 3,200 talents of silver.

91. *Regulus, the Roman Patriot.* The consul Regulus was sent with an army into Africa, where he was defeated, taken prisoner, and confined some years in a dungeon. The Carthaginians being wearied out with the war, sent ambassadors to Rome in order to make peace, and Regulus was allowed to accompany them, hoping he would plead their cause. They however first exacted a promise from him, that if the embassy proved unsuccessful he would return to Carthage, and hinted to him that his life depended on the success of his negociation. Regulus, believing the treaty which the Carthaginians wished to make would be injurious to his country, prevailed upon the Roman senate to reject it, although by so doing his life would be sacrificed. This noble Roman returned to Carthage, where he was punished with the greatest severity. They cut off his eyelids, and he was exposed some days in the strong heat of the sun; he was afterwards confined in a barrel stuck full of nails, whose points entering his flesh, did not allow him a moment's ease ; and to complete their cruelty, they nailed him to a cross, where he expired.

92. *Second Punic War.* From the first Punic war to the Second, was an interval of twenty-three years. During this period Carthage was recruiting her strength, and meditated to revenge her losses and disgrace. She began the second war by besieging *Saguntum*, a city of Spain, in alliance with the Romans. *Hannibal*, one of the greatest generals of antiquity, was the son of *Hamilcar*, the Carthaginian commander in the first Punic war. Hannibal, at the early age of nine years, by the desire

---

91. What is said of Regulus ? What promise was exacted from him ? What advice did he give ? Describe the manner of his death.

92. How long was the interval between the first and second Punic Wars ? Who was Hannibal ? What is said of him ?

of his father, solemnly swore upon the altar, eternal enmity to the Romans. At the age of twenty-six he had the chief command of the army, and having taken *Saguntum*, formed the bold design of carrying the war into Italy. He provided against every difficulty, passed the Pyrenees, and arrived at the Alps, after a toilsome march of five months from his leaving Carthagena in Spain.

Hannibal's Army passing the Alps.

93. *Passage of the Alps by Hannibal.* This celebrated exploit was accomplished in about two weeks. Hannibal followed up the waters of the Rhone, until he arrived at the foot of the Alps; the mountains, with their snowy tops reaching into the clouds, the naked and apparently inaccessible cliffs over which they must pass, the hostile Gauls on the precipices which hung over their heads, ready to check them by rolling down tremendous rocks, were objects well calculated to fill an army with dismay. Hannibal having ascertained that the mountaineers left the pass at night, he with a small party of light troops passed through, and made

---

93. How long was Hannibal in passing the Alps? Describe the dangers of the passage. What number of men did he have after the passage, and how many were lost in it?

himself master of the eminences in the vicinity, and by this means his army gained the first pass; but this was only the commencement of difficulties; sometimes falling into ambush by the treachery of guides, again led through bewildering tracts, and now attacked by large bodies of their enemies. But the resolute Carthaginians pressed onward, and reached the summit on the ninth day. Snow now commenced falling, which increased the danger of the way; but Hannibal arrived on the plains of Italy with 20,000 foot and 6,000 horse, having lost nearly half his army during this perilous enterprise.

94. *Victories of Hannibal.* The first victory gained by Hannibal, after crossing the Alps, was over *Scipio*, who met him near the river *Po*, with a numerous army, soon after he entered Italy. A few days after, he routed another army, under the command of *Sempronius*, with great slaughter. The third army, commanded by *Flammius*, he cut off near Lake Thrasymenus, where the Romans, surrounded by woods and morasses, and hemmed in by their enemies, fought with desperation. Rome was now in the utmost consternation, a dictator was appointed, *Fabius Maximus* being elected to that office. He was sent with an army in quest of Hannibal, but avoided coming into a general engagement with him. This cautious and prudent conduct greatly distressed Hannibal, who frequently offered him battle. The command of Fabius expiring, *Varro*, a man of rash courage, was appointed in his place, who advanced against Hannibal with 90,000 men, the flower and strength of Italy. They fought near *Cannæ*, and the Romans were terribly defeated, leaving forty, some say seventy thousand dead on the field of battle; and it is said that three bushels of gold rings were sent to Carthage, taken from the fingers of the dead Roman knights.

95. *Ending of the Second Punic War.* Immediately after the battle of Cannæ Hannibal sent to Carthage for

94. Describe the first three victories of Hannibal. What is said of the dictator Fabius Maximus? What of Varro? What of the battle of Cannæ?

more troops to complete the reduction of Rome, but owing to the influence of *Hanno*, a powerful demagogue in the senate of Carthage, no assistance was given. Hannibal, however, carried on the war, and kept possession of the finest part of Rome for fifteen years; the Romans, though unable to drive him out of Italy, sent *Scipio* and others into Spain, Sicily, and finally into Africa. Alarmed for the fate of their empire, the Carthaginians recalled Hannibal, who found the affairs of his country in a desperate condition. His army being much inferior to that of the Romans, he endeavored to effect a peace, but Scipio charged the Carthaginians with perfidy and injustice; and both sides prepared for a battle, which was to decide the fate of Carthage and Rome. The hostile armies met on the plains of *Zama*, about five days' journey from Carthage; a memorable battle was fought, and the Carthaginians were totally defeated. A peace soon followed: the Carthaginians agreed to abandon Spain and the islands of the Mediterranean give up nearly the whole of their possessions, and in future undertake no war without the consent of the Romans. Thus ended the second Punic war, 202 years before Christ, after having continued for seventeen years.

96. *Third Punic War.* Fifty years after the close of the second Punic war, the industrious Carthaginians began to recover from the abject state to which that war had reduced them. Cato the Censor, who swayed the decisions of the Roman senate, having occasion to visit Carthage, on his return gave such accounts of its growing power, that he awakened their jealousy, ending all his speeches, it is said, with this expression, " *Carthage must be destroyed.*" At this period the Carthaginians attempted to repel the *Numidians,* who had invaded their territories; the Romans pretending this was a vio-

---

95. What did Hannibal do after the battle of Cannæ? How long did he continue in Rome? Why was Hannibal recalled? Who were defeated at Zama? Why did the Carthaginians agree to have peace?

96. Who visited Carthage? With what expression did he end his speeches? What did the Romans do?

lation of their treaty, made it a pretext for sending an army to Carthage. Conscious of their inability to resist the Romans, the Carthaginians offered every submission, and even consented to acknowledge themselves the subjects of Rome. The Romans demanded 300 young Carthaginians of the first distinction, as hostages for the strict performance of every condition the senate should require. These severe terms were submitted to, and the hostages were given.

97. *Destruction of Carthage.* The Romans having obtained possession of the hostages, the Carthaginians were told that they must deliver up all their arms ; to this they also were obliged to consent. They were then required to remove from Carthage, as the Roman people were determined to demolish the city. This demand was heard by the inhabitants with indignation and despair : they shut their gates, and determined to defend themselves to the last extremity. The delay of the Roman consuls, who did not expect much resistance from a disarmed city, gave time to the inhabitants to make preparations for a siege. The temples, palaces, and open squares, were changed into arsenals, where men and women wrought day and night, in the manufacture of arms. After a desperate resistance for three years, the city was taken by *Scipio*, and was burnt by a fire which raged during 17 days. Such of the inhabitants as disdained to surrender themselves as prisoners of war, were either massacred or perished in the flames. Thus was Carthage, which had existed for 700 years, and containing at the commencement of the war 700,000 inhabitants, reduced to ashes, and even Scipio, the Roman consul, wept over the ruins of the proud rival of his country.

98. *Corruption of the Roman Commonwealth.* The same year in which Carthage was destroyed, Corinth

---

97. What did the Romans require of the Carthaginians? When required to demolish their city, what did they do ? How long did they resist the Romans ? How long had Carthage existed, and how many inhabitants did it contain ?

was taken and Greece was reduced to a Roman province. The power of Rome was now widely extended; her arms everywhere triumphant, and she was freed from the fear of a rival. Her power and splendor drew to her men of learning, taste, ambition, and enterprise, and in short, men of every description, from almost every nation. The descendants of the ancient Romans became few in comparison with the great number who, by some means or other, became citizens or obtained a residence in Italy. While Rome drew art, elegance, and science, from Greece, she drew wealth, luxury, effeminacy, and corruption, from Asia and Africa. In the unequal distribution of this imported wealth, the vices to which it gave rise, the corruption, bribery, extortion, and oppression, which followed, we see the cause of those fatal disorders which extinguish the spirit of liberty, and put a period to the republic.

99. *The Gracchi.* This name is given to *Tiberius* and *Caius Gracchus*, two noble youths, whose zeal to reform the growing abuses and corruptions of the Roman state, drew them into measures destructive of all government and social order. Tiberius, the elder of the brothers, urged the people to assert by force, the revival of an ancient law for limiting property in land, and thus lessen the overgrown estates of the nobility of patricians. A tumult was the consequence, in which Tiberius and 300 of his friends were killed in the forum by the senators. This fatal example did not deter his brother Caius from pursuing a similar course, in endeavoring to maintain by force the privileges of the people against the encroachments of the senate. But, like his brother, he fell a victim to the attempt, with 3000 of his partisans, who were slaughtered in the streets of Rome. From this period, civil disorders followed in quick succession, to the end of the commonwealth.

---

98. When was Greece reduced to a Roman province? What is said of the power of Rome? How did the Roman people become corrupt?

99. Who were the Gracchi? By what means did Tiberius lose his life? What is said of Caius Gracchi?

100. *War of Jugurtha.* The circumstances attending this war, give decisive proof of the corruption of the Roman manners. *Jugurtha*, a grandson of Masinissa, attempted to usurp the throne of *Numidia*, in Africa, by destroying his cousins, *Heimpsal* and *Adherbal*, sons of the deceased king. He murdered the elder, but Adherbal escaping, applied to Rome for aid ; but the senate being bribed by Jugurtha, divided the kingdom between the two. Jugurtha then declared open war against his cousin, besieged him in his capital, *Cirta*, and finally put him to death, and seized the whole kingdom. To avert a threatened war, Jugurtha went to Rome, plead his own cause in the senate, and once more, by bribery, prevailed upon them to free him from all charge of criminality. A perseverance in a similar course of conduct, roused the vengeance of the Romans, who sent an army against him. Jugurtha was taken prisoner, led in chains to Rome, and confined in a dungeon, where he was starved to death, 103 years B. C.

101. *Social and Civil Wars.* A confederacy of the states of Italy against Rome, to obtain the rights of citizenship, occasioned the *Social War*, which raged for several years, in which 300,000 men are said to have perished. It was ended by giving the rights of citizenship to all the confederates who would peaceably return to their allegiance. The *Civil War* commenced 88 years B. C., between *Marius* and *Sylla*. These men being leaders of the Republic, became rivals and enemies, and carried on a bloody warfare against each other. It was attended with the most horrible massacres of the citizens ; and from the time of Sylla, Rome never saw another moment of freedom. In the civil war, 33 persons who had been consuls, 200 senators, and 150,000 Roman citizens, perished, and thousands were left to

---

100. Who was Jugurtha? Who Adherbal? By what means did Jugurtha obtain the kingdom? What finally became of Jugurtha?

101. What occasioned the *Social Wars* in Italy? How many men are said to have perished? Who were Marius and Sylla? What is said of the Civil Wars?

7*

drag out a miserable existence, without friends or means of subsistence. Rome, the mistress of the world, was compelled to submit to her blood-thirsty tyrants; and her cruelties to Carthage and other fallen enemies, were visited upon her own head.

102. *Caius Marius.* This celebrated Roman was a plebeian by birth, and his parents were poor. He was a man of very great stature, strength, and bravery. Having passed through the lower grades of life, he was elected seven times to the office of consul. He distinguished himself in the war against Jugurtha. After the defeat of that king, Rome was invaded by an army of 300,000 barbarians; Marius being consul, defeated them in two engagements, in which the barbarians lost 100,000 killed, and 90,000 prisoners. In the following year a total overthrow of the *Cimbri* took place, in which 140,000 were slaughtered by the Romans, and 60,000 taken prisoners. Marius, with his colleague, Cattullus, then entered Rome in triumph. *Sylla,* who had now become formidable by his great victories over Mithridates, a powerful monarch in the East, now refusing to obey Marius, returned to Italy, and drove him from Rome. Marius was afterwards taken prisoner and condemned to death. The executioner, who entered his dungeon, was so intimidated by the stern voice and countenance of the fallen general, who demanded, if " he dared kill Caius Marius," that he threw down his sword, and declared he found it impossible to kill him. The governor considering the fear of the executioner such an omen in favor of Marius, that he released him.

103. *Return of Marius to Rome.* Marius having been released, fled to Africa, and while wandering near Carthage in a melancholy manner, he received orders from the pretor who commanded there, to retire. He prepared to obey, and said to the messenger, " Tell your

---

102. Who was Caius Marius? Relate his victories. Who drove Marius from Rome? How was the life of Marius saved?

103. To what place did Marius flee? Who was Cinna? What did Marius and Cinna do?

master that you have seen Marius sitting among the ruins of Carthage." Sylla, having left Rome to complete his eastern conquest, Cinna, a partisan of Marius, who had been left behind, applied to the army, which, with a general consent, agreed to nominate him consul, and follow him to Rome. While thus engaged in the cause of Marius, tidings were brought that Marius and his son, escaping from numerous perils, had returned to Italy, and were on the road to join him. Their army soon increased, and they entered Rome like conquerors. Their enemies were inhumanly sacrificed, and Rome was filled with blood. Marius made himself consul, with Cinna, and died the month after, in a fit of debauchery, at the age of seventy.

104. *Sylla, the Dictator.* This bloody and revengeful tyrant was a Roman, of noble family. He served at first under Marius, and afterwards distinguished himself by his victories in the East. After the death of Marius, Cinna having been vanquished, Sylla entered Rome without resistance. The senate and people now found that they had exchanged one brutal tyrant, for another still more bloody. He caused lists of people he disliked to be put up in public places, offering rewards to such as would kill them. These lists of proscription were daily renewed, and whoever favored a proscribed person, although his own father or brother, was himself devoted to death ; while those who destroyed their friends were rewarded. The streets were daily filled with dead bodies, and 7000 citizens, to whom Sylla had promised pardon, were suddenly massacred in the circus, and the insulted senate then sitting near, were compelled to hear their groans. Having compelled the people to appoint him *perpetual dictator*, he continued in this office for three years without control, when to the astonishment of mankind, he resigned it of his own accord. He retired to

---

104. Who was Sylla ? What did he do to those whom he disliked ? To what office did he compel the people to appoint him ? How long did he continue in this office ? What did he do afterwards ?

his country-seat, where he wallowed in the most debasing vices, and soon perished of a most loathsome and painful disease, 78 years B. C., in the 60th year of his age.

105. *Catiline's Conspiracy.* About 63 years before the Christian era, a most dangerous conspiracy broke out, headed by Catiline, who was descended from a very illustrious patrician family of great antiquity. He had been brought up amid the disorders of a civil war, and had been the instrument of the cruelties of Sylla, to whom he was devoted. Destitute of morals or religion, a reputed murderer, he bore a character of the foulest infamy. By his extravagance he contracted vast debts, and being unable to pay them, he grew desperate, and aimed at nothing less than the highest and most lucrative employments. For this purpose, he associated with those young Romans whose excesses had ruined their fortunes, and rendered them the contempt of every discerning person in the city. These abandoned wretches formed a horrid conspiracy, to murder the consuls and the greater part of the senators, and then seize upon the government. This plot was daily strengthened by the young persons who had been brought up in luxury, but now lacked the means to support their extravagances, and in hope, that by a revolution in the state, they should receive a share of the public treasure.

106. *Discovery of Catiline's Plot.* Several women of the first families in Rome, of profligate character, were likewise engaged in Catiline's conspiracy. *Cicero*, the celebrated orator, then consul, found means to bribe *Fulvia*, a lady of illustrious family, whom she dishonored by her profligacy and intimacy with one of the chief conspirators. From this woman Cicero obtained such information as enabled him to counteract all Catiline's projects. Soon after, Cicero accused Catiline, while he

---

105. Who was Catiline? Describe his character. Who were his associates, and what conspiracy did they form?
106. How was Catiline's plot discovered? By whom was he accused in the senate? What did Catiline do, and what became of him?

was in the senate, of his impious plot; but he endeavored to clear himself of the charge. Finding he could not convince the senators of his innocence, he left Rome immediately and retired to Gaul, where his partisans were assembling an army. Five of the principal conspirators were arrested and executed immediately. Catiline having collected his partisans, was attacked by a superior force, and though he fought desperately, was killed, with all his troops.

107. *Julius Cesar and the First Triumvirate.* After the death of Catiline, Julius Cesar rose into notice by his military services in various parts of the Roman empire. When a young man he was proscribed by Sylla, who dreaded his abilities and ambition: " There is many a Marius," said he, " in the person of that young man." Cesar, however, knowing the danger of his situation, conducted prudently, and courted popularity without that show which gives alarm to a rival. *Pompey*, distinguished for his talents and military fame, and *Crassus*, for his great wealth and liberality, were competitors for the government. Cesar, by his address, had the power to reconcile these professed enemies, and to unite them to himself. These three men formed the design, in which they succeeded, of governing the state, and agreed that nothing should be transacted in the republic, without their joint approbation; this form of government was called the *First Triumvirate.* The *triumvirs* divided the foreign provinces among themselves; Pompey received Spain and Africa, Crassus took Syria, which was the richest, and Cesar took Gaul.

108. *Invasion of Britain by Cesar.* Cesar having conquered the numerous tribes in Gaul and Germany, he turned his arms towards Britain. The inhabitants at that time were in a barbarous state: they were, however, brave and warlike. Landing at Deal, Cesar attacked them, but was opposed with zeal and courage.

---

107. What is said of Julius Cesar? What did he do with regard to Pompey and Crassus? How was the First Triumvirate formed?

The irregular skill and courage of these barbarians were, however, no match for the disciplined Roman legions; Cesar defeated them, and bound them to submission during his absence to Gaul. After a winter's residence he returned to Britain with a greater force, and prosecuting his victories, brought a considerable part of the island under the Roman dominion, 54 years B. C. It is related by historians, that Cesar, in his expeditions into Gaul, Germany, and other places, during the space of ten years, conquered 800 cities. He also subdued 300 different nations or tribes, and defeated in different battles three millions of men; of which about a million were slain in battle, and an equal number made prisoners.

109. *Rivalship between Pompey and Cesar.* Crassus, having been killed in the war in Syria, Pompey and Cesar, each aspired to the supreme command. The senate and nobility of Rome sided with Pompey. Cesar relied on his veteran troops, and the common people, whom he had won by his liberality. Pompey, by his influence with the senate, caused them to pass an order, commanding Cesar to disband his troops by a certain day. Cesar, upon this, passed the Alps, and halted at Ravenna, from whence he wrote to the senate, informing them that he would lay down his command, if Pompey would do the same; but if that general kept his command, he for his part knew how to maintain himself at the head of his legions. He concluded his letter by saying, "If I have not justice immediately done me, I will march to Rome." The senate, apprehensive of his designs, passed a decree, branding with the crime of parricide any commander who should dare to pass the Rubicon (the boundary between Italy and the Gauls) with a single cohort, without their permission.

---

108. Where did Cesar land in Britain? What is said of the natives? At what time was Britain brought under subjection to the Roman power? What is related of Cesar's expeditions?

109. Who were on the side of Pompey? On whom did Cesar rely? What order did the senate pass respecting Cesar? What reply did Cesar send the senate? What decree did the senate pass?

ANCIENT HISTORY. 83

Cesar passing the Rubicon.

110. *Cesar's passage of the Rubicon.* When Cesar, with his army, having arrived on the banks of the Rubicon, he is said to have paused before passing it, impressed with the greatness of the enterprise, and its fearful consequences. "If I do not pass this river," said he to one of his generals, "I am ruined; and should I pass it, what multitudes shall I ruin!" After considering a little, and the animosity of his enemies presenting itself to his mind, he plunged into the river, and cried out, "Let us go whither the omens of the gods, and the injustice of our enemies, call us. The die is cast." The army having crossed the Rubicon, Cesar tore his robe in the presence of the tribunes of the people, and implored the protection of his soldiers, when they all cried out with loud acclamations, that they were ready to die in the service of their general. The quickness of Cesar's movements astonished his enemies. Pompey not being in force to meet him, fled from Rome, and Cesar, soon after, entered the city in triumph.

111. *Cesar's pursuit of Pompey.* The monarchs in the East having declared for Pompey, who had fled

---

110. What did Cesar say when on the banks of the Rubicon? What when passing the river? What is said of his soldiers?

thither, he was able to collect a numerous army. His cause was considered that of the commonwealth, and he was daily joined by crowds of the most distinguished nobles and citizens of Rome. He had at one time 200 senators in his camp, among whom were *Cicero* and *Cato*, whose approbation alone was equal to a host. Cesar having defeated Pompey's lieutenants, in Spain, returned to Rome, where he stayed but eleven days, being anxious to bring Pompey to a decisive engagement. He followed him into Greece, and did every thing to provoke a general battle. The hostile armies met on the plains of *Pharsalia*. The contest was now calculated to excite the deepest interest; the two armies were composed of the best troops in the world, and were commanded by the two greatest generals of the age, and the prize contended for, was nothing less than the Roman empire.

112. *Battle of Pharsalia.* The army of Pompey consisted of more than 50,000 men; Cesar's force was less than half that number, but were much the best disciplined. As the armies approached, the two generals rode from rank to rank to animate their soldiers. The signal was then given for battle, and the contest on both sides was long and bloody, and seemed for some time doubtful. Pompey's cavalry charged with great vigor, and obliged the enemy to give ground. Cesar instantly advanced with his reserved corps, who attacking Pompey's troops with their pikes, threw them into the greatest disorder. Cesar pursued his advantage with so much vigor, that the army of Pompey was entirely routed. The battle lasted from early in the morning till noon. Cesar lost but 1,200 men, while the loss of Pompey was 15,000 killed, and 24,000 prisoners. Cesar,

---

111. Where did Pompey collect an army? By whom was he joined? Where did Cesar follow Pompey? Where did the hostile armies meet, what is said of them, and for what did they contend?

112. What was the force of Pompey, and of Cesar? Give an account of the battle, and the losses on each side. What was the conduct of Cesar after the battle?

on this occasion, showed his usual clemency, humanity, and moderation. He set at liberty the Roman knights and senators, and incorporated into his army most of the prisoners. The baggage of Pompey was brought to him, containing numerous letters of his enemies, which, without opening them, he threw into the fire.

113. *Death of Pompey.* Fleeing from the field of battle, Pompey found means to escape to *Lesbos*, where he had left his wife, *Cornelia*, who, expecting her husband as master of the world, was told, that if she wished to see Pompey with one ship, and that not his own, she must hasten. Their meeting was tender and distressing. With one small galley they embarked for Egypt, to seek the protection of *Ptolemy*, whose father Pompey had befriended. The ministers of the young king wishing to court the favor of Cesar, basely proposed to receive and murder their guest. Accordingly, a boat was sent to the galley, as if to take him on shore. Cornelia, looking after him, as the boat moved onward, saw the assassin stab him through the body, and her shriek of agony was heard upon the shore. The murderers cut off his head, and threw his body on the sand: his freedman burnt it and buried the ashes, over which the following inscription was afterwards placed: " He whose merits deserve a temple, can now scarce find a tomb." Cesar, who pursued Pompey to Egypt, had the head of his rival presented to him, but he turned his face from it with horror, and ordered a splendid monument to be erected to his memory.

114. *Cesar's Expedition into Egypt.* At the time Cesar was in Egypt, the throne of that country was claimed by both Ptolemy and his sister, the celebrated *Cleopatra*. The claims of Ptolemy had been upheld by the Roman Senate, and Cleopatra banished. She now laid her claim before Cesar, who, captivated by her charms, decided the contest in her favor. A war en-

---

113. Where did Pompey flee? Relate the manner of his death. What did Cesar do after the death of Pompey?
114. What is said of Egypt? What of Cleopatra? What

sued, in which Ptolemy lost his life, and Egypt submitted to the Roman arms. Cesar for a while abandoned himself to pleasure, in company with Cleopatra, but was aroused by intelligence of the revolt of Pharnaces, the son of Mithridates, and some of the Asiatic provinces. Cesar subdued him with the greatest ease, and in his letter to the Roman senate, he expressed the rapidity of his conquest in three words: *Veni, vidi, vici,* that is, " I came, I saw, I conquered."

115. *Death of Cato.* After the battle of Pharsalia, the remaining followers of Pompey, under Scipio, Cato, Juba, and others, retired to Africa. A kind of senate was formed at *Utica,* and a little body of people collected, to whom Cato gave laws. Cesar sent an army into that country, and entirely defeated their military force. Cato at first intended to have stood a siege at Utica, but finding the inhabitants could not be relied upon, he changed his resolution, and advised his friends either to escape by sea, or submit to the mercy of Cesar. He embraced them with much tenderness, and discoursed on moral subjects, of which this was the theme : " The virtuous are the only happy and free, and the wicked are ever wretched and slaves." He afterwards laid himself down, and with deep attention read Plato's Dialogue on the Immortality of the Soul. He requested that his sword might be brought to him; his friends implored him not to lay violent hands on himself, but continue among them as their guardian and protector. On receiving his sword, he said, "I am now my own master." He then read the book twice over, and fell into a sound sleep. Upon waking, he made some inquiries respecting his friends: he then retired to a room alone and stabbed himself: the wound not being immediately fatal, was sewed up; but Cato coming to himself, tore open the wound with indignation, and expired. This event finished Cesar's war in Africa.

---

did Cesar do? State the expression he used in regard to his conquests.

115. At what place was a new senate formed? What did Cato do? Relate the manner of his death.

116. *Triumphs of Cesar.* The war in Africa being ended, Cesar returned to Rome, and celebrated a magnificent triumph, which lasted four days. The first was for Gaul; the second for Egypt; the third for his victories in Asia; and the fourth for his victories over Juba and Cato. He rewarded his soldiers with great liberality, and treated the people with rare and expensive shows; and to remove every cause of jealousy, he bestowed the honors of the state on Pompey's friends, equally with his own adherents. By these means he became popular, and the multitude cheerfully yielded up their liberties to their great enslaver. After the final overthrow of Pompey's party in Spain, he was hailed as the "Father of his country." The senate and people vied with each other in acts of servility and flattery; he was made a consul for ten years, created *perpetual dictator*, received the title of *Imperator*, or *Emperor*, and his person was declared sacred.

117. *Cesar's Administration and Improvements.* Finding himself in peace, Cesar turned his attention to the improvement of his empire. He labored to reform abuses, and introduced order into all departments of state. He affected moderation in the enjoyment of his power, though he was evidently eager of its possession; he however turned it to a good account. He adorned Rome with magnificent buildings, drained the Pontine marshes, and improved the navigation of the Tiber. He also reformed the calendar, and with the assistance of the most able astronomers, regulated the year according to the course of the sun. Two months were added to the calendar, and the whole year divided into 365 days. He also added one day to every fourth year, in the month of February, and that year was named *Bissextile*, or leap year. The reckoning of time from his regulation, was called the *Julian* account of time.

---

116. Relate the different triumphs Cesar celebrated. How did he treat the people? What title did he receive?

117. To what did Cesar turn his attention? What did he do with regard to the calendar?

118. *Conspiracy against Cesar.* Though many of the people felt greatly obliged to Cesar for his clemency and liberality, yet they detested the name of king—a title they thought he was about to assume. The fresh honors which the senate continued to heap upon him, excited the envy and jealousy of his enemies. A conspiracy was now formed against him by no less than sixty senators, in order to put him to death. At the head of it were *Brutus* and *Cassius*, men whose lives had been spared by Cesar, at the battle of Pharsalia. Cesar loved Brutus, loaded him with favors, and adopted him as his son. Brutus, though " loving Cesar much, loved Rome more ;" and being guided by what he believed would be for his country's good, joined the conspirators. Cassius thirsted for revenge against an envied and hated superior. The conspirators deferred the execution of their plot till the *"Ides of March,"* a day on which it was supposed that Cesar would be declared king.

119. *Assassination of Cesar.* The Ides of March having arrived, Cesar, while proceeding to the senate-house, met the augur, who had forewarned him of the dangers of that day. " The Ides of March are come," said Cesar. " True," replied the augur, " but they are not yet past." As soon as he had taken his place in the senate, the conspirators came near, under the pretense of saluting him, and presenting petitions. On a signal agreed upon, the conspirators all drew their swords and rushed upon him. Cesar defended himself with great vigor, till seeing Brutus among the assailants, he uttered the exclamation, " And you, too, my son Brutus ;" when, muffling up his face with his robe, he sunk down near the statue of Pompey and expired, having received 23 wounds. Thus fell Julius Cesar,

---

118. What excited a conspiracy against Cesar? Who were the conspirators? When did they intend to execute their plot?

119 What is said respecting the augur? Relate the circumstances of Cesar's death. At what age and at what time was he assassinated?

the master of the world, in the 56th year of his age, 14 years after he commenced his career of conquests in Gaul, and 44 years before the commencement of the Christian era.

120. *Speech of Antony. Flight of the Conspirators.* The Roman people were struck with horror at the murder of Cesar. Although he had made himself master of their lives and liberties, he was generally popular. *Mark Antony*, Cesar's friend, who was at that time consul, summoned the senate. The two parties of which it was composed, agreed that no inquiry should be made concerning Cesar's death, and that his funeral should be performed at the public expense. Antony, who was selected to deliver the funeral oration, artfully exerted the whole power of his eloquence to work on the passions of the multitude. He read Cesar's will in the presence of the people, in which it was discovered that he had left to every Roman citizen a considerable legacy. He then displayed his bloody robe, and his image in wax, in which were discovered the 23 wounds received at his death. When he found the people agitated with grief and anger, he swore by the gods of Rome to avenge his death, and conjured the people to favor him in doing his duty. The populace were now inflamed with rage and indignation against the conspirators, who, to escape from their fury, fled from Rome.

121. *Second Triumvirate.* Cesar, by his will, had appointed *Octavius*, his sister's grandson, his heir, who arrived at Rome soon after his uncle's death. Availing himself of his titles, Octavius gained the senate to his interest, and divided with Antony the favor of the people. The difference between these rivals being settled, it was agreed to admit *Lepidus*, the governor of Gaul, and possessor of immense riches, to a share of the government. These three persons invested themselves with the su-

---

120. What is said of Mark Antony? Relate the circumstances of his funeral oration. How were the people affected?

121. Who formed the second triumvirate? How long did they have the supreme command? What did they do?

preme power for five years, and thus formed the *second triumvirate.* They divided among themselves the provinces, and agreed that all their enemies should be destroyed; and each sacrificed his friends to the vengeance of his associates. Antony consigned to death his uncle; Lepidus, his brother; and Octavius, his guardian and his friend, *Cicero,* the celebrated orator In this horrible proscription, 300 senators and 3,000 knights were put to death.

122. *Death of Brutus and Cassius.* Antony and Octavius having deluged Rome with blood, now turned their arms against Brutus and Cassius, who had fled to Greece, and raised an army of 100,000 men, to restore the commonwealth. The two armies met near *Philippi,* and after a dreadful conflict of two days, the fate of the empire was decided by the total defeat of the republican army. Brutus and Cassius, the last Roman republicans, seeing all was lost, stabbed themselves, it is said, by the same weapons with which they had killed Cesar. The head of Brutus was sent to Rome, and laid at the foot of Cesar's statue; his wife, *Portia,* the daughter of Cato, hearing of his death; determined not to survive him, and when every weapon was removed from her reach, killed herself by swallowing burning coals.

123. *Antony and Cleopatra.* Antony, when at Tarsus, summoned Cleopatra, the queen of Egypt, to answer for her conduct in poisoning an infant brother, and favoring the party of Brutus and Cassius. Cleopatra came to Tarsus in a galley decorated with gold; the sails were made of purple silk, and the oars were inlaid with silver. A pavilion of cloth of gold, was raised upon the deck, under which appeared the queen, robed like Venus, and surrounded by the beautiful young women of her court, representing Nymphs and Graces. Incense was

---

122. Where did Brutus and Cassius flee to? Who was defeated at Philippi? What became of Brutus and Cassius?

123. For what did Antony summon Cleopatra before him? Relate the circumstances of her voyage. What is said of Antony?

burnt on deck : the oars kept time to soft and delightful music, and the whole scene was enchanting. Antony was conquered: he forgot to decide upon her cause, gave up the pursuit of ambition, neglected all his affairs, and abandoned himself to pleasure with the beautiful and licentious queen. He lavished on her the provinces of the empire, for which he was declared an enemy to the Roman people.

124. *Death of Antony and Cleopatra.* Antony having divorced his wife, Octavia, the sister of Octavius, war was declared against him. In the struggle between Antony and Octavius, the strength of the East and West was arrayed against each other. Antony's fleet consisted of 500 ships. Octavius had but half the number of ships, but they were better built and manned. The hostile fleets came to a decisive engagement, near *Actium*, on the coast of Epirus. Victory was sometime doubtful, till Cleopatra fled, with the Egyptian squadron, in the heat of the engagement. Antony abandoned the rest of the fleet, and followed her to Alexandria. Here the base Cleopatra betrayed the cause of Antony, who killed himself in despair. Octavius was desirous of conveying Cleopatra to Rome, in order to grace his triumph ; but she prevented it by causing herself to be bitten by an asp. From her death, Egypt became a Roman province, 30 years before the Christian era.

125. *Reign of Octavius, or Augustus Cesar.* The battle of Actium decided the fate of the commonwealth ; and Octavius, now named *Augustus*, was master of the Roman empire. He wisely avoided the vain show of power, and it was his policy to change the nature, rather than the form of government. He had the address to rule as a king, and yet preserve the appearance of a republican. The empire embraced the best part of Europe, Asia, and Africa. The revenues were immense, and a great army was kept on foot, distributed in the va-

---

124. What is said of the struggle between Antony and Octavius ! What of the engagement near Actium ? What became of Antony and Cleopatra ?

rious provinces. The emperor and his chief counsellors were eminent patrons of learning and the arts. The *Augustan age* of Roman literature, has been the admiration of all succeeding ages. In token of universal peace, the temple of Janus was shut. In the 26th year of the reign of Augustus, and according to the best authorities, *four* years before the time assigned for the Christian era, our *Lord and Saviour Jesus Christ* was born at Bethlehem in Judea.

126. *Character and Education of the Romans.* The Romans under their kings, and in the first ages of the republic, were distinguished for their virtuous and rigid severity of manners. The private life of the citizens was frugal, temperate and laborious. The Roman mothers bestowed the utmost attention to the formation of the mind and character of their offspring. They esteemed this duty sacred; and these, with the necessary occupations of their household, the highest traits of female merit. Next to the care bestowed on the morals of their children, a great degree of attention was given to their language, that they might speak correctly; and the honors of the state were given to those who distinguished themselves by their eloquence. The exercises of the body were also strictly attended to, in order to endure fatigue, and confer strength and agility. It was owing to the virtuous and manly principles which were instilled into the minds of the Roman youth, that all the greatness and prosperity of Rome is to be ascribed.

127. *Industry of the illustrious Romans.* The first magistrates and generals cultivated their fields and thrashed their grain with their own hands. *Cincinnatus,* the saviour of his country, was taken from the plough, when chosen dictator. *Marcus Curius,* who drove Pyrrhus out of Italy, was possessed of but one small

---

125. What is said of Octavius? What of the state of the empire? At what period was our Saviour born?

126. State the character of the Romans during the first periods of their national existence. To what is their greatness and prosperity to be ascribed?

farm, which he cultivated himself. The elder *Cato*, who rose to all the honors and offices of the state, went to work in the fields with his slaves, and sat at the same table and partook of the same food. *Scipio Africanus*, after having defeated four of the Carthaginian generals, conquered the great Hannibal, and rendered Carthage tributary to Rome, labored on his farm. The celebrated *Lucretia*, a noble Roman lady, employed herself in spinning with her female servants. Probity, simplicity, and the love of labor, were virtues as common at that period as they were rare in succeeding ages.

128. *Religion.* The religion of the Romans was nearly the same as that of the Greeks. Their priests did not form a distinct order of the state, but were selected from the most honorable citizens. The priests were of two kinds—those that were common to all the gods, and those that were appointed to the service of some particular divinity; as, the " priest of Jupiter," the " Vestal virgins," who guarded the sacred fire in the temple of Vesta. There were also priests appointed to preside over feasts, processions, &c. The *pontifices*, fifteen in number, were judges in sacred things, and directed what should be done in cases where there was no law. The *pontifex maximus* was the supreme arbiter, or high priest. There were also fifteen priests, whose office it was to keep the *Sibylline books*, in which it was said the future history of Rome was written. These books were obtained in the time of Tarquin the Proud, from a *Sibyl*, or woman supposed to be inspired. They were kept in a stone chest, under the capitol, and consulted in times of great calamity.

129. *Government.* The government among the Romans was at first a monarchy, next a republic, in which

---

127. What is said of the first Roman magistrates and generals? What of Cincinnatus? Marcus Curius? The elder Cato? Scipio Africanus, and Lucretia?

128. What is said of the religion of the Romans? Of their priests? Who were the Vestal virgins? The Pontifices? Who the pontifex maximus? What is said of the Sibylline books?

the aristocratic power prevailed. This power was finally overthrown by the people, who became corrupt. A state of anarchy prevailed, which, according to the common course of things, settled down to a despotism, under the Cesars. The kings of Rome were not absolute or hereditary, but limited and elective. They could not enact laws, make war or peace, without the consent of the senate and people. Their badges were a white robe, a golden crown, and an ivory scepter. They sat in a chair of state, made or adorned with ivory, and were attended by twelve *lictors*, or officers, carrying *fasces*, which were a bundle of rods, with an ax in the center. The consuls, after the banishment of the kings, were put into their places, to perform the duties of royalty. They were two in number, and held their office for one year. At first, they had the same badges of authority, excepting the crown.

130. *Roman Senators.* The senate was composed of 100 old men, and afterwards of 200 or more. They were the council of the king, and by them most of the business of the state was transacted. They were at first nominated by the kings, but were afterwards chosen by the consuls, and at last by the censors. They were distinguished by a particular dress, and had separate seats at the public spectacles. This body usually assembled three times a month, but were often called on other days for special business. On account of their age, gravity, and the paternal care they had of the state, they were called *patres*, or fathers. The *patrician* families were descended from these fathers. The senate, notwithstanding many usurpations on their authority, continued to have, on many points, great authority and influence, in every period of the Roman state.

---

129. What were the forms of government among the Romans? What power did the kings have? What is said of the consuls?

130. Who formed the senate, and how were they chosen? How were they distinguished, and how often did they meet? What families descended from them?

131. *Other Roman Magistrates.* The next in rank to the consuls, were the *prætors*, who took their places when vacant, and were appointed to administer justice, and call assemblies of the senate and people. They also presided at certain public games. Their number varied much towards the end of the republic, and under the emperors. The *tribunes* of the people were officers whose duty it was to guard and protect the *plebeians*, when the patricians became oppressive. They were without tribunal or guards, and without a seat in the senate house; yet they had the power, by a single veto, to suspend or annul the decrees of the senate, and the decisions of the consuls. Their persons were declared sacred; but their authority was confined to the limits of a mile from the city. They were chosen annually. Their number was, at the first, five, afterwards ten. The *pro-prætors* and the *pro-consuls* usually governed the provinces of the Roman empire. The *quæstors* were elected by the people, to take care of the public revenue.

132. *Roman Citizens and Assemblies.* The Roman citizens were not merely the inhabitants of Rome and its environs, but the privilege of citizenship was granted to other parts of Italy, and afterwards to foreign cities and towns in the empire, and this privilege was some times bought with money. The power of the people in Rome was expressed in their assemblies, called the *comitia*. The comitia were summoned to pass laws, elect magistrates, decide concerning peace and war, and try persons accused of certain crimes. The comitia continued in power for upwards of 700 years, when that liberty was abridged by Julius Cesar, and afterwards by Augustus, both of whom shared with the people the right of creating magistrates. Tiberius

131. Who were next in rank to the consuls? What did they do? What was the duty of the tribunes, and what power had they? Who were the pro-prætors, pro-consuls, and quæstors?
132. Who were Roman citizens? What is said of the comitia? How long did the comitia continue to be assembled?

Cesar deprived the people altogether of the right of election.

133. *Arts and Sciences.* During the first ages of the Roman republic, they were without all the elegant improvements of life. War, politics, and agriculture, were the only arts they studied, because they were the only arts they esteemed; and, though a sensible and energetic people, they were rude and illiterate. But, upon the downfall of Carthage, the Romans, having no enemy to dread from abroad, felt secure; and having leisure, they began to cultivate the arts. When they conquered Greece, it put them at once into the possession of every thing rare, curious, or elegant, in the arts and sciences. Asia, which they next conquered, offered all its stores; and the Romans, from being the most simple, soon became acquainted with the arts, the luxuries and refinements of the whole earth.

134. *Roman Poets, Historians, &c.* Virgil, called the "prince of the Latin (or Roman) poets," was born near Mantua, about 70 years B. C. He was well skilled in all the various branches of learning. Notwithstanding he was the pride and admiration of the Roman people, he was uncommonly modest and bashful. When about the age of forty-five, he began his most celebrated work, the *Æneid,* a poem, in twelve books, which engaged his attention for eleven years. It has for its subject the settlement of *Æneas,* in Italy, after his flight from Troy. Virgil died before he had corrected it, and ordered it to be burnt; but this was prevented by Augustus, the Roman emperor. The *Georgics,* said to be the most perfect and finished of all Latin compositions, was a poem of Virgil, in four books, and treats principally of agricultural pursuits.

---

133. What were the arts the Romans studied at the first? When did they begin to cultivate the arts?

134. What is said of Virgil? What was his most celebrated work, and what was its subject? What is said of the Georgics? Who was Horace, and for what was he distinguished? What is said of Livy? Sallust? Tacitus?

Horace, a celebrated poet, received instruction from the best masters in Rome; after which, he completed his education in Athens. He followed Brutus from Athens; but after the battle of Philippi, he abandoned the military life, and returned to Rome, where he devoted himself to literature and poetry. He is distinguished for his *Odes* and *Satires*, and was an Epicurean in sentiment. He was the companion of Virgil, and died eight years before Christ.

Livy, the first of Roman historians, was born at Padua. The work which has brought his name down to all succeeding ages, is his history of the Roman empire. This originally consisted of 142 books, of which only thirty-five remain. The loss of the others is irreparable. His history everywhere bears marks of probity, integrity, and impartiality. He died about 17 years after the Christian era.

Sallust was a Roman senator, and, by embracing the cause of Cesar, was made governor of Numidia, in Africa. He composed a history of Rome, of which only a few fragments remain. His only compositions extant are his history of Catiline's conspiracy, and the wars of Jugurtha, king of Numidia. No one was better acquainted with the vices which prevailed in Rome during his time, and no one condemned them more severely, although a vicious man himself. He died about 35 years B. C.

Tacitus was born about 60 years *after* the Christian era. He wrote the history of some of the Roman emperors, who were the most cruel and abandoned tyrants that every disgraced the human race. Among other works, one respecting the Germans is very valuable; and his writings abound with just sentiments.

Pliny the *Elder*, and the *Younger*, were also historians of note, after the Christian era.

135. *Cicero, the Roman Orator.* Marcus Tullius Cicero, one of the greatest orators of antiquity, was born about 107 years B. C. His father was a Roman knight, and took great care of his education. He was naturally of a weak and delicate constitution and he visited Greece

on account of his health. On his return, he soon distinguished himself above all the speakers of that age, and was raised to offices of dignity. One of his most celebrated orations was against *Verres*, who had been prætor in Sicily, where he was guilty of rapine and cruelty. When in the office of consul, he had the skill and address to suppress the horrid conspiracy of Catiline; and for this great service, he was honored with the title of the *father of his country*, and "second founder of Rome." In the great contest between Cesar and Pompey, he joined the latter, and after the battle of Pharsalia, returned to Rome, and was received into favor by Cesar. When the *triumvirs* succeeded to the government of Rome, after the death of Cesar, Cicero was proscribed. As he was fleeing in a litter towards the sea, he was overtaken, beheaded, and his head and right hand carried to Rome.

136. *Domestic Life and Manners.* At the period when the Roman empire was fully established, the day was spent, in Rome, by the higher and lower ranks of the people, as follows: the morning was devoted to visiting the temples, and attending the levees of the great, and the patricians visited each other. From the levee, they proceeded to the forum, either for business or pleasure. At noon, the hour of dinner, they partook of a slight repast, and of which it was not customary to invite any guests to partake. After dinner, the youths repaired to the *Campus Martius*, where they engaged in athletic exercises and sports till sunset. The elder class retired an hour to repose, and then passed the afternoon in literary and other conversation with their friends: others went to the theaters, or to the shows of the circus or amphitheater. After these occupations, it was customary to go to the baths. From the bath they went immediately to supper, which was their principal meal,

---

135. Who was Cicero? When consul, what conspiracy did he suppress! Relate the manner of his death.
136. How was the day spent in Rome by the people? After dinner what was done? When was their principal meal?

ANCIENT HISTORY. 99

and taken about the ninth or tenth hour, counting from sunrise. They sometimes partook of a portion of food in the morning and after supper, but it was not considered a regular meal.

137. *Diet, and Luxurious Habits.* The diet of the earlier Romans consisted of milk and vegetables, with a coarse kind of pudding, which served for bread. They rarely indulged in meat, and wine was almost unknown. But when they became rich, by the conquest of other nations, their vices and luxurious habits were introduced. The luxury of the Roman suppers far exceeded every thing known among the moderns. Cookery became a science, and the number and costliness of the dishes was scarcely credible. All parts of the empire were ransacked, and no expense was spared to gratify the appetite, and many things were esteemed only in proportion to their cost. Thus the tongues and brains of Maltese cranes, peacocks, and rare singing birds, &c., were esteemed great delicacies, and were procured at an enormous expense. Gluttony was sometimes carried to such an excess, that emetics were taken, to throw off from the stomach one full meal, in order to make room for another.

138. *Public Amusements.* Theatrical amusements, though condemned by the early Romans, at length became popular. There were many public games connected with their religion, where much licentiousness was allowed; the shows exhibited in the circus were contests of strength and agility, mock fights, combats of wild beasts, chariot and horse-races. Criminals were condemned to fight with wild beasts; others did so for hire. Great numbers of lions, leopards, bears, and ele-

---

137. What was the diet of the earlier Romans? What was it when they became rich? To what an extent was their gluttony sometimes carried?

138. What is said of the theatrical amusements of the Romans? Their public games? Shows exhibited in the circus, and the gladiatorial shows? What is said of Trajan? Of the coliseum?

phants, were sent from the provinces, for the amusement of the people. Pompey, on one occasion, treated them with the spectacle of 500 lions, which were dispatched in five days. The *gladiatorial shows* had great attractions for the Romans. Not only the populace, but senators, and Roman ladies of distinction, were eager to behold these brutal scenes. The *gladiators* were persons who fought with weapons, in a public circus, or amphitheater, for the gratification of the audience. Great numbers of men were killed on these occasions. Trajan, the emperor, exhibited games for one hundred and twenty-three days, when 10,000 wild beasts were killed, and 10,000 gladiators fought. Amphitheaters were erected for the convenience of the spectators, one of the most celebrated of which was the *Coliseum*, being capable of containing 100,000 persons. The ruins of this structure are still to be seen.

139. *Military Affairs.* The education of the Romans, and all their institutions, were calculated to encourage a military spirit. It was their perfect discipline, making a great multitude act as one man, that rendered their armies victorious. The *Roman legion*, so celebrated for its arrangement and discipline, varied at different periods from 3,000 to 11,000 men. The legion, when in order of battle, was drawn up in three lines : the first consisted chiefly of young men ; the second line was formed of men of middle age ; the third line consisted of veterans of tried valor. The men in the first two lines were armed with a heavy *javelin*, or spear, about six feet in length, a sword, and a shield. The head of the javelin consisted of a point of steel, of a triangular shape, 18 inches in length, and was commonly thrown from 8 to 12 yards distance, and was a terrible weapon in the hand of a Roman. When these were discharged, they

---

138. What made the Roman armies victorious? What is said of the Roman legion? Describe the javelin. What is said of the light-armed troops? State the manner of besieging fortified places. What is said of the art of intrenchment?

rushed upon the enemy with two-edged swords. Those in the third line were armed with a long spear, sword, and buckler.

The light-armed troops used slings, bows and arrows, and threw light javelins. They advanced before the rest of the army, and annoyed the enemy as much as possible: they retired on the approach of the main body, and rallied in their rear. A body of cavalry was attached to each legion.

In besieging fortified places, the Romans used the *battering-ram*, which was the most effective when applied against a wall. It was formed of a long beam, armed at one end with iron, in the shape of a ram's head. It was suspended in such a manner, that 100 men, by violently thrusting it forward, could break down almost any wall which it could be made to reach.

The art of *intrenchment* was carried to great perfection, especially by Julius Cesar, who was able, with 60,000 men, to defend himself successfully in this manner against an army of 240,000 Gauls.

140. *Military Triumphs.* The highest military honor to which a Roman could attain, was the honor of a triumph. This was a grand solemn procession through the city to the capitol, granted to those generals who, by hard-earned victories and great achievements, had added to the Roman territories, or had delivered the state from threatened danger. The procession passed through the most public streets; musicians led the way; oxen, for sacrifice, with gilt horns and ribbons, and the priests, with their ceremonial dresses, next followed; then the standards taken from the enemy; then carriages, laden with their arms and spoils: the captives followed, in chains. The triumphant general was next in order. He was clothed in a robe of purple and gold, with a crown of laurel on his head, and other decora-

---

140. What was the highest military honor granted to a Roman? Describe a triumph. How was the triumphant general clothed?

9*

tions. He stood in a gilded chariot, drawn by white horses; his friends and relatives accompanied him, and his principal officers were on horseback beside his chariot. His victorious army, also crowned with laurels, came last, singing songs of victory

MODERN HISTORY.

PERIOD I.

DISTINGUISHED FOR THE ESTABLISHMENT OF CHRISTIANITY

Emblems of Christianity.

FROM THE CHRISTIAN ERA TO THE REIGN OF CONSTANTINE THE GREAT

(306 YEARS.)

141. *The Coming of Jesus Christ.* "The fullness of time" having arrived, Jesus Christ, the Saviour of Mankind, was born in Judea. It is supposed by the learned, that he was born four years *before* the common date of the Christian era. Our Saviour made his appearance when the whole world was in a state of peace,—the temple of *Janus*, in Rome, being shut, which was always open in time of war. For more than 700 years this temple was closed but three times. An account of the life of Jesus Christ and the doctrines which he taught, is given to us by divine inspiration, in the books of the New Testament. The Christian religion, under the ministry of the apostles, spread with great rapidity, when the universal wickedness of mankind is considered. The

---

141. At what time is it supposed our Saviour was born? What was the state of the world at this time? What is said respecting the coming of our Saviour?

coming of our Saviour has had an influence upon all civilized nations, and will alter more and more the aspect of all human affairs. When the true spirit of his religion shall universally prevail, this world will become a paradise.

142. *State of the Roman Empire.* At the commencement of the Christian era, the Roman empire comprehended most of the known world. By the conquest of the world, Rome was filled with the riches of the conquered nations. Ambassadors from remote kingdoms daily arrived, to do homage, to court favor or alliance. With the wealth, the Romans imported the manners, luxuries, and vices, of the nations they subdued. The higher classes became indolent, proud, and ambitious; the lower classes were distinguished for a servile spirit, and indifference to the national prosperity. Many of the forms of a free government remained, but force and bribery prevailed at every election, and the populace took part with that candidate for office who could best pay for their favor and support. The Roman people having abandoned their virtuous principles, their liberties were of course destroyed; and in order to exist as a nation, it was necessary to have a despotic government. The history of the Romans fully shows, that freedom and liberty cannot exist among any people whose morals are corrupted, whatever may be their forms of government.

143. *Conquest of Britain.* The first authentic history respecting Britain, commences with its invasion by the Romans, under Julius Cesar, 55 years before the Christian era. Cesar, having conquered Gaul, next turned his arms towards Britain, the inhabitants of

---

142. What was the state of the Roman empire at the commencement of the Christian era? What is said of the higher and lower classes? What of the government? What of the liberties of the people? What does the history of the Romans show?

143. When did Julius Cesar invade Britain? How long was it a Roman province? What is said of Caractacus? Of Boadicea? What did the Roman conquest introduce into Britain?

which, at this period, were considered barbarians. When Cesar lan led, he was opposed with great bravery and courage ;_but the disciplined legions of Rome were more than a match for the irregular skill and bravery of savages, and most of the island, after a while, fell under the Roman power, and continued a Roman province for more than 400 years. The Britons were not, however, easily kept under subjection. In A. D. 51, during the reign of Claudius, Caractacus, a British king, having made a brave resistance, was carried in chains to Rome. Ten years after, Queen *Boadicea* obtained some advantages against the Romans, but was finally defeated in a great battle, in which 80,000 Britons perished. The final conquest of Britain was accomplished by *Julius Agricola*, in A. D. 80. By the Roman conquest, the arts and sciences, and finally the Christian religion, were introduced among the Britons.

144. *Caligula and Nero.* The Roman people having generally become corrupted, most of their rulers were of the same character. Some of their emperors were monsters of wickedness and cruelty. Of these, *Caligula* and *Nero* were the most distinguished. Caligula commenced his reign with mildness and clemency, but soon became proud, wanton, and cruel. He built a temple to himself, and ordered his head to be placed on the images of the gods. He appeared in public places in the most indecent manner, and his conduct towards his own sisters was most shameful. He often amused himself by putting innocent people to death ; and he took such delight in cruelty, that he wished " that all the Roman people had but one neck, that he might dispatch them at a single blow." This tyrant was murdered by his servant, A. D. 11, after a reign of about four years.

Nero, like Caligula, began his reign by acts of kindness, affability, and popularity; but he soon threw off the mask. He caused to be put to death his mother, his fa-

---

144. Who were Caligula and Nero? What is said of Caligula? Relate his wish! What is said of Nero? Why did he set Rome on fire? Relate the circumstances.

ther, his wife, his preceptor, and all who were distinguished for birth, riches, courage, and virtue, who stood in the way of his pleasures or inclinations. In order to have a representation of the burning of Troy, he caused Rome to be set on fire in various places: the conflagration continued for nine days, and most of the city was consumed to ashes. Nero, to enjoy the scene, placed himself in a high tower, and sang on his lyre the destruction of Troy In order to avert the odium of this crime, he charged it upon the Christians, and caused a dreadful persecution against them, in which St. Paul was put to death. A conspiracy was formed against Nero, and he was condemned to death. In order to prevent his execution by his enemies, he killed himself, A. D. 68, in the 32d year of his age, having reigned 13 years.

145. *Invasion of Judea.* Judea became a province of the Roman empire about two years after the birth of Jesus Christ. As the Jews rebelled on every slight occasion, *Vespasian* was sent by Nero into Judea with a powerful army, accompanied by his son Titus. Having conquered the most of Galilee, and while advancing upon Jerusalem, Vespasian heard of the death of Nero, Galba, and others, and of his own election to the throne. Departing, therefore, for Rome, he gave orders to his son to besiege Jerusalem. Titus lost no time in carrying his father's orders into effect. Jerusalem was strongly fortified by nature and art. It was surrounded by three walls, and numerous towers surmounted them, which were high and strong. The circumference was nearly four miles. Titus was desirous of saving the city; but all his offers of peace were scornfully rejected. He then entered upon the siege, and determined not to leave it till he had razed the city to its foundations.

146. *Siege of Jerusalem.* When Titus laid siege to Jerusalem, A. D. 70, the city was full of inhabitants, by reason of the many thousands who had come there from

---

145. When did Judea become a Roman province? Who was sent to invade Judea? What is said of Jerusalem?

distant parts, to keep the passover. The city was well supplied with provisions and men, and being strongly fortified, it was, to appearance, well able to resist every effort of its enemies. But the "days of vengeance," foretold by divine inspiration, were now at hand. The city was filled with tumult, disorder, and contention, and when the Jews were not fighting the Romans from their walls, they were killing each other. In their rage and madness, they burned each other's store-houses, which were full of provisions. This produced such a famine, that the inhabitants were compelled to eat old shoes, leather, carrion, &c., and thousands perished of hunger. A Jewish lady suffered so extremely by hunger that she killed her son, and ate his flesh. After a blockade of six months, Jerusalem was taken by storm, the temple, the pride of the Jewish nation, was reduced to ashes, and the city buried in ruins. It is estimated that upwards of a million of the Jews perished in the siege.

147. *Dispersion of the Jews.* From the destruction of Jerusalem by Titus, the Jews have been scattered, according to the prediction of Moses, from one end of the earth to the other. From this period they have been " without a king, without a prince, and without a sacrifice and altar." After Jerusalem was destroyed, Vespasian ordered all the Jewish lands to be sold for his own use, and imposed a tribute on all the Jews within the empire. Their preservation as a distinct people, through eighteen hundred years of awful suffering and disgrace, a " reproach and a by-word," may be considered as a standing miracle in evidence of the truth of divine revelation. Our Saviour, in speaking of the Jews, declares : " They shall fall by the edge of the sword, and shall be led away captive into all nations,

146. What is said of Jerusalem, when Titus laid siege to it? Describe the state of the city within. How was the city taken, and how many Jews perished ?
147. What became of the Jews, after the destruction of Jerusalem ? What is said of their preservation as a distinct people ? To what nations has Jerusalem been subjected ?

and Jerusalem shall be trodden down of the Gentiles, till the time of the Gentiles be fulfilled." Jerusalem is still trodden down by the Gentiles. It was first in subjection to the *Romans*, afterwards to the *Saracens*, then to the *Franks*, next to the *Mamelukes*, and now to the *Turks*.

148. *Spread of Christianity.* The apostles and evangelists, as we learn from the scriptures and historical fragments, early went abroad among the distant nations, and preached the gospel to multitudes in all parts of the known world. The extension of the Roman empire, and the persecution of the Christians, were the means of rapidly extending the knowledge of Christianity; so that, before the destruction of Jerusalem, Christianity was extended throughout the world. The labors and sufferings of the apostles, and other early Christian teachers, in spreading the gospel, are almost incredible; and many of them lost their lives in the cause. The opposition the Christian religion met with, did not hinder its progress. The " blood of the martyrs was the seed of the church." Notwithstanding all the attempts to put it down, it finally prevailed throughout the Roman empire, and reached, at last, the throne of the Cesars.

149. *Persecution of the Christians.* Historians usually reckon ten general persecutions, the first of which took place A. D. 64, under Nero, who, when he burnt the city of Rome, charged it upon the Christians. First, all those who openly avowed themselves Christians, were apprehended, and by them were discovered an immense multitude, all of whom were condemned. Their death and tortures were aggravated by cruel derision and sport: many were torn to pieces by lions and other wild beasts; some were covered with the skins of wild beasts, and torn by dogs; others were fastened to crosses, and wrapped in combustible garments, which

---

148. What caused the extension of Christianity? What is said of the labors and sufferings of the apostles and others? What of the opposition Christianity met with ?

149. When did the first persecution take place? Describe the manner. How long did the last persecution continue? How many perished in Egypt?

were set on fire in the night, to give light to spectators. Nero offered his gardens for this spectacle, and exhibited at the same time the diversions of the circus. During a space of two centuries, in ten successive instances under the Roman emperors, these persecutions

Martyrdom of Christians by Lions.

were repeated, and the suffering and loss of life exceed calculation. The last persecution continued for ten years. In Egypt alone, 144,000 Christians died by the violence of their persecutors, besides 700,000 who died through the fatigues of banishment, or the public works to which they were condemned.

150. *Christian Martyrs.* The first Christians counted it an honor to suffer for their religion, and many of them gave up their lives with joy for the sake of their Lord. In one instance, the Emperor *Valens* gave orders to have the Christians in Edessa slain on a certain day, while they were at their devotions. The emperor's officers being compassionate men, gave private notice to the Christians not to assemble on the day appointed, so that they might escape death. The Christians thanked the

---

150. Did the first Christians suffer willingly? What is said of the Emperor Valens, and his officers? Relate the account of a woman and child.

officers for their advice, but rather than neglect their duty, repaired to the church, and resolved to suffer martyrdom. As the troops were put in motion to destroy them, a woman with a child in her arms broke through their ranks, when the officer ordered her to be brought before him, and asked where she was going? She replied, "to the church, whither others were making all the haste they could." "Have you not heard," says the officer, "of the emperor's order to put to death all found there?" "I have," says she, "and for that cause I make the more haste." "And whither," said the officer, "do you lead that child?" "I take him," replied she, "with me, that he also may be reckoned among he martyrs."

151. *Christian Fathers.* The term *Father* is applied to those ancient authors who have preserved in their writings traditions of the Church; some of the most distinguished were the following: *Clemens Romanus*, who was born at Rome, and a fellow-laborer with St Paul. He was a zealous defender of the faith, and his writings, which have come down to us, are esteemed very valuable. 2d. *Ignatus*, the bishop of Antioch, wrote a number of epistles to the churches. In A. D. 107, he was sent to Rome by Trajan, thrown to wild beasts and devoured. 3d. *Polycarp*, a companion of Ignatus, was a pastor of the church in Smyrna for eighty years, he also suffered martyrdom at Rome. 4th. *Justin Martyr*, distinguished for his powers and learning, was born in Palestine. He wrote two *apologies*, or defences of Christianity, addressed to the Roman emperor and senate; he also fell a martyr, by being beheaded. He was converted to Christianity about A. D. 132. 5th. *Irenæus*, a Greek, employed his pen principally against heretics: five of his books remain. He suffered death A. D. 202. 6th. *Clemens Alexandrius*, was born as Alexandria, in

---

151. To whom is the term Father applied? What is said of Clemens Romanus? Of Ignatus? Polycarp. Justin Martyr, Irenæus, Clemens Alexandrius, Tertullian, Origen, Cyprian, Ambrose, Jerome, Augustine, and John Chrysostom?

the second century : three of his works are existing. 7th. *Tertullian* was by birth a Carthaginian, and was distinguished for his great learning. 8th. *Origen* was born at Alexandria, A. D. 185. He was the author of numerous works. 9th. *Cyprian*, the bishop of Carthage, was distinguished as an orator. 10th. *Ambrose* was born in Gaul, A. D. 333, and was bishop of Milan. 11th. *Jerome* translated the bible into Latin : he died near Jerusalem, A. D. 420. 12th. *Augustine* was born in Africa ; his writings formed a body of divinity, which was in use for a number of centuries in the Christian church : he died A. D. 430. 13th. *John Chrysostom* was born at Antioch, A. D. 354. He was elected bishop of Constantinople, and was considered one of the ablest of preachers.

152. *Trajan, the Emperor.* Trajan, who was a native of Seville, in Spain, is esteemed one of the greatest and most virtuous of the Roman emperors. He was the greatest general of his age, and accustomed himself to hardships ; he often marched at the head of his troops on foot, over extensive regions. He was distinguished for his affability, his simplicity of manners, and his merciful and generous disposition. The senate conferred on him the title of *Optimus*, or best, and for more than 200 years they hailed every new emperor with the exclamation : " Reign fortunately, as Augustus, and virtuously, as Trajan." During his reign the boundaries of the Roman empire were more extensive than either before or afterwards. He subdued the *Dacians*, a nation north of the *Danube*, and in commemoration of this event a stately column was erected, which is still to be seen in Rome, and is one of the most remarkable ancient monuments in the city. He died in A. D. 117, after a reign of upwards of 10 years, aged 62.

153. *Successors of Trajan.* Trajan was succeeded by *Adrian*, his nephew. This emperor undertook to

---

152. What is said of Trajan ? What exclamation did the senate use ? What nation did Trajan conquer ? What is said of the column commemorating this event ?

visit all the provinces of the empire: in this expedition he spent thirteen years. While in Britain he erected a turf wall across the island, to protect the Britons from the incursion of the Picts. In his progress he reformed abuses and rebuilt cities. He was succeeded by *Antoninus Pius*, who reigned 23 years, and was distinguished for his public and private virtues. His successor was his son-in-law, *Marcus Aurelius Antonius*, surnamed the *Philosopher*. He is esteemed the best model of pagan virtue among the Roman emperors; he reigned about 19 years, and died A. D. 169. From this period the emperors were, with a few exceptions, either weak or vicious, and some of them monsters of cruelty. The empire was too large to be governed properly; barbarous and successful enemies began to oppose them from without, while they were torn by cruel factions within. Patriotism, virtue, and the sciences, were almost extinct.

154. *Partition of the Empire.* Diocletian, the Roman emperor, began his reign A. D. 284, and two years afterwards he admitted to the government of the empire his general, *Maximian*. About eight years from this time they took two colleagues, *Galerius* and *Constantius*, and bestowed upon each the title of Cesar. This was a novel state of things; the empire was in four divisions with two emperors and two Cesars, each nominally supreme. Diocletian, however, was the master-spirit that controlled the whole. In this state the government was administered for a few years, when the two emperors *voluntarily* resigned their authority into the hands of the two Cesars. Diocletian retired to his native country, Dalmatia, where he built a palace and amused himself in cultivating his garden. He declared he enjoyed more happiness in his quiet retirement, than when he was emperor of the world.

155. *Constantine, the first Christian Emperor.* On

---

153. Who was Adrian? What is said of Marcus Aurelius Antonius? What of the emperors who succeeded him?
154. How did Diocletian manage the government of Rome? What farther is said of Diocletian?

the death of Maximian, who had resumed the throne, Constantine, the son of Constantius, had no other competitor than Maxentius; the contest between these two was decided by the sword—Maxentius perished, and Constantine remained sole master of the empire. It is related by historians, that when Constantine was marching at the head of his army against Maxentius, he saw the appearance of a cross in the heavens, inscribed with these words, "*By this conquer;*" and that in consequence of this vision, and the success that followed his arms, he embraced Christianity. However this may be, Constantine became the avowed friend and supporter of Christianity. He put an end to the persecution of the Christians, also to combats of the gladiators, and other barbarous exhibitions; and the Roman government, from being a cruel persecutor of Christianity, became its professed protector.

156. *Government of the Emperors.* After the dissolution of the Roman republic, all the institutions of the government were made to support despotic authority. Taxes and impositions of every nature were laid and collected by sole authority of the emperor. The quantity and rate was fixed by a census made over all the provinces, and part was generally paid in money, and part in the produce of the lands—a burden often found so grievous as to put a stop to cultivation. All merchandise was also highly taxed. The government supported numerous spies, who conveyed all sorts of intelligence from the remotest parts of the empire to Rome. It is stated that the principal reason why the despotism of Nero and other monsters was so quietly borne by the people, lay in the fact, that a great part of them were fed by the emperors, from the distribution of corn, meat. and money, among the populace.

---

155. How did Constantine obtain the mastery of the empire? What do historians relate respecting the appearance of a cross? What did Constantine do?

156. What is said of the Roman government? Of the taxes? The spies? Why did the people endure the despotism of Nero and others?

PERIOD II.

DISTINGUISHED FOR THE CONQUEST OF THE ROMAN EMPIRE

Northern Barbarians advancing upon the Roman Empire.

FROM THE REIGN OF CONSTANTINE TO THE BIRTH OF MAHOMET.

(263 YEARS.)

157. *Reign of Constantine.* The Christian religion, which had stood the trial of ten fiery persecutions, was seen at once to prevail over the whole Roman empire. Constantine commanded that in all the provinces the orders of the bishops should be exactly obeyed; a privilege of which they afterwards made a bad use. By his order the pagan temples were demolished, or converted into Christian churches; the exercise of the old priesthood forbidden, and the idols destroyed. Large and costly buildings were erected for Christian worship. The clergy were honored with great favors, and enriched with great endowments. Many additions were made to the forms of worship—the dress of the clergy was pompous, and the whole of the Christian service exhibited a scene of worldly grandeur and parade. Constantine

---

157. What did Constantine order to be done? What is said of the clergy? Who assembled at Nice, and for what purpose?

MODERN HISTORY. 115

also assembled a general council of Christian fathers, at *Nice,* in order to repress the heresies which now began to appear in the church.

158. *Corruption of Christianity.* When the profession of the Christian religion was attended with danger; while dungeons, racks, and flames, were threatening the disciples of Christ, they had no source of consolation but in the gospel. This they found sufficient to enable them to meet death in all its horrid forms, and consequently their lives were pure and heavenly. But when a profession of Christianity was considered honorable, and was a means of advancement in the state, many unworthy and unprincipled persons found means to introduce themselves into the church. The government of the church underwent a great change, being connected with the state; the emperor assumed the title of a bishop, and regulated its external affairs. By these means, Christianity was degraded, and the virtues of humility, self-denial, and brotherly kindness, which so distinguish the religion of Christ, were but little known.

159. *Removal of the seat of the Empire from Rome to Constantinople.* In A. D. 329, Constantine wishing to found a new capital, removed to *Byzantium,* where he built a capitol, an amphitheater, many churches, and other public works. Having dedicated that city to the God of martyrs, and named it after himself, he transferred his court thither, and made it the seat of government. By this means he made it the rival of Rome, in population and magnificence. From this period the two cities began to look upon each other with jealousy, which eventuated in the division of the empire into the *Eastern* and *Western.* Whatever might have been Constantine's motives in removing the seat of government, it weakened exceedingly the already tottering empire. By a division of the military force under the government

---

158. What effect did persecution have upon Christians? How was it when the profession of Christianity was honorable? What is said of the government of the church?

159. When did Constantine found a new capital? What effect did this have upon the empire?

of his sons, the northern barbarians, who fought with superior numbers, and were often defeated, began now to prevail against the Romans.

160. *Julian, the Apostate.* Julian, the Roman emperor, began his reign about A. D. 360 ; he is generally called the *apostate*, because, after having received a Christian education, he cast off its profession, and restored the pagan worship. He was possessed of considerable talent, and of many heroic qualities, but was the slave of superstition, being addicted to the studies of magic and astrology. He endeavored to make Christianity an object of ridicule, and those who professed it he removed from public offices, closed their schools, and took various methods to humble and oppress them. The Saviour he always distinguished by the name of *Galilean.* In a war with the Persians he was mortally wounded by a lance. As he was expiring, he filled his hand with blood, and casting it into the air, exclaimed, " O, Galilean! thou hast conquered."

161. *Attempt to rebuild the Temple at Jerusalem.* Julian, in order to give the lie to our Saviour's prophecy, attempted to restore the Jews to their city, temple, and worship. If he had succeeded in this object, he would have converted it into an argument against the truth of the Christian religion. He therefore resolved to erect, on Mount Moriah, a stately temple ; and at the call of their supposed great deliverer, the Jews, from all of the provinces of the empire, repaired to Jerusalem. Although the emperor's orders were obeyed with enthusiasm by the whole people, they entirely failed of attaining their object. A heathen writer states, " while Alypius, assisted by the governor of the province, urged with vigor and diligence the execution of the work, horrible balls of fire, breaking out near the foundations with frequent attacks, drove them to a distance, and the un-

---

160. Why was Julian called the apostate ? What is said of him ? Relate the manner of his death.
161. What was the object of Julian in restoring the Jews to their city, &c. ? How was he prevented ?

dertaking was abandoned." This remarkable event is fully attested by the various historians of the age.

162. *Barbarians.* This name was generally applied by the ancient Greeks and Romans to most nations except their own. At the first, it was applied to those persons who spoke inelegantly, or with harshness and difficulty. The barbarians who effected the conquest of the Roman empire, may be divided into three classes. 1. Those of Europe; 2. those of Asia; and, 3. those of an intermedial origin. The barbarians of Europe were divided into many tribes, of whom the Goths and Vandals were the most celebrated. The *Intermedial Barbarians*, or the Scythians and Samaritans, were a mixed race of the Asiatic and European tribes; their complexion, customs, and manners, partook of the different nations. The *Barbarians of Asia*, or the Tartars, were of a brown complexion. They were shepherds, and kept constantly moving about with their cattle, and encamped under movable tents; they had many wives, and their principal military force consisted of cavalry. In this class the Huns, Alains, and Turks, are generally placed.

163. *Of the Goths.* The name of *Goths* is generally given to those tribes or nations in the northern parts of Europe, who directed their arms against the Roman empire, and introduced disorders, anarchy, and revolutions, into the west of Europe. They were said to be of Asiatic origin, and were originally a colony of Scythians, from the borders of the Black and Caspian seas. They established themselves in *Scandinavia*, a name given by the ancients to the tract of territory which contains the modern kingdoms of Norway, Sweden, Denmark, &c. From this country they are sometimes called *Scandinavians.* The modern nations of Europe are

---

162. To whom was the name barbarian applied? Who were the three classes that conquered the Roman empire? What is said of them?

163. To what nations is the name of Goths applied? Why are they sometimes called Scandinavians? For what were the original Goths distinguished?

mostly a mixed race, compounded of the Goths and the nations they conquered. The original Goths were distinguished by a savage ferocity of manners, and their institutions; but as they extended their conquest their manners became much improved, by adopting many of the manners and customs of the nations they conquered.

164. *Religion of the Goths, or Scandinavians.* The Goths held to three principal doctrines of religion. "To serve the Supreme Being with prayer and sacrifice; to do no wrong or unjust action; and to be intrepid in fight." *Odin,* the principal deity of the Scandinavians, was represented as a terrible and severe god, the Avenger and the Father of Carnage. The favorites of Odin were all those who die in battle, or, what is equally meritorious, died by their own hand. The timid wretch who allowed himself to perish by disease or age, was deemed unworthy of the joys of paradise. These joys were fighting, ceaseless slaughter, and drinking beer out of the skulls of their enemies, &c. These notions had a great effect upon their character. The Scandinavian placed his sole delight in war; he entertained an absolute contempt of danger and death. and his glory was estimated by the number he had killed in battle.

165. *Vandals.* The Vandals, Suevi, and others, left their native land, on the shores of the Baltic, at the commencement of the fifth century, and came down upon Italy. Here they were defeated with great slaughter. They then retired into Germany; from whence the *Vandals* traversed Gaul and penetrated into Spain, fixing themselves at first, in the southern parts; but soon after, crossing the straits, they arrived in Africa, and ravaged the Roman provinces. They founded a kingdom upon the ruins of Carthage: they then embarked for Italy, and

---

164. What were the three principal religious doctrines of the Goths? Who was their principal deity, and how was he represented? What were represented to be the joys of the Scandinavian paradise?

165. Where did the Vandals emigrate from, and at what period? Where did they found a kingdom? By whom were they overthrown?

took Rome by assault, and avenged the Carthaginians, six hundred years after their overthrow. The Vandals became proverbial for their rage for devastation: after they had ravaged Rome, they returned to Africa, and continued a monarchy for 100 years, which was finally overthrown by *Belisarius*, a celebrated Roman general, in A. D. 534.

166. *Ancient Germans.* The Germans, as well as the Gauls, were branches of the original nation called *Celts*, who inhabited most of the countries in Europe, south of the Baltic, before they were invaded by the Scandinavians. They are described by ancient authors, as men of great stature, of a fair complexion, and fierce countenances. They were robust, being inured to cold and hardships, with little clothing in winter, and scarcely any in summer. In battle, their first onset was almost irresistible, but their strength and ardor were soon exhausted. The first inhabitants of Europe, like other savages, subsisted on the flesh of wild beasts, fish, fowls, and the fruits of forest-trees, particularly acorns. As they advanced in population, they raised cattle for a subsistence.

167. *Druidical Religion.* The religion of the Celtic nations was *Druidism*; the priests of which were called *Druids*. This religion, like that of the Scandinavian, acknowledged a god who delighted in bloodshed. It taught the immortality of the soul, and a contempt for danger and death. It is said that they neither had temples nor idols, but worshiped their god in a consecrated grove, which was the place appointed for prayer and sacrifice, and which none but the priests were allowed to enter. Their chief sacrifices were human victims, probably prisoners taken in war. The Druids concealed the mysteries of their worship, and thus gave great sanctity to their character. They had the greatest influence over the minds of the people, so that the Romans had

---

166. What is said of the Germans and Gauls? How are they described? What did the first inhabitants subsist on?

167. Who were the Druids? What did the druidical religion teach? What is said of the manner of worship? Their sacrifices? What did the Romans do to secure their conquests?

no other way of securing their conquests over the Celtic nations, than by exterminating the Druids.

168. *Poetry and Learning.* The Gothic nations were greatly attached to warlike music and poetry. Hence they had an order of men called *bards*, who composed poems in honor of brave men, and sung them on public occasions. All the first laws, customs, and religious rites, were rehearsed or recorded in verse; and songs and poems were their only histories. The inhabitants of northern Europe neglected and even despised the use of letters. For a long period, the Druids or priests pretended to have all the learning of those rude ages, but would not commit their knowledge to writing. The prejudice against learning continued down to the ninth century after the Christian era; the Emperor Charlemagne, at that period, could not write his own name, and many of the nobility, for ages afterwards, made *their marks*, and set their seals, instead of their proper signatures, to written instruments.

169. *Sacking of Rome by Alaric.* The Goths, under the conduct of the famous *Alaric*, filled all Greece with the terror of their arms, and spread their devastations to the very walls of Constantinople. He afterwards laid siege to Rome, but was induced to retire from its walls by receiving from the inhabitants 5,000 pounds of gold, 30,000 pounds of silver, and almost an incredible quantity of other valuable articles. But the doom of the city was not far distant. In A. D. 410, Alaric again appeared under the walls of Rome, and reduced this great city, which had long sat mistress of the world, to the greatest distress. Through the treachery of the Roman guard, one of the gates was silently opened, and the inhabitants were awakened at midnight by the sound of the Gothic trumpet. For six days the fierce tribes of Germany and

---

168. Who were the bards? How were the first laws, histories, &c., preserved? What is said of the Druids? What of the Emperor Charlemagne?

159. What is said of Alaric, and the Goths? What induced Alaric to retire from Rome? How did Alaric get into Rome and what did his soldiers do?

Scythia devastated the city, and indulged their cruelty and ferocity without pity or restraint.

The Goths, under Alaric, ravaging Rome.

170. *Ravages of Attila, the Hun.* A few years after the sacking of Rome by Alaric, the *Huns*, under their leader, *Attila*, commenced their sanguinary ravages. This people are supposed to have originated from the eastern part of Asia; their incursions were extremely desolating, and their ferocious king, Attila, was called the "*Scourge of God.*" He first invaded the East, which he ravaged at pleasure; the Emperor Theodosius, at Constantinople, however, bought his favor by paying tribute. He now turned to the West, and invaded Gaul, with an army of 500,000 men. He was here defeated by the Romans, with the loss of 160,000 men, which checked his progress for a time. He, however, not long afterwards, invaded Italy, and compelled the Emperor Valentinian to purchase a peace. Attila dying suddenly, the earth was delivered from a warrior, who never suffered Europe to enjoy repose.

171. *Extinction of the Western Roman Empire.* The end of the Roman empire in the West, took place by the

---

170. What is said of the Huns, and what was their king called? Give an account of the invasion of Attila.

taking of Rome, by *Odoacer*, prince of the *Heruli*, in A. D. 476. The last Emperor, Romulus Augustus, had his life spared upon condition of resigning the empire to Odoacer, who assumed the title of *King of Italy*. Thus the empire of Rome passed from the hands of its ancient masters, into the possession of those called barbarians, who had so long harassed it by their invasions. As an empire, it had existed more than 500 years, computing the time from the battle of *Actium*. The whole period of its duration, from the founding of the city by Romulus, was more than twelve hundred years. The ruin of the Roman empire, the most powerful the world ever saw, was the result of its moral corruption, combined with its great extent of territory. Rome, having become a mass of luxury, weakness, and profligacy, fell an easy prey to the surrounding barbarous nations.

172. *Reign of Theodoric the Great.* The kingdom of the Heruli lasted but about twenty years. The nation of the *Ostrogoths*, or *Eastern Goths*, under their prince, *Theodoric*, invaded Italy. After a struggle of four years, Odoacer surrendered all Italy to the conqueror, and Theodoric (commonly surnamed the Great) was acknowledged the sovereign of the country, and fixed his residence at Ravenna. He reigned about thirty-three years, and has the reputation of being an able and virtuous prince. The successors of Theodoric, in the Gothic kingdom of Italy, were seven in number; they were succeeded in the sovereignty by the *Lombards*, another Gothic nation. The Goths, at the time of their taking Rome, under Alaric, had partially embraced Christianity, and though they retained a portion of their barbarian manners, when they settled in Italy, were at least as virtuous as the native citizens.

---

171. What caused the extinction of the western Roman empire? How long had it existed as an empire? And how long from the founding of Rome by Romulus?

172. Who was Theodoric, where did he fix his residence, and what was his character? What is said of the Goths at the time of their taking Rome?

173. *Eastern Roman Empire.* The eastern empire, sometimes called the *Greek Empire*, although it suffered much from the ravages of barbarous nations, yet it resisted their attacks and existed more than *eleven centuries* from the time of its foundation by Constantine. The empire was in the meridian of its glory in the sixth century, during the long reign of Justinian, (sometimes called the Great,) who published a code of laws prepared by a great lawyer of that age. This code is regarded as the foundation of the science of law in modern Europe. After the removal of the seat of Empire, there arose a rivalship between the Bishop or pope of Rome, and the patriarch of Constantinople, each contending for the supremacy. This controversy finally ended in the entire separation of the *western* or *Roman*, and the *eastern* or *Greek churches.* Justinian built the church of *St. Sophia*, which is now a Turkish mosque, in Constantinople.

174. *Belisarius.* During the reign of Justinian, *Belisarius*, a celebrated general in the eastern empire, revived in a degree the fading glory of the Roman name. He defended the empire against the Persians, recovered Africa from the Vandals, and carried their king prisoner to Constantinople. Belisarius defeated the Goths in Italy, and for a while restored Rome, the ancient capital, to the Empire. This success, however, excited the jealousy of Justinian, and he was recalled to Constantinople, and the Goths again nearly overran Italy. Belisarius was once more sent to expel the Goths, and when he had nearly accomplished this object, he was again recalled. He died, after a life of military glory, having experienced much from royal ingratitude, A. D. 564.

175. *Conquest of Italy by the Lombards.* In A. D.

---

173. What was the eastern empire sometimes called? How long did it exist from Constantine? Who published a code of laws, and what is said of them? Who contended for the supremacy in the church, and how did the controversy end?

174. Who was Belisarius, and what is said of him? Why was he recalled to Constantinople?

568 the *Lombards*, another Gothic tribe, expelled the Ostrogoths from the sovereignty of Italy, and were masters of the greater portion of it for more than three hundred years. This tribe gave a permanent name to the northern section of Italy. The occasion of their entrance into the country was the invitation to invade it by *Narses*, the general of Justinian, the emperor, to avenge the wrongs which he suffered from that monarch, by being recalled from Italy. Several attempts were made by Maurice, the eastern emperor, assisted by a number of barbarian chiefs, to expel the Lombards, but without much effect. An anarchy took place after the death of one of the Lombard kings, which continued for ten years, during which time Italy was governed by thirty dukes. One of the kings, in A. D. 584, confirmed the dukes in their authority, on condition of paying him half their revenues, and serving under his command in time of war. This is considered by some as the origin of the *feudal system*, which will be hereafter described.

176. *State of the World on the Extinction of the Western or Roman Empire.* By the fall of the western empire, the arts and sciences declined; darkness and barbarism began to prevail in many parts of the Roman world. It was at this period that Italy was so overrun with the Gothic nations, that the *Latin tongue* ceased to be spoken. Christianity, during this period, was considerably extended, particularly in Gaul, Britain, and Scotland, and among some of the barbarous tribes beyond the Danube. These conversions, however, seemed to consist in but little more than the adoption of some of the outward forms of Christianity; such as baptism, making the sign of the cross, &c. Religious errors and corruptions abounded, and but very little of the

---

175. Who expelled the Ostrogoths? How long were they masters of Italy? When did an anarchy take place, and how was Italy governed after that event?

176. What effect did the fall of the western empire have? What is said of the extension of Christianity during this period?

genuine spirit of Christianity seemed to prevail. By the destruction of the Roman power, many of the provinces of the empire being obliged to manage their own affairs, became independent, particularly Spain, Britain, and France.

177. *Of Spain.* Spain was anciently called *Hesperia*, or Western, on account of its situation, as being the extreme west known to the ancients. It was also called *Iberia*, from the river Iber, now the Ebro. The name *Hispania*, or Spain, is said to be derived from a word meaning, *abounding with rabbits*, these animals formerly being very numerous in Spain. The original inhabitants were *Celts*, of the same race with those of France. The fertility of the soil induced the Phœnecians, who were the first navigators, to open a trade with Spain, and they built the city of *Gades*, now Cadiz, about nine hundred years before the Christian era. About 500 years before Christ, it was partly subdued by the Carthaginians, who held possession for about three centuries. The Romans then succeeded as masters, in whose power it remained for six hundred years. After the Romans, the northern barbarians held possession, till displaced by the Moors.

178. *Of Britain.* The island of Britain, before it was known to the Romans, was inhabited by a very rude and uncivilized people. They went nearly naked, or clothed only with the skin of beasts, having their bodies painted with various colors; and it is said that the country was named from a word in its language, which signified *painted*. All ancient authors agree that the first inhabitants of Britain were a tribe of *Gauls*, or *Celts* from the neighboring continent. *Caledonia*, now called Scotland, was so little known to the Romans,

---

177. What was Spain anciently called? What was the name Hispania, or Spain, derived from? Who built the city of Gades or Cadiz? State the names of those nations who have had possession of Spain.
178. What is said of the inhabitants of Britain, before it was known to the Romans? What was Scotland formerly called? What was the ancient name for Ireland?

11*

and its inhabitants so little civilized, that they called it *Britannia Barbara*, or Barbarous Britain. *Hibernia* was the ancient name for Ireland. Julius Cesar began the Roman dominion in Britain, which continued till A. D. 426, when the Romans withdrew their forces, in order to defend themselves at home, from the incursions of the Gothic nations.

179. *Of England.* The ancestors of the English, who subdued the Britons, are generally known by the name of *Saxons*. A tribe of this people was called *Angles*, a term formed from *eng*, a Saxon word, which signified a meadow, or plain. The Angles inhabited the low lands along the banks of the Elbe and Weser, and on the borders of the Baltic sea. After this tribe obtained possession of the south part of Britain, it was called from them *Eng*-land, and hence the word *English*. When the Romans left the island, the Britons being left without protection, they were greatly harassed by their former enemies, the *Scots* and *Picts*, inhabiting the northern part of Britain. In their distress they applied to the Saxons, one of the most warlike tribes of Germany, for assistance. The first body of Saxons arrived in the year 449, and joining the Britons, defeated the Scots and Picts in a bloody battle.

180. *Saxon conquest of England.* The Saxons being pleased with the country which they had defended, determined to make it their future residence. For this purpose they sent for additional troops. Being now sufficiently strong, they began a quarrel with the Britons about their provisions and promised rewards, and enforced their demands by fire and sword. The Britons, roused to indignation against their treacherous allies, made a desperate war upon them; they were, however,

---

179. Who were the ancestors of the English? What is said of the word Angles? What country did the Angles inhabit? When the Romans left Britain, by whom were the English harassed, and what did they do?

180. What is said of the Saxons? How did they obtain possession? How many petty kingdoms did they establish and what were they called?

defeated, and the Saxons, under *Hengist*, established their kingdom in England. The Saxons now came over in large bodies, and established seven petty kingdoms, called the *Heptarchy*, which, after a series of wars and revolutions, which lasted 200 years, were united in one kingdom under Egbert, in A. D. 827.

181. *Introduction of Christianity into Britain.* The religion of the ancient Britons was *Druidism*, being similar to that of the Goths, or Scandinavians. Christianity is supposed to have been introduced into Britain during the age of the apostles. It is certain, however, that it had made some progress as early as the second century of the Christian era. The Saxons, when they conquered England, were pagans; and wherever they established themselves, endeavored to extirpate Christianity. They murdered the Christian clergy, and destroyed their places of worship. In A. D. 570, *Ethelbert*, one of the Saxon kings, married a daughter of the king of France, who was a Christian, and it was agreed in the marriage contract, that she should enjoy the free exercise of her religion. In A. D. 597, Pope Gregory sent Augustine, with forty other monks, to instruct the inhabitants of England in the Christian religion; and from this period it gradually gained the ascendancy, till the seventh century, when it became the religion of all the inhabitants.

182. *Of France.* France, anciently called *Gaul*, at the period of the dissolution of the western Roman empire, was divided between the *Visogoths*, *Burgundians*, and *Franks*. This last tribe is supposed to have been of German origin. Under their king, *Clovis*, in A. D. 481, the Franks obtained possession of the country by degrees, and from this people, Gaul obtained the name of *France*. Clovis, in his contest with the Germans, in

---

181. What was the ancient religion of the Britons? When is it supposed Christianity was introduced? Who did Ethelbert marry, and what is said of the marriage agreement? What is said of Augustine?

182. What was France anciently called, and how divided? Who was Clovis, and why did he profess Christianity?

A. D. 496, invoked assistance from the god of *Clotilda,* a Christian princess he had married three years before. Being victorious, he became a professed believer in Christianity, and, with 3,000 of his subjects, was baptized on Christmas day, the same year. His religion, however, had but little influence over him, as in 13 years afterwards he murdered most of his relatives. He made Paris the seat of his kingdom, and his immediate successors were in general a race of weak and wicked men.

183. *Of the Arabs, or Saracens.* The Arabs, in all ages, have lived as wanderers in a state of independence; they never have been subdued by any of the great conquerors of the world, although generally at war with their neighbors. They derive their origin from *Ishmael,* and have, in a remarkable manner, fulfilled the Divine prediction concerning their ancestor: " He shall be a wild man, his hand against every man, and every man's against him, and yet he should dwell in the presence of all his brethren." Before the time of Mahomet, the Arab religion was a mixture of idolatry and Judaism. The *Saracens* were a people who inhabited the northwest part of Arabia, and this name was applied to most of the Arabian tribes, who before this period had been induced by the hope of plunder to forsake their deserts.

Arabia had afforded an asylum to the persecuted Christians of different sects; and at the end of the sixth century, Christianity, though in a very corrupt form, had become the prevailing religion in some parts of the country. This was the state of Arabia when *Mahomet,* the successful impostor, appeared, whose religion has had such a mighty influence on the destinies of mankind.

---

183. What is said of the Arabs? From whom did they derive their origin? What was the prophecy concerning Ishmael? Who were the Saracens?

PERIOD III

DISTINGUISHED FOR THE ESTABLISHMENT OF THE MAHOMETAN RELIGION.

Mahometanism offered to Mankind.

FROM THE BIRTH OF MAHOMET TO THE CROWNING OF CHARLEMAGNE

(231 YEARS.)

184. *Of Mahomet.* Mahomet was born at Mecca, a city in Arabia, near the Red Sea, A. D. 569. He was descended from a noble family, but his circumstances were mean, and his education scanty; he however possessed great natural talents, by which he was able to exercise great influence over the passions and affections of men. At an early age he lost his parents; his uncle then became his guardian, and under his care he was instructed in the business of a merchant, and several times accompanied the caravans into Syria, by which his knowledge of men was extended. At the age of 25 he entered into the service of *Cadijah,* a rich and noble widow of Mecca, whom he soon after married; and by this means he became possessed of wealth and

---

184. Where was Mahomet born, and at what time? What was his education and talents? How came he possessed of wealth and power? How did he pretend to have received the Koran?

power. Ten years after his marriage, he put on the appearance of great sanctity, retired every morning to a cave near Mecca, where he pretended to hold conferences with the angel Gabriel, who delivered to him portions of the *Koran*, (the Bible of the Mahometans,) containing revelations from God, which his prophet (Mahomet) was to make known to the world.

185. *Of the Koran.* The Koran, while Mahomet lived, was kept alone in loose sheets. His followers say he had no hand in inditing it, but that it was delivered to him from God by the angel Gabriel, who communicated to him a verse or two at a time, during the course of 23 years. During this period, the Mahometans say that God himself repealed and altered several doctrines and precepts which the prophet had before received and recorded. This accounts, say they, for the contradictions, disorders, and confusions, visible in the work. By this piecemeal revelation, Mahomet had the advantage, whenever he happened to be perplexed with any thing, of obtaining a new revelation. The religion of the Koran is a system of Asiatic sensuality, intermixed with some of the precepts of Christianity, and rites of Judaism. Moses and Jesus Christ are admitted to be prophets; but Mahomet is the greatest of all, and no other is to be expected after him. Mahomet taught a belief in *one God*, in the resurrection and final judgment, and in God's *eternal decrees*. As Mahomet was rather an illiterate man, he is supposed to have employed one *Sergius*, a monk, who had a principal hand in composing the Koran.

186. *Mahometan Paradise.* The religion of Mahomet was made popular with the eastern nations, by the nature of the rewards which he promised his followers. In this particular the paradise of the Mahometans differed in some respects from that of the Gothic nations

---

185. What do the followers of Mahomet say respecting the Koran? How do they account for the contradictions visible in it? What is said of the religion of the Koran? What did Mahomet teach?

in Europe. This latter people delighted in war and bloodshed, and to these scenes their ideas of a future state corresponded. The eastern, or Oriental nations, in their burning climate, considered happiness to consist in luxurious enjoyment and repose. Hence, Mahomet informed those who were believers, that after death they would enter into pleasant gardens and shady groves, where cool fountains and rivers of water continually flow; there were also rivers of milk, wine, and honey; also the tree of happiness, laden with all kinds of fruit of surprising bigness, and of tastes unknown to mortals. In these delightful gardens they would be attended by the *houris*, or maidens of surpassing beauty.

Flight of Mahomet from Mecca to Medina.

187. *Flight of Mahomet.* In the year 609, Mahomet having matured his system, began to announce himself as a prophet sent from God, and to publish his religion. For several years his efforts were confined to the city

---

186. What made the Mahometan religion popular? How was the Mahometan paradise distinguished from that of the Gothic nations? . In what did the eastern or Oriental nations, suppose happiness to consist?

of Mecca. His first converts were his wife, his slave, his pupil, and a friend. After a while, ten of the most respectable citizens of Mecca were won over to his faith. These were the only triumphs of his religion for fourteen years. In A. D. 622, Mahomet met with so much opposition in Mecca, that he was obliged to flee to Medina, in order to save his life. This flight is called by the Mahometans the *Hegira*, and is regarded by them as their grand epoch, being the period from which they compute their time.

188. *Propagation of Mahometanism.* Mahomet was received with enthusiasm by 500 of the richest citizens of Medina; the people embraced his faith, swore allegiance, and repeated the Mahometan creed : " *There is but one God, and Mahomet is his prophet.*" To those who demanded of him a miracle in proof of his mission, he replied, that God had sent Moses and Jesus, with miracles, and yet men would not be obedient to his word; he now, therefore, had sent him, in the last place, to force men to do his will by the power of the sword. From the time of his establishment at Medina, Mahomet placed himself at the head of an army of his converts, and propagated his religion by the sword, and before his death was master of all Arabia.

Mahomet divided his spoil among his followers, and from all sides the roving Arabs were allured to the standard of *religion* and *plunder*. In order to reconcile the timid to the dangers of war, he taught that those who were killed in battle, would have died at that very moment, had they remained at home in their houses: the time of every man's life being fixed by the decree of God. " The sword," says Mahomet, " is the key of heaven and hell; a drop of blood shed in the cause of God, or a night spent in arms, is of more avail than

---

187. Who were the first converts of Mahomet? What is said of his flight from Mecca?

188. What expression contains the Mahometan creed? What reason did Mahomet give for not performing miracles? How did he propagate his religion? What did he say of his followers that were killed in battle?

two months of fasting and prayer, and whoever falls in battle his sins are forgiven."

189. *Death of Mahomet.* Having conquered all Arabia, Mahomet next turned his arms towards Syria, against which he was proceeding with an army of 20,000 foot and 10,000 horse, when he was poisoned by a Jewish female. The poison is said to have been put into a shoulder of mutton, which Mahomet tasting, but not liking, spit out. He survived for a time, yet it finally killed him. The girl being asked why she did it, replied, "that she had a mind to try whether he was a prophet; for if he was, he would certainly know that the meat was poisoned; and if he was not, it would be a good thing to rid the world of so wicked a tyrant." He died at the age of 63, and was buried on the spot where he expired. His remains were afterwards removed to Medina, whither countless numbers of pilgrims to Mecca, often turn aside to bow in devotion before the simple tomb of the prophet.

190. *Successors of Mahomet.* Mahomet was succeeded by *Abu-beker,* who is styled the *calif,* a word signifying, in the Arabic language, *successor.* He continued a career of conquest, defeated the Greek emperor, took Damascus, and died in the third year of his reign. At his death he bequeathed the scepter to the brave *Omar,* who, with the assistance of his general, in one campaign deprived the Greek emperor of Syria, Phoenecia, Mesopotamia, and Chaldea; the next campaign, the whole of the empire of Persia was reduced to the Mahometan dominion and religion. His army, under Amrou, took Alexandria, and subdued Egypt. Amrou being requested to spare the *Alexandrian library,* wrote for directions concerning it to Omar, who returned the following answer, well suited to a barbarian and fanatic :

---

189. What was the cause of Mahomet's death? What reason did the girl give for doing it? Where was Mahomet finally buried?

190. By whom was Mahomet succeeded? What is said of Omar? What answer did he give respecting the Alexandrian library? What is said of this library?

"If these writings agree with the Koran, they are useless, and need not be preserved; if they disagree with it, they are pernicious, and ought to be destroyed." This great library, said to contain from 500,000 to 700,000 volumes, was burnt, and was the greatest loss to literature recorded in history.

191. *Mahometan, or Saracen Empire.* In less than half a century, the Mahometans, or Saracens, (as the followers of the prophet were called,) raised an empire more extensive than what then remained of the Roman. In 100 years from the flight of Mahomet, the dominions of his successors extended from India to the Atlantic, comprehending the widely extended dominions of Persia, Syria, Asia Minor, Arabia, Egypt, the north of Africa, and Spain. *Ali*, one of the Mahometan sovereigns, removed the seat of government to Cufa, on the Euphrates; and in A. D. 768, it was removed to *Bagdad*, which became one of the most splendid cities of the world, being the seat of the Saracen empire, and so continued for nearly 500 years, when it was taken by the Tartars, in A. D. 1258. At this time the califate was abolished, and the empire of the Saracens may be considered as terminated.

192. *Conquest of Spain by the Saracens, or Moors.* In the early part of the eighth century, Spain was invaded by the Saracens, or Moors, from Africa, and in A. D. 713, they gained the great battle of *Xeres*, in which *Roderick*, the Gothic king, was slain. Previous to the invasion of Spain, the Saracens extended their conquests into the north of Africa, near Spain, conquered the *Moorish* tribes along the coast, and adopted them into the Mahometan family. From Africa, the Saracens extended their conquests into Spain, and from this circumstance they were called *Moors*. In a few years,

---

191. Give an account of the extent of the Mahometan, or Saracen empire What is said of Bagdad?

192. When was Spain invaded by the Moors? Why were the Saracens of Africa called Moors? Who established an independent kingdom in Spain, and what was the name of the capital?

the Moors overran the most of Spain, and for some time it was governed by the viceroys of the Saracen califs. In 755, *Abderrahman* established an independent kingdom, and fixed the seat of his government at *Cordova*, which became a place of great splendor and magnificence, and for two centuries was the capital of a splendid monarchy, which, at this period, was the most enlightened state in Europe, being distinguished for its attention to the arts and sciences.

193. *Christian Kingdoms in Spain.* When the Moors had conquered the greater part of Spain, the Gothic, or, as they are now called, the Christian forces, retired to the mountains of the *Asturias*, and founded a kingdom in 718. From this time they gradually recovered other parts of the country. For several centuries, there were frequent struggles between the Christians and Moors. Several distinct Christian kingdoms were established during this period, the most considerable of which were *Castile, Leon, Arragon*, and *Navarre*. As the several provinces of Spain were wrested from the Moors at different times, and by different leaders, almost every province was formed into a separate kingdom. By conquest, marriages, &c., these petty kingdoms were gradually diminished, until about A. D. 1479, when all the Spanish crowns were united in one, by the marriage of Ferdinand and Isabella, the former, monarch of Arragon, the latter, of Castile. It was during their reign, that the Moors were driven from *Grenada*, the only possession they had left in Spain.

194. *Defeat of the Saracens, by Charles Martel.* The Saracens, having conquered the greater part of Spain, next turned their arms against France, and all Europe was threatened with subjugation to the Mahometan dominion and religion. *Charles Martel*, who held in his

---

193. Where did the Christian forces retire, on the invasion of the Moors? What Christian kingdoms in Spain? Under what monarchs were they finally united?

194. By whom were the Saracens defeated? What were the consequences of this event?

hands the government of France, by his genius and great exertions, rescued the empire from destruction. He brought the Moors to a general engagement, near *Poictiers*, and, notwithstanding their numbers and bravery, defeated them with immense slaughter. They afterwards rebelled, but were again defeated and driven out of France. By this event, the terror with which the Saracens filled Europe, was greatly removed; and it is a remarkable fact, that after this defeat, they made no farther attack upon the northern nations.

195. *State of the Eastern Empire.* During the period of the Saracen conquests, the eastern empire retained a portion of its ancient grandeur. Constantinople, the capital, though splendid and refined, was a constant scene of rebellions and conspiracies, and the members of the imperial family committed a series of the most horrid and atrocious crimes. One emperor was put to death in revenge for murder and incest; another was poisoned by his queen; a third was assassinated in the bath, by his own domestics; a fourth tore out the eyes of his brothers; the Empress *Irene*, who commenced her reign in A. D. 788. deposed and murdered her only son. At this period, there was a most violent controversy respecting the worship of images in the churches; and these disputes were often settled by the sword. The Empress Irene assembled a council of 350 bishops, at Nice, who established the worship of images, and pronounced the most dreadful curses against all those who should make any opposition.

196. *Arabian Literature.* The Arabians were early distinguished for their love of poetry. The book of Job, the earliest poetic composition of which we have any knowledge, was written in Arabia. I was customary, before the time of Mahomet, in the fairs at Mecca, to have poetical contests; and the poem to which the

---

195. What was the state of the Greek empire, during the period of the Saracen conquests? What is said of the Empress Irene?

196. What is said of the book of Job? What is said of the poetical contests? What is said of Haroun al Raschid?

prize was awarded, was written on asbestos, in letters of gold, and hung up in their sacred buildings. These poems are distinguished for deep feelings, exalted imagination, rich imagery, and violent breathings of love and revenge. The brightest period of Arabian history commenced with Mahomet: the golden age of the Mahometan literature was during the reign of *Haroun al Raschid*, who flourished about A. D. 800. This prince invited to Bagdad learned men from all countries, and paid them princely salaries. He caused the works of the most famous Greek authors to be translated into Arabic. *Al Mamum*, who ruled soon after, offered the Greek emperor 10,000 pounds of gold, and a perpetual peace, if he would send him the philosopher Leo, to instruct him.

197. *Arts and Sciences.* At the time when the whole civilized world appeared to be approaching towards a barbarous state, the Saracens employed themselves in collecting and diffusing knowledge in the three divisions of the world. Besides the Academy at Cordova, the Saracens had fourteen others, of a superior class, in Spain. Soon after the beginning of the tenth century, students traveled from various European countries to the Arabian schools in Spain, in order to gain a knowledge of mathematics, medicine, and other sciences. The figures which we now use in arithmetic, were introduced into Europe by the Saracens,—letters of the alphabet being previously used. They had an extensive knowledge of medicine, zealously studied botany, and may be considered as the inventors of chemistry. They were also distinguished for their knowledge of history, geography, geometry, and astronomy. This is proved from the various terms used in these sciences, which are derived from the Arabic. In A. D. 802, the calif at Bagdad sent *Charlemagne* a present of a striking clock, in order to court his alliance.

197. What is said of the Saracens' diffusing knowledge? Of their academies? Of their libraries and students? What did they introduce into Europe?

198. *Attack on Constantinople. Greek Fire.* While the Saracens were extending their conquests, the eastern, or Greek empire, was also invaded by them, and suffered the loss of several valuable provinces; particularly Syria, and its provinces in Africa, which have ever since, for the most of the time, remained under the dominion of the Mahometans. In 673, the Saracens besieged Constantinople, but were compelled to retire. They renewed their attacks for seven years in succession, but were defeated each time, by *Callinicus*, who invented an inextinguishable fire, called the *Greek fire*, by which he destroyed their ships. This liquid fire was composed of such materials, that water, instead of quenching, quickened this powerful agent of destruction. It was a period of more than 400 years, before the secret of its composition was obtained from the Greeks. The Mahometans at length discovered and stole it. It continued to be used in war, till the discovery of gunpowder, in the fourteenth century.

199. *The Feudal System.* The feudal system had its origin among those barbarous nations, the Goths, Lombards, &c., who overran the countries of Europe on the decline of the Roman Empire. It was adopted by Charlemagne, and eventually by most of the princes of Europe. When a northern chief or king made a conquest of a Roman province, the lands, after he had taken out his share, were distributed by lot to his principal chiefs, who served under his orders. These lands were held in entire sovereignty by the different chieftains, with this condition, that in time of war, they were to render their military services to the king. This bond of union being feeble, the king oftentimes found it difficult to obtain assistance from his chiefs or nobles, and his kingdom frequently exhibited a scene of anarchy, turbulence, and strife.

---

198. When did the Saracens besiege Constantinople? What is said of the Greek fire? How long was it used?
199. Where did the feudal system have its origin? How was the system introduced?

200. *Of the Barons or Lords.* The example of the king in distributing lands was imitated by his chiefs, who also, under similar conditions, distributed portions of their estates to their dependents. Every freeman or soldier, upon receiving his allotment of the conquered lands, bound himself to appear in arms against the common enemy, whenever his leader should call upon him for this purpose. The grantor of land was called *lord*, or *baron*, and they who received the grant, were called *vassals.* The same service which a vassal owed his lord, was due from the lord to the king. Possessed of a large tract of country, and residing at a distance from the capital, these barons, or lords, erected strong castles or fortresses in places difficult of access: they oppressed their dependents, slighted the civil laws of the state, and were often in a condition to set the authority of the king at defiance. In the reign of Stephen, of England, when the feudal system was at its height, not less than one thousand castles had been erected in the southern part of the island.

201. *Of the Serfs, or Villeins.* The most numerous and useful class of the community, were the common people who cultivated the lands, and were called *serfs,* or *villeins.* They were in a miserable state of servitude, and no better than slaves, being transferred from one lord to another, like cattle and the implements of husbandry. The barons often contended with each other, and settled their disputes by the sword: "the people became familiarized to violence and blood, to despotism and injustice; intellectual and moral improvement was suspended, the arts and sciences were banished, and the light of Christianity was obscured." Never was there a period in the annals of Europe, so

200. In what respect did the chiefs imitate the king? Who were lords, and who vassals? What is said of the barons, or lords?
201. Who were the most numerous class of the community? What were they called, and what was their condition? What is said of the era of the feudal system?

filled with atrocious actions, as from the seventh to the eleventh century, the era of the feudal system.

202. *Decline of the Feudal System.* At the commencement of the twelfth century, the unhappy state of things, brought on by the prevalence of the feudal system, began to abate, and government, laws and manners, began to have influence on the minds of men. Some of the principal causes of the decline of the system, were the Crusades; the formation of cities into communities with special privileges; the extension of commerce; the increase and distribution of wealth, and the diffusion of knowledge. The establishment of standing armies had a great effect. By this means, the king was able to crush the power of the nobles, and reduce them to order and obedience. The feudal system, however, still exists in some degree, in some parts of Europe, particularly in Russia and Poland, and in some parts of Germany.

203. *Bishop of Rome.* When Christianity first prevailed throughout the Roman empire, Rome was the seat of government. From this circumstance the bishop and church at Rome obtained a kind of pre-eminence over all others. The authority of the bishop of Rome seems to have been first established by *Phocas*, the emperor of Constantinople, who in A. D. 606, conferred on Boniface III., the title of *Universal Bishop*, and at the same time declared the "*Church of Rome to be the head of all other churches.*" The bishop of Rome is also called the *Sovereign* or *Roman Pontiff*, or High Priest, and the *Pope:* this latter term is derived from a Greek word, which signifies *father*, and accordingly, the pope is considered by the Roman Catholics, as the father and head of all Christians, and the regular successor of the Apostle Peter. They believe that Peter was the first pope or bishop of Rome: they also believe the pope to

---

202. What were the principal causes of the decline of the feudal system? Where does the feudal system, in a degree, now exist?

303. By whom was the church of Rome declared to be the head of all others? What is the bishop of Rome called? State the belief of the Catholics?

be *infallible*, that is, he cannot err, when he addresses himself to the faithful on matters of doctrine, &c.

204. *Temporal power of the Popes.* At the time when Childeric, a weak prince, occupied the throne of France, Pepin, the son of Charles Martel, was his prime minister. The latter, who aspired to the throne, referred the question to Pope Zachary, whether he or Childeric was best entitled to the crown. Zachary decided in favor of Pepin, who, accordingly, ascended the throne, after having deposed Childeric, who was sent to end his days in a monastery. Pepin thus became the first of a race of kings, who occupied the throne of France for two hundred and thirty-six years. As a reward to the Roman pontiff, Pepin, in A. D. 755, conferred on Stephen, the successor of Zachary, several rich provinces in Italy, by which gift he was established as a *temporal monarch.*

205. *Charlemagne.* Pepin was succeeded in the government of France by Charles, who is distinguished in history by the name of *Charlemagne,* or *Charles the Great.* He was by far the greatest monarch of his age, and was distinguished as a conqueror and statesman. He was engaged in war during most of his reign. He successively encountered the Saracens, Huns, and Saxons, with whom he had a bloody war of 30 years duration. Although allied to the king of the *Lombards* by marriage, yet at the request of the pope, he made war upon him, drove him from the throne, and put a final period to the Lombard dominion in Italy, A. D. 774. Charlemagne was accustomed to visit Italy yearly: when in Rome for the last time, on Christmas, then the first day of the new year, being at mass on his knees before the altar, the pope came suddenly behind him, and placed on his head the crown of the Cesars. This act was followed with loud acclamations, and Charlemagne was consecrated *Emperor of the West,* A. D. 800.

---

204. By what means was the Roman Pontiff established as a temporal prince?

205. What is said of Charlemagne? By whom was he crowned emperor of the West? Relate the circumstances.

PERIOD IV.

DISTINGUISHED FOR THE PREVALENCE OF THE DARK AGES

Monastic System.—Dark Ages.

FROM THE CROWNING OF CHARLEMAGNE TO THE FIRST CRUSADE.

(295 YEARS.)

206. *Reign of Charlemagne.* The empire of Charlemagne, when he was crowned *Emperor of the West*, comprised France, the Netherlands, Germany, Switzerland, a great part of Italy, and part of Spain. He had no permanent capital, though *Aix-la-Chapelle* was, for a long time, his favorite residence. Charlemagne, though living in a dark age, was an eminent patron of learning, and endeavored to dispel the great ignorance which then prevailed. He manifested his zeal for religion by compelling those whom he subdued, to receive Christian baptism, on pain of being either made slaves, or of suffering death. His private character is said to have been amiable and respectable ; he brought up his sons to manly exercises, and his daughters to spinning and housewifery, and took delight in appearing ornamented with the productions of his wife and daughters. This

---

206. What countries did the empire of Charlemagne embrace? What is said of Charlemagne, and when did he die?

illustrious monarch died A. D. 814 in the 72d year of his age.

207. *Danish invasion of England.* England, which had been divided into a number of petty sovereignties, during more than two centuries, became one entire kingdom, in A. D. 827, under Egbert, nearly 400 years after the first arrival of the Saxons in England. The English, now so happily united, enjoyed their prosperity but a short period. The piratical *Danes*, or *Normans*, who had molested the English coasts for fifty years, now became more troublesome. The Danes, then comprehended under the general name of Normans, were of Gothic origin, and were driven by Charlemagne into Denmark: from this *northern* part of Europe, they made their incursions; hence the name *Normans*. In their course, they carried off the goods, the cattle, and even the wretched inhabitants; and then returning to their vessels, sailed to some other quarter, which was not prepared for their reception. The Danes at length became so formidable, that they obtained possession of some of the principal places, and established themselves in the country.

208. *Alfred the Great.* While the Danes were ravaging England, *Alfred*, called the Great, the sixth king of England, for a time successfully defended his country. In one year he defeated the Danes in eight battles, when a new irruption of their countrymen forced him to solicit a peace, which these pirates interrupted by new hostilities. The forces of Alfred were so weakened and dispirited, that he was abandoned, and compelled to seek his safety for many months, in an obscure part of the country, disguised in the dress of a peasant, and living in a herdsman's cottage as a servant. It is said, that on one occasion, the herdsman's wife ordered him to take care of some cakes that were baking by the fire,

---

207. When did England become one kingdom? Who were the Danes, and what is said of them?

208. What is said of Alfred? With whom did he seek refuge? Relate the anecdote of Alfred and the herdsman's wife.

but he forgot his trust and let them burn ; for this she scolded him severely, telling him he would be ready enough to eat, though he would not take the pains to turn them.

The herdsman's wife scolding at King Alfred.

209. *Successes of Alfred.* The Danes having been made careless by their successes, the followers of Alfred gained some advantages over them. Alfred hearing of this, resolved to make a vigorous effort to obtain his crown. He entered the Danish camp in the disguise of a harper, and excited so much interest by his musical talents, that he was introduced to *Guthrum*, the Danish prince, and remained with him for some days. Having obtained a perfect knowledge of their camp and unguarded state, he returned to his followers, and with a large force attacked the Danes, and obtained a complete victory. Alfred then proposed to Guthrum, that he and his followers should embrace the Christian religion, and join the English in opposing the ravages of the Danes. This proposition was accepted ; Guthrum and his men were baptized, and settled in England, A. D. 880.

---

209. By what means did Alfred get into the Danish camp? What is related of Guthrum, the Danish prince, and his followers?

MODERN HISTORY. 145

210. *Character of Alfred.* Alfred was one of the greatest and best sovereigns that ever sat on a throne. The institutions which he founded, are to this day the glory of the British nation. He was equally excellent in his private and public character, and was distinguished for his personal accomplishments, both of body and mind, and is considered the greatest legislator, scholar, and warrior of the age in which he lived. After having restored tranquillity to his distracted kingdom, he employed himself in cultivating the arts of peace, and in raising his people from the depths of ignorance, barbarism, and wretchedness. He invited learned men from every quarter of Europe to reside in his dominions, established schools, and is said to have founded the University of Oxford. According to various historians, he divided England into countries, composed a code of laws, established trial by jury, and for the instruction of his people, translated a number of works into the Saxon language.

211. *Conquest of England by the Danes.* After the death of Alfred his wise institutions were but feebly enforced by his successors—disorders sprung up, and the nation again began to return to their former barbarism. The Danes renewed their invasions, and harassed the kingdom for a long series of years. In 981, *Swein,* king of Denmark, assisted by the king of Norway, invaded England with a great fleet, won several important battles, and would have destroyed London, had not *Ethelred,* the king, purchased their departure with a large sum of money. In the year 1002, great numbers of the Danes, on a given day, were massacred all over the kingdom: to revenge this barbarous massacre, Swein again attacked England with a powerful army, and after a series of struggles, the English were

---

210. State the character of Alfred. What did he do for his kingdom?
211. After the death of Alfred, what was the state of England? What kings invaded England? At what time were the English conquered?

13

conquered, and submitted to the Danish king, *Canute*, A. D. 1017.

212. *Canute and his Successors.* Canute having conquered England, became the most powerful monarch of his time, being now sovereign of Denmark, Norway, and England. Some of his courtiers affected to think his power uncontrollable, and that all things would be obedient to his command. In order to make them ashamed of their folly, he placed himself in a chair by the sea side, while the tide was rising. As the waters approached, he commanded them to retire and obey the voice of the mighty Canute; but the sea still advanced, and when it began to wet his feet, he turned to his courtiers and reproved them for their impious flattery.

Canute died in 1035, and the English throne descended to his two sons, who died soon after their father. The kingdom now returned to the Saxon line of kings, in the person of Edward, who had been an exile for forty years; he died, however, immediately on his arrival in England, and Edward, surnamed the *Confessor*, succeeded to the throne. The king died without children, and is said to have bequeathed the crown to his kinsman, *William, Duke of Normandy*, in France. The English nobles and clergy, however, elected and proclaimed *Harold*, the son of the Earl of Kent, as king of England.

213. *Norman Conquest.* (*Battle of Hastings.*) William of Normandy now resolved to maintain his claim to the crown of England, by force of arms. He made the most formidable preparations, and was aided by many sovereign princes, and was accompanied by a great body of the nobility of the European nations,

---

212. Of what countries was Canute the sovereign? What did he do to shame his courtiers? Who were the successors of Canute? Who was William, Duke of Normandy, and who was Harold?

213. By whom was William of Normandy attended? How were the armies of William and Harold occupied previous to the battle of Hastings? State the result of the battle. What was William called after this period?

who were soldiers of fortune. William lai ded his army, 60,000 in number, on the coast, and met the army of Harold at *Hastings*. On the night previous to the battle, the English, flushed with their recent success over the Norwegians, and being confident of a new victory, spent the night in riot and jollity. The Normans, on the other hand, were occupied in prayer and other religious duties. In the morning, William ordered the signal of battle to be given, and his whole army, singing the hymn of Roland, the peer of Charlemagne, advanced to the attack. After a desperate battle, which lasted from morning to sunset, Harold was slain, and his army nearly destroyed. The Normans lost 15,000 men. William, from this period, was styled *Conqueror*, and came into possession of the throne of England, and was crowned on Christmas day, A. D. 1066.

214. *William the Conqueror.* The character of William was spirited, haughty, and tyrannical, yet not without a portion of the generous affections. He disgusted the English by giving most of the offices of trust and importance to his Norman followers. To prevent the seditious meetings of his subjects, he ordered a bell, called the *Curfew bell*, to be rung every evening at 8 o'clock, to warn the people to put out their lights. He introduced the French language into court, and ordered that all law proceedings should be directed in that tongue. By this means, many words of French origin are now to be found in the English language. He is said to have introduced the *feudal system* into England. By his forest laws he reserved to himself the exclusive privilege of killing game throughout the kingdom. One of the acts of his reign was his accomplishing a general survey of all the lands in the kingdom, their value, the names of the proprietors, and a record of every class of persons on them, &c. This valuable record is called the *Doomsday book*, which is still preserved.

---

214. What was the character of William? What did he do to prevent seditious meetings? What did he introduce into England? What was called the Doomsday book?

215. *State of the Arts, &c., at the Norman Conquest.* By the conquest, great changes were effected in the state of England. Many of the Norman nobility and common people, settled in England, and by them the agriculture of the country was much improved, by the introduction of carts, harrows, sythes, &c. The Norman plough had two wheels, and was drawn by one or more oxen. Great improvements were made in the art of building, particularly churches and monasteries, which were often erected at an immense expense. The clergy and monks at this period, possessed the most wealth and influence, and their zeal was directed towards these objects. It was at this time, that the *Gothic style* of building was introduced. The houses of the common citizens, however, were very mean. Even in London, the houses of mechanics and common burgesses, were built of wood and thatched with reeds or straw, down to the close of the 12th century. Glass windows were seen only in churches, or in the mansions of the rich. The dressing and spinning of wool and flax were practiced before the conquest; but these arts were greatly improved by the *Flemings*, who settled in England after the conquest.

216. *Norman Nobles, or Barons.* William the Conqueror introduced into England the *feudal law;* dividing the whole kingdom excepting the royal domains, into *baronies*, and bestowing the most of them on his Norman followers, under the tenure of military service. The Norman barons introduced much splendor and magnificence into England. Instead of the mean houses in which the English used to spend their nights in feasting and revelry, the Norman barons dwelt in stately palaces, kept elegant tables, and a splendid equipage. As there were no good inns in those times, they were obliged, when traveling, to carry their own bedding and

---

215. What improvements did the Normans introduce into England? What is said of the houses of the common and other citizens? What is said of the Flemings?

216. Who introduced the feudal law into England? What is said of the Norman barons? How was a nobleman, or prelate, attended on a journey?

provisions. A nobleman, or prelate, when on a journey, was attended with a train of servants and attendants, knights, esquires, pages, clerks, cooks, &c. Many of the English nobility, at the present day, trace their descent up to their ancestors, the Norman barons.

217. *Baronial Castles, &c.* During the prevalence of the feudal system, murders, robberies, and violence, were so common, that the barons of England, as in France, erected castles for their residences, of which many remain at the present day. Their situation was generally on an eminence, and near a river. They surrounded these structures with a deep broad ditch, oftentimes filled with water. Before the great gate was an outwork, a strong high wall with turrets upon it, for the defense of the gate and draw-bridge over the ditch. The walls of the castle were eight or ten feet thick, and twenty or thirty feet high. From the top of this wall and from the roofs of the buildings, the defenders discharged arrows, darts, and stones, upon the assailants. Within this outward wall were one or two more, surrounding the chief tower, four or five stories high, with thick walls. This was the residence of the owner of the castle. Under the ground a dungeon was built for the confinement of prisoners. Robbery was so common at times, that no person could travel in safety. The robbers sometimes formed companies, under powerful barons, who shared with them the plunder, and protected them in their castles.

218. *Dark Ages.* Although the Emperor Charlemagne, and Alfred the Great, made many and noble efforts to enlighten their subjects, yet the darkness and superstition of the age proved too powerful for their exertions. After they were removed by death, darkness returned and prevailed throughout Europe, more or less,

---

217. What prevailed during the feudal system? Why were castles built? Give a description of them. What is said of robbers?

218. After the death of Charlemagne and Alfred, what was the state of Europe? What is said of Christianity during these times? **What is said of the clergy, and of the bishops?**

13*

till the fifteenth century. The scarcity of books, in those times, and the nature of their subjects, as legends, lives of the saints, &c., account in part for such a state of things. During this period the human mind appeared debased, and hardly any thing was too irrational or absurd for the credulity of the times. Pure Christianity was but little known, amidst a multitude of idle ceremonies, external pomp and show. The clergy were noted for their luxurious habits, and ignorance. Even the higher clergy were so destitute of the first rudiments of learning, that it was scarcely disgraceful to acknowledge it; and many bishops, who attended councils, &c., could not even write their names to the acts that were passed.

219. *Collection of Relics.* In the beginning of the ninth century, the passion for collecting the relics of the saints arrived at a great height, and many persons of distinction traveled into Palestine in order to obtain them. The bodies of the apostles, and first martyrs, are said to have been dug up, and great quantities of bones and other relics, were brought into Europe, and sold for enormous prices. Numerous impositions were practised in this traffic; and purchasers seem not to have been very nice or scrupulous in their inquiries; and many a devotee has wept over the bones of a dog, or jackall, supposing he had before him the relic of an apostle. These relics were supposed to have the power of healing diseases, working miracles, &c., and so eager were some of the churches to obtain these precious treasures, that they would sometimes possess themselves of them by violence or theft; and these attempts, when successful, were considered as pious and acceptable to the Supreme Being.

220. *Monastic Institutions.* During the first ages of Christianity, the persecutions attending its profession,

---

219. At what time did the passion for collecting relics prevail? Where were these relics obtained, and what were they? What power was it supposed they had? What means did some of the churches take to obtain them?

forced some Christians to retire from the world, and live in deserts and places most private and unfrequented, in hopes of finding that peace and comfort among beasts which was denied them among men. Some very extraordinary persons having retired in this manner, their example gave such reputation to retirement, that the practice was continued when there was no reason for it. After Christianity became the religion of the Roman empire, it was considered to be highly meritorious for a person to abandon all human connections and concerns, and to afflict the body with fastings, penances, &c. To drag out a life of suffering was considered as an act most acceptable to the Deity. The first monks were the followers of *St. Anthony*, of Egypt, who, near the close of the fourth century, formed themselves into a regular body, and engaged to live by certain rules.

221. *Progress of the Monastic System.* The example of Anthony was followed to such an extent, that in a short time the whole East was filled with a set of indolent mortals. In Egypt where the Mahometan religion has prevailed for centuries, the remains of numerous Christian monasteries are still to be seen. From the East, this gloomy disposition passed into Europe, and very soon all Christendom became infected with this superstition; and various orders of *monks* and *friars* were instituted—such as *Dominicans, Benedictines,* &c. This kind of life was not confined to males; females also began to retire from the world, and dedicate themselves to solitude and devotion. These female devotees were called *nuns,* and the establishments in which they were secluded, *nunneries.* At the period of the dark ages, the monastic system arrived at its height: even kings and great lords, unmindful of their duties to

---

220. What first caused Christians to retire from the world? How was it when Christianity was the religion of the empire? Who were the first monks?

221. Where was the example of Anthony followed? What are the names of some of the monkish orders? What are nuns, and nunneries?

society, sought in these abodes an asylum from the cares and temptations of the world.

222. *Corruption of the Monastic System.* The original rules of the monastic life were strict, but they fell gradually into disuse. The monasteries daily increased in wealth, by donations from the rich, who were in the habit, just before death, of bestowing their property on these institutions, supposing that by this means they would secure the salvation of their souls. The monks now found themselves in a condition to claim high stations in worldly society. Many of their monasteries appeared more like the palaces of princes, stored with luxuries, than as the retreats of penitence and mortification. Before the close of the fifth century, the monks became notorious for their licentiousness, and often excited the most dreadful tumults and disorders in various places. In the eighth century, the monastic discipline was extremely relaxed, both in the eastern and western provinces, and all efforts to restore it were ineffectual. The monks were generally lazy, illiterate, profligate, and licentious epicures.

223. *Increase of the Papal Power.* The influence of the pope, during the dark ages, and for a long period afterwards, was far greater than that of any other monarch in Christendom : he claimed authority over kings and kingdoms, and assumed the title of master of the world. If a sovereign offended him, his whole kingdom was liable to be laid under an *interdict*, during which the celebration of public worship was suspended, and the churches shut up ; no sacrament, except baptism and extreme unction, were administered, and the dead were buried in the highways, without funeral rites. In the eleventh century, when Gregory VII. occupied the papal chair, he excommunicated and deposed Henry

---

222. How were the monasteries increased in wealth? What is said of monasteries, and the character of the monks.?
223. What is said of the influence and authority of the popes ? What was an interdict? What did Pope Gregory compel Henry, the emperor of Germany, to do?

IV., emperor of Germany, and compelled him to appear before him as a penitent sinner, and in the depth of winter to pass three days in the open air, with his head and feet bare, before he would grant him absolution. This pontiff said in several of his letters, that "it was his duty to pull down the pride of kings."

224. *Of the Clergy.* The *secular clergy*, during this period, who had the care of parishes, and whose business it was to instruct the people, were destitute of almost every qualification for their sacred office. They seldom preached, for scarcely any of them knew how to read or write. In the 12th, 13th, and 14th centuries, the sacred scriptures were but little known, and many bishops had never seen a Bible during their lives. The sermons of those who undertook to preach, were principally made of legends and absurd stories, relating to the lives and exploits of the saints. By degrees public instruction was mostly given up; and it was generally held, that to repeat a few forms in rapid succession, observe the holy days, go pilgrimages, and to pay tithes, &c., to the clergy, was all that was necessary to make a good Christian.

225. *State of Learning.* In these dark and miserable times, learning was as much corrupted and obscured as religion. The little which existed, was chiefly employed about the life and miracles of the saints, and other subjects of no utility. The questions which commanded attention were of the most trifling and absurd character, and the discussions were specimens of folly. The establishment of monasteries, although pernicious in other respects, performed an important service to literature, and for ages they were the abode of what little learning remained in the Christian world. The monks being confined to the monasteries, had more opportunities for study, and fewer for dissipation, and were not in general sunk so low in ignorance as the secular clergy.

---

224. What is said of the secular clergy? The bishops? What of the sermons of those who preached? What was considered necessary to make a Christian?

225. What was the state of learning? How did monasteries perform service to literature?

But the most important services the monasteries performed, was their being a safe repository for books; and some of the higher order of monks made manuscript copies of the choicest works of Greece and Rome, and by this means almost all the ancient learning and manuscripts which have reached us, were preserved.

226. *Trials by Ordeal.* During the dark ages, trials by *ordeal* were very common, and were sanctioned by the public laws of most countries of Europe. The criminal was ordered by the judge to prove his innocence or guilt by the ordeal of cold water, of boiling water, or red-hot iron. The *ordeal by cold water*, was as follows: the person to be tried was conducted to the church, and most solemnly adjured to confess the fact if he was guilty. If he would not confess, he received the sacrament and then was conducted to a river or lake. The priest then exorcised the water, charging it not to receive the criminal if he was guilty. The criminal was now stripped naked, and bound, and a rope was tied to him: he was then cast into the water; if he floated, he was accounted guilty; but if he sunk to the depth marked on the rope, (sometimes a yard and a half,) he was instantly drawn out and pronounced innocent. In the *ordeal of boiling water*, the criminal was made to thrust his hand and arm into boiling water, and take a ring or stone from the bottom of the vessel in which it was contained. In the *ordeal of hot iron*, he was made to walk bare-footed over red-hot ploughshares, or hold red-hot iron in his hands. History records examples when these experiments were undergone without injury or pain.

227. *Trial by Combat.* The trial by combat originated among the northern barbarians, before the Christian era. Many of these barbarous tribes, when they embraced Christianity, still continued many of the savage customs and laws of their ancestors, although entirely

---

226. By whom were trials by ordeal sanctioned? Describe the ordeal by cold water, the ordeal by boiling water, and the ordeal of hot iron.

227. How did the trial by combat originate? What is said respecting these trials?

contrary to the spirit and precepts of the Christian religion. The *trial by combat* was a mode of settling private disputes and quarrels between individuals, when there was not sufficient evidence to make the case clear. The judge appointed the time for the combat and presided over it. The parties deposited with the judge, bonds or goods, for paying the forfeiture and fees of the court, in case they were cast. The knights fought on horseback, and common men fought on foot. Certain persons, as women, priests, and others, might employ *champions* to fight in their stead. The judicial combat, though sanctioned by high authority, even so late as the last century, in France and England, was a bloody and iniquitous custom, from which, to this day, may be traced the savage custom of duelling.

228. *Peter the Hermit.* Peter the Hermit, the first mover of the Crusades, was a gentleman of Amiens, in France, who left the military profession to become a hermit and pilgrim. He was led to this course by the belief which then prevailed throughout Christendom, at the close of the 11th century, that the world was near its end. He with many others hastened to the Holy Land, in A. D. 1093, that he might terminate his days in a spot which had given birth to the Saviour of the world. Such, however, was the cruel treatment that the Christian pilgrims received from the Turks, who had Jerusalem and the Holy Land in their possession, that Peter returned, to arouse all Europe for the deliverance of the Holy city from the hands of the infidels. Having received the sanction of Pope Urban II., Peter traveled from city to city, and from kingdom to kingdom, and succeeded in arousing all classes of men to undertake this holy warfare.

---

228. Who was Peter the Hermit? When did Peter go to the Holy Land, and for what purpose? Why did Peter return to Europe, and for what purpose?

PERIOD V.

DISTINGUISHED FOR THE CRUSADES

Christendom excited to the Crusades.

FROM THE FIRST TO THE LAST CRUSADE.

(200 YEARS.)

229. *First Crusade.* The attention of all Christendom having been fully aroused, by Peter the Hermit, to the subject of recovering the Holy Land from the infidels, Pope Urban called a general council, at Clermont, in France, A. D. 1095, in order to make a final decision. An immense multitude assembled. Urban and Peter addressed the assembled crowds : the horrors and indignities of the infidel oppressions, the duty of arming in the holy cause, and the reward of those who were slain in fighting the battles of the Lord, were set forth with such effect, that they all, as one man, sent forth the shout, " *It is the will of God! It is the will of God!*" Persons of all ranks now flew to arms with the utmost ardor. Eternal salvation was promised to all who should come forth to the help of the Lord, in this holy warfare. All men

---

229. Where did Pope Urban call a general council, and for what purpose ? Who addressed the multitude, and what did the crowd do ? What was promised to those who engaged in the crusades ? Who engaged in these expeditions ?

now deemed the crusades the road to heaven and were impatient to open the way with their swords to the holy city. Nobles, artisans, peasants, and even priests, enrolled their names ; and to decline this service was considered impious and cowardly. The aged and infirm contributed by presents and money, and many attended in person, being determined, if possible, to breathe their last in sight of the holy city. Even women, concealing their sex under the disguise of armor, attended the camp. Robbers, incendiaries, and murderers, embraced this opportunity to expiate their sins, and secure a place in heaven.

230. *March of the Crusaders.* The middle of August, A. D. 1096, was the time fixed for the departure of the crusaders ; but so eager were the common people to go forward, that they made no suitable preparation for the undertaking, and took their departure early in the spring. *Peter the Hermit* assumed the office of general, and led on an army of 80,000 recruits towards the East. This army was followed by a mixed multitude of 200,000 persons, more like banditti than a regular body of soldiers. Subject to little control, their route was marked with various outrages, particularly against the Jews, thousands of whom they murdered. Their outrages in Hungary and Bulgaria drew upon them a severe retaliation from the inhabitants ; so that not more than one third of this multitude arrived at Constantinople. These were met soon after by the sultan, *Solyman*, on the plain of *Nice*, and almost wholly destroyed, without ever having seen Jerusalem.

231. *March of the main body of the Crusaders.* After the march of Peter, a formidable body of disciplined troops followed, being led on by able and experienced generals. The supreme command was given to *God-*

---

230. Who led on the first crusaders? By whom was this army followed? What became of them?
231. By whom was the main body of the crusaders commanded, and how many were they? Where were the Christians besieged, and by what means did they defeat their enemies?

frey, of Bouillon, duke of Lorrain, and was supported by the most distinguished princes of Europe, who served in the army. When reviewed, in the neighborhood of Nice, they amounted to 100,000 horse and 600,000 foot, including a train of women and children. Having taken Nice and defeated Solyman, they proceeded eastward, and took the city of Antioch. Their successes having alarmed the Mahometan powers, the Christians were besieged in Antioch, by an army of 300,000 men. The most terrible famine prevailed in the army of the crusaders, and their numbers were reduced far below that of the besieging army. Recourse was now had to superstition. A monk declared, that it was revealed to him that he could find where the lance which pierced our Saviour's side was buried; and that when this relic was obtained, it would insure their victory. The lance was found; the crusaders rushed out upon the infidels, who fought bravely and obstinately, till the Christian soldiers cried out, that the saints were seen fighting on their side. This gave them resistless might: the infidels fled in confusion, with the loss of 69,000 men, while that of the crusaders did not amount to one sixth of that number.

232. *Taking of Jerusalem.* The army of the crusaders, by the sword, famine, and pestilence, was reduced to about 60,000 men, when they arrived at Jerusalem. They, however, made the most incredible exertions to obtain possession of the city, and after a siege of forty days, took it by storm. The whole of its Mahometan and Jewish inhabitants were put to death. The crusaders were guilty of the most shocking barbarities: the inhabitants were massacred without mercy, and without distinction of age or sex. These ferocious conquerors and blind enthusiasts, after this terrible slaughter, marched over heaps of dead bodies, towards the holy sepulcher, and, while their hands were polluted with the

---

232. How many crusaders arrived at Jerusalem, and how did they take it? What did they do, after taking possession? Who was proclaimed king of Jerusalem?

blood of so many innocent victims, sung anthems to the common Saviour of mankind. *Godfrey* was now proclaimed king of Jerusalem, by the troops, and he soon after defeated the sultan, with an immense army but after having reigned one year, he was compelled to give up his kingdom to the pope's legate.

233. *Second Crusade.* The crusaders divided Syria and Palestine into four separate states, and having accomplished their object, began to return to Europe. The Turks began now to recover their strength: and the newly-formed Christian states in Asia found it necessary to solicit aid from Europe. The second crusade set out from the West in 1146, to the amount of 200,000 French, Germans, and Italians, led on by *Hugh*, brother to the king of France. These met with the same fate which attended Peter the Hermit. The garrison of Jerusalem now became so weak, that the monks armed themselves for its defense: hence arose the military orders of *Knights Templars,* &c. The pope now employed St. Bernard to preach up a new crusade in France; and *Louis VII.,* of France, and *Conrad III.,* of Germany, with 300,000 of their subjects, were persuaded to engage in this expedition. The Germans were cut to pieces by the sultan at Iconium; the French were totally defeated near Laodicea; and the two monarchs, after many disasters, returned with shame to their dominions.

234. *Third Crusade.* The occasion of the third crusade was the conquest of Jerusalem by the illustrious *Saladin,* nephew of the sultan of Egypt, in A. D. 1187, after it had been in the possession of the Christians about 90 years. Pope Clement, alarmed at the success of the infidels, stirred up a new crusade, in which

---

233. When did the second crusade set out? How many men, by whom commanded, and what was their fate? Who was employed to preach up a new crusade? Who went on this expedition? What is said of them?

234. What was the occasion of the third crusade? What sovereigns engaged in it, and what is said of them? Who defeated Saladin? What was done to Richard, on his return?

three sovereigns took the field with their subjects, namely: *Philip Augustus*, of France, *Richard I.*, of England, and *Frederic Barbarossa*, of Germany. This latter sovereign defeated the Turks in a general battle, but he soon after died, and his army dwindled away. Richard and Philip took *Ptolemais;* but they soon quarreled, from a jealousy of each other's glory, and Philip returned in disgust to France. Richard (surnamed the *Lion-hearted*) nobly sustained the contest with Saladin, whom he defeated near *Ascalon;* but on account of dissensions in his camp, and the reduction of his army by famine and fatigue, he thought it prudent not to attempt the siege of Jerusalem, but concluded a truce with Saladin for three years. While returning home to England, he was arrested in Germany, and kept in prison till he was ransomed with an immense sum by his subjects.

235. *Fourth Crusade.* In 1202, *Baldwin*, count of Flanders, collected an army to act against the Mahometans, in a fourth crusade. It is said, however, that his real object was not the extirpation of the infidels, but the conquest of Constantinople, the head of the eastern Christian empire. Baldwin arrived at Constantinople at a time when there was a dispute respecting the succession to the throne. After one or two revolutions in the government, the allied army of the French and Venetians determined to seize the city on their own account. This, after a severe struggle, was effected. The army of the invaders consisted of but 20,000 men, while there were in Constantinople 400,000 men capable of bearing arms, and the city was at this time the largest and most splendid in the world. To the infamy of the followers of Baldwin, they destroyed most of the noble monuments of genius which had been preserved from ancient times. In no conquered city, it is thought,

---

235. Who engaged in the fourth crusade? What is said to have been his real object? Did he effect it? What is said of the followers of Baldwin? What became of Baldwin and his empire?

was there ever so much booty obtained. Baldwin was elected emperor, but was murdered after reigning a few months: the imperial dominions were then shared among his principal followers. From the time of Baldwin, the spirit of crusading remained at rest for nearly half a century, when it revived under *Louis IX.*, of France

236. *Chivalry, or Knighthood.* Chivalry was an institution which had for its principal object the correction of the evils which prevailed in the state of society during the prevalence of the feudal system among the European nations. Chivalry attained its greatest height and perfection during the time of the crusades; and during the several centuries it prevailed, it had a very great influence on the opinions, habits, and manners of mankind. The origin of this spirit may be traced to the manners and customs of the *Gothic* nations, among whom the profession of arms was the only employment esteemed honorable. Chivalry was distinguished for a romantic spirit of adventure; a love of arms, and the rewards of valor; and eagerness to protect the oppressed; to avenge wrongs; high sentiments of honor and religion; and especially a devoted and respectful attachment to the female sex.

237. *Education of Knights.* The sons of noblemen who were destined for chivalry, at the age of seven years, entered on a course of education, which was to prepare them for the performance of its duties and enjoyments of its honors. They were educated at their father's castle, or that of some nobleman in the vicinity. From the age of 7 to 14 the name given to these boys was *valet*, or *page:* they were kept in active employment, and became accustomed to the duties of obedience and courtesy, by waiting on the master and mis-

---

236. What was the object of chivalry, and when did it attain to its greatest height? What was the origin of this spirit, and for what was it distinguished?

237. At what age did the knights begin their education? When was the name varlet or page given? What was their employment, and what were they taught?

14*

tress of the castle, at home or abroad. By the ladies of the castle they were taught at the same time the rudiments of religion and devotion to the female sex, and the first impressions made on their minds were those of love, gallantry, honor, and bravery. They were taught that the only means of attaining the highest honors, were respectful devotion to the ladies, and skill and courage in warfare. In order that they might practice in some degree the instructions they received, it was customary for each youth to select some young, accomplished, and virtuous lady, at whose feet he displayed his gallantry, and who undertook to refine and polish his manners.

238. *Of the Esquires.* At the age of fourteen, the pages received the title of *armiger*, or *esquire*, and were then authorized to bear arms: his education, however, was not completed until he was twenty-one years of age. The esquire prepared the repast in the morning; at dinner, he, as well as the pages, attended at the table, and presented to the lord and his guests the water used for washing. The knights and esquires never sat at the same table, not even in the case of a father and son. The esquires often made the beds of their lords; each of them had their respective duties, such as the squire of the chamber, the carrying squire, &c. They practiced every exercise by which strength and activity could be given to the body; they learned to endure hunger and thirst, and accustomed themselves to wield the sword, thrust the lance, strike with the ax, and to wear armor; no exercise, however, was more important than that of horsemanship.

239. *Of the Knights.* The full dignity of knighthood was seldom conferred on a squire before the age of twenty-one. To prepare for this honor they were obliged to submit to severe fastings, to spend nights in

---

238. At the age of 14, what title did the pages receive? What were the duties of the esquires? What were their exercises?

239. How was the esquire prepared for the dignity of knight-

prayer in a church, to receive the sacrament, to bathe, to put on white robes, confess their sins, and hear sermons, in which Christian morals were enforced and explained. The candidate then took an oath, consisting of 26 articles, in which, among other things, he swore he would be a good, brave, loyal, just, generous, and gentle knight, a champion of the church and clergy, a protector of the ladies, and a redresser of the wrongs of widows and

A Knight in Armor.

orphans. While on his knees he received from the hands of the knights and ladies the various parts of his armor, and in the last place his sword. The concluding sign of being *dubbed*, or adopted into the order of knighthood, was a slight blow given by the lord, on the neck or cheek; he was then proclaimed a knight, " in the name of God and the Saints."

240. *Character, &c. of the Knights.* The character of a true knight, although containing many defects, was distinguished by much that was praiseworthy and noble. His whole course was directed by a regard to religion;

---

hood? What did he take an oath to be? What was the concluding sign of being adopted a knight?

240. What is said of the character of the knights? What were his privileges?

though it must be confessed, that the religion of the times consisted more in form, than in spirit. The knight was distinguis'.ed for his perfect fidelity to his word, his modesty, generosity, and courtesy. By being dubbed a knight, he was invested with many privileges and dignities which were not limited to his own country, but extended throughout a great part of Europe. He had a right to roam through the world in search of adventures, and was authorized to propose a trial of skill with the lance, to all of his own order he met, and to combat them with fury, if they did not acknowledge the lady to whom he had devoted himself, to be the most beautiful in the world. In war, when the sovereign led his army to the attack, his never-failing injunction was, "Let every one think of his mistress."

241. *Of Tournaments.* Tournaments were military exercises, performed by two parties of knights or cavaliers. No amusement was so delighted in, by the gallant knights or beauteous ladies, by kings, the nobility, and gentry, as these images of war. These exhibitions were often splendid, far beyond any thing seen at the present age, especially at coronations, the marriage of princes, victories, &c. No knight who had blasphemed God, or offended the ladies, or had been false or ungrateful, was allowed to enter these contests At the tournament, the space inclosed within the lists was surrounded by sovereign princes, nobles, knights of renown, and all that rank and beauty had distinguished among the fair. Covered with armor, and known only by their emblazoned shields, the combatants rushed forward to a strife, without enmity, but not without danger The ladies were the supreme judges of the tournaments, and victory little less glorious, and perhaps, at the moment, more deeply felt than in the field, since no battle could assemble such witnesses of valor.

242. *Orders of Knighthood.* The orders of chivalry,

---

241. What were tournaments? What is said of these exhibitions? What knights could not enter these contests? **Describe them.**

or knighthood, were of two general descriptions viz religious and military. Some of the religious orders were those of Templars, St. James, Alcantrava, the lady of Mercy, and St. Michael. In the religious orders, the *cavaliers*, or knights, were bound by the three great monastic vows of chastity, poverty, and obedience. The military orders were imitations of the religious. Those of the *Garter*, the *Golden fleece*, and *St. Michael*, in France, were clearly of chivalric origin : many others, which now exist in Europe, cannot boast of such a descent. All these various orders had particular rules, by which they professed to be governed, but they varied with the spirit of the times. The *Knight Templars*, who became quite famous, were founded by *Baldwin*, king of Jerusalem, for the defense of the holy sepulcher, and protection of the Christian pilgrims. After the ruin of Jerusalem, about 1186, they spread themselves throughout Europe, and flourished for a considerable period, but as their prosperity increased they became corrupted, till their vices were such, that the order was suppressed.

213. *Effects of Chivalry.* Absurd as chivalry was in some respects, it had a powerful influence in changing the manners of society in a barbarous age. It refined the manners, promoted the social intercourse, and softened in many respects, the horrors of war. By thinning the ranks of robbers and ruffians, it added to the safety and order of society. A nice sense of honor, and a strict regard to truth, was cherished by its maxims. But perhaps the most important effect of this institution, was the delicate and respectful attention paid to woman, whereby they were delivered from the degradation so common in savage and barbarous nations. In short, it was a great corrector of the evils of the feudal system, haughtiness, tyranny, oppression, and misrule. It can-

---

242. What were the names of some of the religious orders of knighthood ? By what vows were they bound ? What is said of the military orders ? What of the knight Templars ?

243. What was the influence of chivalry ? What was one of the most important effects of this institution ?

not be denied, however, that the principles of chivalry, like other institutions, were much superior to the practice of its professors, and that it fell far short of preserving purity. The poetry and tales of those times, afford evidence of a low state of morals.

244. *Henry II. of England.* Henry II., the first of the Plantagenets, being descended by his grandmother from the *Saxon kings,* and by his mother from the *Norman family,* succeeded to the throne, to the great satisfaction of the nation. He was the most powerful sovereign in Christendom : in addition to England he owned, by inheritance and marriage, nearly one half of France, and afterwards claimed Ireland by conquest. Some of the most remarkable circumstances in his reign, relate to his contests with *Thomas Becket,* archbishop of Canterbury. During the preceding reign, the power of the clergy had increased to a great height; they were also very corrupt in their morals, and committed, without restraint, the most enormous crimes. It is related, that it was proved, in the presence of the king, that more than one hundred murders had been committed by ecclesiastics, not one of whom had been punished. Henry resolved to reform these abuses, but he met with the most determined opposition from Becket, who contended that the clergy were not subject to the civil power.

245. *Murder of Becket.* After a long series of contests with this haughty prelate, Henry was so exasperated by his audacious conduct, that he rashly exclaimed, in the midst of his courtiers : " What ! is there none that will avenge me of that insolent priest ?" Four knights of his household, taking this expression to be a hint for the primate's death, proceeded to the cathedral, and assassinated Becket before the altar. Nothing could exceed the consternation of the king at this event;

---

244. What is said of Henry II.? What is said of the clergy, and what was proved against them ? Who opposed Henry in reforming abuses ?

245. Relate the cause and manner of Becket's death. What did Henry do ? What did the pope do respecting Becket, and what is said respecting his tomb ?

and in order to avert the resentment of the pope, did penance at the tomb of Becket, with fasting and prayer, and even presented his bare shoulders to the monks, to be scourged by a knotted cord. Becket was canonized by the pope, as a saint, by the title of *St. Thomas, of Canterbury*, and miracles were pretended to be wrought at his tomb; and at the jubilee, which was observed once in fifty years, 100,000 pilgrims are said to have been present on a pilgrimage to his tomb.

246. *Magna Charta*. John, the king of England, having made Pope Innocent III. his enemy, by appropriating some of the treasures of the church to his own purposes, felt the weight of the papal power. His kingdom was laid under an interdict, he was excommunicated, and his subjects absolved from their allegiance. The wretched monarch was brought into submission, and on his knees he solemnly agreed to hold his kingdom subject to the authority of the pope. His subjects thus trampled upon and sold, resolved to maintain their rights. The barons assembled, and binding themselves by an oath to a concert of measures, demanded from the king a ratification of the charter of privileges granted by Henry I. John refused, till resort was had to the sword; by this means he was compelled to yield to their demands, and on the 19th of June, 1215, signed that solemn charter, called the *magna charta*, or the *great charter*, which is considered the great bulwark and foundation of English liberty.

This charter consisted of fourteen specifications, of which the following were the most important, viz.: that no aid or money should be drawn from the people, unless in a few special cases, without the consent of the great council of the nation; that no person shall be tried on suspicion alone, but on the evidence of lawful witnesses; and that no person shall be tried or punished,

---

246. What was the cause of John, king of England, having the kingdom laid under an interdict? How did the barons obtain a charter? What was it called, and how considered? What were some of the provisions of the charter?

except by the judgment of his peers, (persons of the same rank with himself,) and the law of the land. John granted at the same time, the *charter of the forest*, which abolished the exclusive right of the king to kill game all over the kingdom.

247. *Of the Inquisition.* The formidable tribunal, called the *Inquisition*, was instituted about the year 1204, by Pope Innocent, in order to punish and examine heretics, as all those who differed from the Roman church were called. The increase of the *Waldenses*, at this period, seems to have been the immediate cause of the establishment of the inquisition. The Waldenses were the followers of *Peter Waldo*, a merchant of Lyons, in France, who being animated with uncommon zeal for the advancement of piety and Christian knowledge, began, in 1180, as a public teacher, to instruct the multitude. His efforts were crowned with great success, and spread into the neighboring countries. In order to crush this heresy, as it is called, the pope issued orders to the Catholic princes and people to extirpate heretics, to search into their number and quality, and transmit a faithful account thereof to Rome. Hence they were called *inquisitors*, and gave birth to the terrible tribunal called the *inquisition*.

248. *Establishment of the Inquisition.* At first the inquisitors had no tribunals, but they soon, however, had power given them to punish, in any manner they thought proper, all those brought before them. *Dominic*, a descendant from an illustrious Spanish family, and founder of the order of *Dominicans*, was appointed the chief inquisitor. From his early years, he was educated for the priesthood, and is represented to have been fiery and bloody in his disposition and character. In the course of a few years the system was brought to matu-

---

247. When was the inquisition instituted, and for what purpose? Who were the Waldenses? Who were the inquisitors?

248. What is said of Dominic, the inquisitor? At what time was the inquisition generally held? What is said of this tribunal?

rity; and branches of the "Holy Inquisition" were established in almost every province in Europe, where people were suspected of heresy. Their tribunals were held in the night, or in some retired apartment, from which the light of day was excluded. No man, however exalted his station, was secure from their summons. The hour of midnight was generally selected to demand the presence of an accused person. Wherever this tribunal exercised its full power, the people stood in so much fear of it, that parents delivered up their children, husbands their wives, and masters their servants, to its officers, without daring to murmur, or make the least resistance. Few who once entered the gloomy walls of the inquisition, ever returned; or if they were released, they never dared to whisper what they had seen or heard within those prisons of death.

249. *Scriptural Plays.* Before the invention of the art of printing, it was quite common in most countries of Europe to have the various scenes described in the Bible, acted out by theatrical companies, who visited the various towns and villages for that purpose. Not only were the first parents of mankind, the patriarchs, apostles, angels and demons, represented on the stage, but even representations of God the Father, of Christ, and of the Holy Ghost. Such was the passion of the people for these religious shows, (or *mysteries* as they were usually called) they became important subjects for regulation by law. Sometimes a single play occupied several days; and not unfrequently embraced the story of both he Old and New Testament, from the creation to the lay of judgment. Such was the ignorance of the comnon people at this period, that many persons derived most of their knowledge of the transactions recorded in the Bible, by means of these plays.

250. *Genghis Khan.* In the beginning of the thir-

---

249. At what time were Scriptural plays performed in Europe? What was represented? How long did they sometimes continue? What is said of the ignorance of the people at this time?

15

teenth century, *Genghis*, the son of a barbarian chief, who reigned over a few hordes of Tartars, appeared as a conqueror, in the heart of Asia. The death of his father induced a revolt of his subjects, and at the age of thirteen, Genghis fought a battle with the rebels ; he was, however, compelled to flee, but his youthful spirit acquired him renown. By degrees he gained control, until he was proclaimed the *Great Khan*, or prince of the Moguls and Tartars. He led a vast army against the Chinese—passed the great wall, and destroyed a multitude of cities ; and the Chinese emperor, in order to have him depart, agreed to pay him tribute. In the second expedition, he conquered the northern part of China, and added it to his dominions. With 700,000 Moguls and Tartars, he now advanced towards the dominions of the Mahometan sultan in the West. In his advance towards Europe, nations and kingdoms were laid waste and destroyed ; and it is said, that five centuries were not sufficient to repair the ravages of four years. Genghis Khan died in the midst of his conquests, A. D. 1227, and his successors conquered near the whole of Asia, and a portion of Europe.

251. *End of the Saracen Empire.* Bagdad continued to be the seat of the Saracen empire 490 years, during which time it sustained several obstinate sieges, and was the scene of many bloody revolutions. The later califs, in the decline of the Saracen empire, were not the warlike sovereigns which their predecessors had been. They thought only of securing their ease and pleasure. *Al Mostasem*, the last calif, exceeded all others in pride and display. When he appeared in public, he was usually veiled, in order to attract the attention of the people, whom he considered unworthy to look at him. On these occasions, a great price was given for the privilege to stand at a window, or in a

---

250. Who was Genghis Khan ? Where did he make his conquests ? What is said of his ravages ?

251. How long was Bagdad the seat of the Saracen empire ? What is said of Al Mostasem, the last calif ? When was Bagdad taken, and by whom ?

balcony, for the purpose of seeing him as he passed, and scarcely any thing could exceed the eagerness of the people to catch a sight of their sovereign. In A. D. 1258, Bagdad was taken by *Hulaku,* the grandson of Genghis Khan, and Al Mostasem was confined in a leathern sack, and dragged about the city till he expired. Hulaku gave up the city, which contained immense treasures, to be pillaged by his troops, for seven days. By this event the empire of the Saracens was terminated.

252. *Empire of the Assassins.* This singular sect (from which the word *assassin* is derived) was formed in the eleventh century, the object of which was to expel the Mahometan religion and government, by establishing an empire of their own. The founder of this society, which for more than a century and a half filled Asia with terror and dismay, was *Hassan Ben Sahab.* In possession of a strong fortress in Persia, Hassan organized his band of followers, whose daggers spread the terror of his power throughout Asia. All those governors and princes who would not submit to his authority, were generally assassinated by his devoted followers. After a reign of 35 years, Hassan saw his power extended over a great part of the Mahometan empire, which continued under his successors, till they were overthrown by the Tartars.

253. *Method of making Assassins.* Hassan had three classes of followers, the third of which were the blind and willing instruments of their superiors, and, regardless of their own lives, executed their bloody mandates. If they perished in executing their orders, it was represented to them that they would immediately enter paradise. When the chief had noticed any youth whom he wished to employ as an assassin, he invited him to a feast, and placing himself beside him, he conversed on

---

252. When was the sect of the assassins formed, and for what object? Who was its founder? How long did his society, or empire, exist?

253. How many classes of followers did Hassan have, and what is said of the third class? Give an account of the deception practiced to make assassins.

the happiness reserved for the faithful, and contrived to administer an intoxicating draught, which caused a deep sleep. He was then carried to a beautiful garden, prepared for this purpose, where, when awakening, he found himself surrounded with every thing delightful to the senses or imagination; bowers of roses, airy halls, murmuring brooks, the richest of viands, and the choicest of wines, sparkled from golden cups; beautiful maidens, or houries, and blooming boys, were the inhabitants of this delicious spot, which ever sounded with the melody of birds, and the most enchanting music. The happy youth really believed himself in paradise, and the language of his attendants confirmed the delusion. When nature began to yield, through excess of enjoyment, the sleeping draught was again administered, and he was conveyed back to his chief. His imagination was filled with what he had seen, and he longed for the hour when death, in obeying the commands of his superiors, should dismiss him to paradise.

251. *End of the Crusades.* The crusading spirit, which had begun to languish in Europe, was revived, for the last time, by Louis IX., of France, a monarch distinguished for his heroic and amiable virtues, but deeply affected by the unworthy superstition of the times. After three years preparation, he set out for Palestine, with his queen, three brothers, and nearly all the knights of France, A. D. 1248. He had greatly encouraged the hearts of the Christians, in Palestine, by sending troops thither before his own departure. Louis began his enterprise by invading Egypt, and after losing one half of his army by sickness, he was defeated and taken prisoner by the Saracens. Having ransomed himself and his followers, he proceeded to the Holy Land, where he remained for some time, and then returned to France, and for thirteen years reigned with wisdom. But the crusading frenzy again seized him; he embarked on another crusade against the *Moors*, in

---

251. By whom were the crusades revived for the last time? Give an account of his expeditions.

Africa, and while besieging *Tunis*, he, and the greater part of his army, perished by pestilence.

255. *Effects of the Crusades.* These barbarous expeditions agitated, convulsed, and distressed every family in Europe, for two hundred years. It is computed, that during the time of the crusades, more than two millions of Europeans were buried in the East; and those that survived were soon incorporated with the Mahometan population, in Syria, and in a few years no traces of the Christian conquests remained. Though these expeditions were attended with a great amount of misery, yet they were followed with some beneficial effects. Many of the nobility were obliged to sell their lands, in order to procure the means to convey their troops to a foreign land; and in this way the lower classes began to acquire property, influence, and a spirit of independence. Kings, likewise, raised money by selling to towns the right of electing their own magistrates, and being governed by their own municipal laws. The crusaders, by traveling in the East, particularly in the vicinity of Constantinople, became acquainted with many arts and sciences, which, on their return, they introduced into their own countries. By the frequency of voyagers to convey troops to Palestine, the art of navigation rapidly improved, and consequently commerce was much extended.

Notwithstanding some benefits may have arisen to the European nations on account of the crusades, yet it cannot be denied, that they caused an immense degree of suffering. The path of the fanatical crusader was everywhere marked with blood : under the sacred name of religion, every excess and crime was committed.

---

255. How many Europeans is it supposed were buried in the East during the crusades ! Describe the effects of the crusades.

PERIOD VI.

DISTINGUISHED FOR DISCOVERIES AND INVENTIONS.

Mariner's Compass.   *Printing.*   *Gunpowder*

FROM THE LAST CRUSADE TO THE DISCOVERY OF AMERICA.

(222 YEARS.)

256. *Conquest of Wales.* Wales is said to have been first inhabited by the Britons, who fled thither from the Saxons, in A. D. 675. Edward I., of England, who had been engaged in the last crusade to the Holy Land, with Louis, the French king, on his return formed the design of uniting the whole of the island of Great Britain into one dominion. *Llewellyn*, the prince of Wales, was surprised and slain, with 2,000 of his followers. His brother, Prince David, who had formerly received great favors from Edward, was made prisoner by the English, and executed as a traitor, for defending his country. The Welch nobility submitted to the conqueror, and the principality was annexed to the crown of England, A. D. 1282. It is said that Edward promised to give the Welch a prince, who should be born in their country. His eldest son, then an infant,

---

256. By whom is Wales said to have been first inhabited? By whom were they conquered? By whom is the title of the Prince of Wales borne?

was born at Caernarvon, and in consequence received the title of *Prince of Wales*, which has ever since been borne by the eldest sons of the British monarchs.

257. *War between the English and Scots.* On the death of Alexander III., who left no son, *Bruce* and *Baliol* were competitors for the throne of Scotland, and Edward was chosen umpire to decide the contest between the two rivals. The crown was adjudged to Baliol, who promised to hold it as a vassal to the king of England. He, however, soon after renounced his allegiance, which was the occasion of a war, which lasted, with some intermission, upwards of seventy years. Edward invaded Scotland with a large army, defeated the Scots with great slaughter, and carried Baliol prisoner to London, and compelled him to abdicate the throne. The Scots were afterwards roused to arms, for the recovery of their independence, by that renowned hero, *William Wallace*, but after gaining a series of victories, they were defeated in the battle of *Falkirk*. The heroic Wallace was betrayed, and was put to death by the English in a cruel manner. The Scots found a second champion and deliverer in *Robert Bruce*, who expelled the English from the country, and was raised to the throne of his ancestors, A. D. 1306.

258. *Swiss Republics. William Tell.* The establishment of the Swiss republics was occasioned by the tyrannical conduct of the emperor of Germany, in 1307. The Swiss having petitioned him against the oppressions of his governors, he, in resentment, increased their burdens, which was the cause of a conspiracy and revolt. *Gesler*, the governor, in order to ascertain the spirit of the people, ordered his hat to be placed on a pole, and homage paid to it, as to himself. *William Tell* refused,

---

257. Who were the competitors for the throne of Scotland? What became of Baliol? By whom were the Scots roused to arms for the recovery of their independence? Who expelled the English?

258. How were the Swiss republics established? What is said of Gesler and William Tell?

and when seized for disobedience, was directed to shoot an arrow at an apple placed on the head of his son, or else be dragged, with his child, to immediate death. Being an excellent marksman, he cleft the apple without injuring his son. Gesler perceiving another arrow under his cloak, asked for what purpose that was intended. Tell heroically replied, " To have shot you to the heart, if I had killed my son." The people soon flew to arms; three of the cantons only, at first, combined to assert their freedom, and with a small army defeated an immense number of their enemies. The rest of the cantons, by degrees, joined the association. Their freedom cost them 60 battles.

259. *Wickliffe, the English Reformer.* John Wickliffe was born in 1324, and was professor of divinity, at Oxford, for many years. England was at this time completely under the dominion of the papal power; the country, at this period, swarmed with monks, of the Mendicant order, and the clergy were generally corrupt, proud and indolent. This state of things aroused the spirit of Wickliffe, who commenced writing against the monks, and the tyranny of the pope and the bishops. He declared that the gospel was a sufficient rule of life, without any other, and that if a man was truly penitent before God, he need not confess his sins to the priest. He also asserted, that the Bible ought not to be kept exclusively in a language the common people could not understand. He accordingly translated the whole Bible into the English language, for their use. For these proceedings he was seized as a heretic, but owing to his popularity with the nobles and people, he was suffered to die in peace, A. D. 1385. The malice of his enemies was so great, that forty years after his death, his bones were burnt, and the ashes thrown into the river. His *doctrines,* however were not destroyed; they prevailed, more or less, till they were firmly estab-

---

259. Who was John Wickliffe, and when was he born? What was the state of England at this time? What did Wickliffe do? What was done with Wickliffe's bones, and what is he often called?

lished in Europe, by the Reformation of Martin Luther, for which Wickliffe, in a degree, had prepared the way, and from this circumstance he is called "*the morning star of the Reformation.*"

260. *Insurrection of Wat Tyler.* By the propagation of the sentiments of Wickliffe, an increase of the spirit of independence prevailed among the people, who now began to understand their rights, and of course had more of a disposition to maintain them. About the year 1380, a poll-tax of three groats was imposed upon every person above the age of 15 years, male and female. This created universal discontent among the lower classes, on account of its injustice, as the poor were obliged to pay as much as the rich. A brutal tax-gatherer, having demanded payment for the daughter of *Wat Tyler*, a blacksmith, whom the father had asserted to be below the age specified, was proceeding to improper familiarities with her, upon which the father dashed out his brains with his hammer. The people, justifying this action, flew to arms throughout the kingdom, and 100,000 men were assembled near London, in order to redress their grievances. Tyler, however, was killed, while in a conference with the king, and his followers were compelled to submit and return to their homes.

261. *War between the houses of York and Lancaster.* The houses of *York* and *Lancaster* were both descended from Edward III.,—that of York from his third son, and that of Lancaster from the fourth. As the reigning king was subject to fits of insanity, and was also a weak prince, Richard, duke of Gloucester, of the house of York, his uncle, was appointed *Protector* of the kingdom. *Margaret*, the queen of the deposed king, and

---

260. What effect did the propagation of Wickliffe's sentiments have upon the people? Relate the account of the tax-gatherer and Wat Tyler. What followed?

261. What is said of the houses of York and Lancaster? What is said of Richard, duke of Gloucester, and Queen Margaret? What of the roses? What is said of the wars between these parties?

her adherents of the house of Lancaster, appealed to arms, in order to obtain their rights. The whole nation took the side of one or the other, and each party was distinguished by a particular badge or symbol. That of the house of York was a *white rose*, and that of Lancaster a *red* one : hence this contention was styled the quarrel of the *two roses*. War commenced between the parties in 1455, and continued for thirty years, and was signalized by twelve sanguinary pitched battles, and marked with great barbarity. During the contest, more than 100,000 men were killed, including 80 princes of the blood, who fell on the field, or were executed on the scaffold. Henry, the only survivor of the house of Lancaster, gave battle to Richard, the bloody usurper, on *Bosworth field*, where the latter was killed, his army defeated, and Henry was acknowledged king. Henry marrying into the house of York, the two houses became united, and thus terminated this bloody controversy.

262. *Wars between England and France.* The contests of the English kings for the crown of France, occupy a considerable space in the history of both countries. Philip, king of France, died, leaving three sons, and one daughter, who was married to the king of England. All his sons died without leaving male heirs. Edward III., king of England, now laid claim to the throne, on account of his being the son of the daughter of the French king. The French opposed his claim, and placed the brother of their king on the throne. Edward, in support of his claim, invaded France with an army of 30,000 men, gained the famous battle of *Cressy*, in which *cannon* were for the first time used in war, A. D. 1346. Ten years after this event, Edward, the Black Prince, (son of Edward III.,) so called from the color of his armor, gained the victory of *Poictiers*, and took John, king of France, prisoner, and led him in

---

262. Why did Edward, king of England, lay claim to the throne of France? Who first used cannon in war, where, and in what year? What is said of the Black Prince?

triumph to London. The French, however, vigorously pursued the war, during the captivity of their sovereign.

263. *Joan of Arc, the Maid of Orleans.* The English triumphed repeatedly in France, and by their victory at *Agincourt*, they threatened the capital itself. The English undertook the siege of *Orleans*, a place of the utmost importance, and pushed their designs so successfully, that the affairs of Charles, the French prince, seemed almost desperate, when they were suddenly restored by one of the most marvelous incidents found recorded in history. *Joan of Arc*, otherwise called the *Maid of Orleans*, a country girl, who was a servant at an inn, presented herself before the French king, professing to be divinely commissioned to deliver her oppressed country, and raise the siege of Orleans. Her mission was pronounced, by an assembly of divines, to be supernatural; and, at her own request, she was arrayed in complete armor, mounted on a white horse, and appeared at the head of the French army, which, fired with enthusiasm, courageously attacked the English, and drove them from the walls, and, by her heroic exertions in the field, effected the salvation of her country. She, however, fell into the hands of the enemy, who condemned her to death for witchcraft, and, to their disgrace, burnt her alive at Rouen, in 1430.

264. *Founding of the Turkish Empire.* While the empire of the Saracens, under their califs, was drawing near to its close, the power of the *Turks* was rising into importance. They derive their origin from a tribe of *Huns*, or *Scythians*, who dwelt in *Tartary*. They were forced, by the tribes in the south, to abandon their country, and pushing their course eastward, some settled around the Caspian sea, and others in Asia Minor. They became Mahometans, and, in 1037, conquered Persia, ravaged the neighboring countries, and made themselves masters of Palestine. Their establishment

---

263. Who besieged Orleans? How was the siege of Orleans raised? What became of Joan of Arc?

264. Where do the Turks derive their origin? Who was Ottoman, and what title did he assume?

as a separate empire is dated A. D. 1299, at the time when *Ottoman,* the calif or prince of the Turks, fixed his seat of government at Byrsa, in Asia Minor, and assumed the title of *Sultan.* From this time they were known as the Ottoman race and sovereignty. Being near Constantinople, they gradually encroached upon the Greek empire, till it fell into their possession.

265. *Of Tamerlane.* Tamerlane was a prince of the *Usbeck Tartars,* and a descendant of *Genghis Khan.* Having conquered Persia, and most of the East, he turned his arms westward. At this period, *Bajazet,* one of the successors of Ottoman, was besieging Constantinople: the Greek emperor implored the assistance of Tamerlane against his enemy. Tamerlane gladly accepted the invitation, and sent a message to Bajazet, commanding him to abandon the siege, and restore the prisoners he had taken. This message roused his indignation: he left the siege and marched against this new enemy, but was defeated by Tamerlane, after a dreadful battle, which lasted three days, in which it is said that nearly a million men were engaged, and 300,000 slain. The victorious career of the Turks was suspended by this event. Bajazet was taken prisoner, and, it is said, was shut up in an iron cage, by his conqueror, and carried about to grace his triumphs. Tamerlane made *Samarcand* the seat of his empire, and there received the homage of all the princes of the East. For a while this place was the seat of learning and the arts; but after the death of Tamerlane, it relapsed into its former barbarism.

266. *Taking of Constantinople by the Turks.* After the death of Tamerlane, the Turks resumed their purpose of destroying the Greek empire. Constantine was the name of the last emperor of the East, as it was also

---

265. Who was Tamerlane? How came Tamerlane to make war upon Bajazet? What is said of Bajazet? Where was the seat of Tamerlane's empire?

266. Who was the last emperor of the East? What is said of him? What of the conquest of the city? How long did the eastern Roman empire exist?

of the first. The Turks had so encroached upon his dominions, that they became very much reduced. The indolent inhabitants of Constantinople made but a feeble preparation for defense. Constantine, however, with a spirit worthy of the former days of the empire, endeav-

Taking of Constantinople by the Turks.

ored to animate the fainting hearts of his degenerate subjects, to defend the last remains of their possessions. He applied to the western monarchs, and solicited the aid of his Christian brethren; but the powers of Europe looked on with indifference. The city was assailed by sea and by land, and the walls were battered down with cannon. The emperor was slain, and the city taken. The imperial buildings were preserved, and the churches converted into *mosques*, or Turkish places of worship. The city was given up to spoil for three days, in which the soldiers were permitted to commit every enormity. The capture of Constantinople took place A. D. 1453, and by this event the eastern Roman empire was extinguished, having existed upwards of *eleven hundred years*.

267. *Invention of the Mariner's Compass*. The invention, during this period, of the *mariner's compass*, that of *gunpowder*, and especially the art of *printing*, gave a new direction to the affairs of men, and will

continue to affect the destinies of future ages. The mariner's compass is said to have been invented about the year 1300, by Gioia, a mathematician, at Naples. It did not, however, come into general use till the year 1400. The Chinese lay claim to the honor of this, as well as several other discoveries and inventions; but not much reliance can be placed on their statements. Before this discovery, mariners scarcely ever ventured out of sight of land; but since, man has ventured to quit his timid course along the shore, and steer boldly into the deep. It has opened to him the dominion of the sea, and presented a new world to his view, destined to become the abode of civilization and Christianity.

268. *Gunpowder. Firearms.* The invention of gunpowder has done much towards softening the ferocity and diminishing the chances of war. War is now more a matter of calculation than formerly. In ancient times, a man whose brute force was superior to those around him, had the advantage over those of a weaker frame; but by this invention a comparatively weak man is placed upon an equal footing. *Roger Bacon,* a learned English friar, or monk, who died at Oxford, 1292, understood the secret of the composition of gunpowder, and it is said that he was the inventor. Its application to warlike purposes is said to have been first suggested by *Swartz,* a monk of Cologne, about the year 1330. Sixteen years afterwards, Edward III., of England, at the battle of *Cressy,* used four pieces of artillery. The invention of portable firearms seems to have originated in Germany. They were at first made so long and heavy, that they were placed on props when fired. The first gunlock was invented in 1517, and the term *firelock* was given to the invention.

---

267. What time was the mariner's compass invented? What is said of the Chinese?

268. What effect has the invention of gunpowder had upon war? Who is said to have been the inventor? What is said respecting portable firearms?

269. *Art of Printing.* The art of printing with movable types is said to have been discovered by *John Guttenburg* and others, at Mentz, in Germany, A. D. 1436. Guttenburg, having expended nearly all his property in the invention of this art, was about to abandon it, when *John Faust*, likewise a citizen of Mentz, came to his assistance, and they brought the art to a considerable degree of perfection. The servant of Faust discovered the art of casting singly each type or character. The oath of secresy being taken by all their workmen, the art was concealed till 1462, when Mentz was taken and sacked; the workmen engaged in printing were dispersed and by this means the art was spread over Europe. From remote antiquity, a kind of block-printing has been practiced among the Chinese; but it bears but little resemblance to that important art discovered in modern Europe, from which benefits of such magnitude have arisen to mankind.

270. *Moorish kingdom of Grenada.* The conquest of Spain by the Saracens, or Moors, is noticed in sections 191 and 192. The Christian princes in Spain had gradually recovered the various kingdoms or provinces in that country, till the kingdom of *Grenada* alone remained under the government of the Moors. This kingdom was situated in the southern part of Spain, bordering on the Mediterranean, and was surrounded by a lofty range of mountains on the land side, which inclosed a deep, rich, and fertile valley. The city of Grenada lay in the centre of the kingdom, and was, perhaps, the most splendid city of the age, and the remains of its ancient grandeur still astonish the beholder. So beautiful was this region, so pure the air, and so serene the sky, that the Moors imagined the paradise of their prophet to be situated in that part of heaven which overhung the kingdom of Grenada. This kingdom, with the territo-

---

269. By whom was the art of printing discovered, and at what time? What is said of Guttenburg, and of John Faust? How was the knowledge of the art spread over Europe?

270. Where was the kingdom of Grenada? What is said of it?

ries under its protection, previous to its conquest, contained 14 cities and 97 fortified towns, besides numerous places defended by formidable castles. The capital was surrounded by a wall, three leagues in circuit, and fortified with a thousand and thirty towers.

271. *Conquest of Grenada.* The Christian princes of Spain had left the Moors in quiet possession of Grenada, on condition of their paying an annual tribute of 2,000 pistoles of gold, and 1,600 Christian captives. In the year 1478, when the Spanish courtier arrived to demand the customary tribute, Hassan, the Moorish monarch, replied: "Tell your sovereign, that the kings who used to pay tribute are dead. Our mint at present coins nothing but cimetars and heads of lances." Of course, war followed this declaration. For a period of ten years, the Moors bravely defended their country: their towns were taken, one after another, although they disputed every advance of their enemies with the utmost resolution. After a series of almost uninterrupted disasters to the Moorish arms, their capital was surrounded by the Christian forces under *Ferdinand* and *Isabella.* The resources of the city now being cut off, famine stared the inhabitants in the face. The Moorish prince, *Boabil,* despairing of all relief, was forced to surrender Grenada to the Spaniards. This event, which took place in January, 1492, put an end to the dominion of the Moors in Spain, after it had existed nearly eight hundred years.

272. *Portuguese Discoveries.* The discovery of the mariner's compass awakened a spirit for maritime discovery, and several nations turned their attention to navigation and commercial enterprise. Previous to this period, the Venetians took the lead in commercial pur-

---

271. On what condition did the Moors have quiet possession of Grenada? What answer did Hassan give to the Spanish courtier? Who conquered Grenada? How long had the dominion of the Moors continued in Spain?

272. Who took the lead in commerce, before the discovery of the mariner's compass? Where did they trade, and by what route? What is said of the Portuguese?

suits. For a long time they had the whole trade of India, which they carried on by way of Egypt and the Red Sea, or through the inland routes of Asia: and the immense wealth they acquired by it, excited the envy and enterprise of other nations of Europe. Many began anxiously to inquire, whether *another route* could not be found to India by water, which would be less tedious and expensive. The Portuguese devoted the most attention to this subject, and to them is justly due the honor of leading the way in those enterprises, which have been attended with such important results to mankind. Under the patronage of Prince Henry, son of their king, the Portuguese navigators discovered the *Azores*, *Madeira*, and *Cape Verd* islands, and explored the shores of Africa, to the coast of Guinea. The fame of these discoveries attracted the learned, the curious, and enterprising, from various nations, to Lisbon.

273. *Of Columbus.* Christopher Columbus was born in the city of Genoa, about 1440. His father was a wool-comber, and gave him as good an education as his limited means would allow. He early showed a great fondness for navigation, and, at the age of fourteen, began to navigate the Mediterranean, and about the year 1470, he repaired to Lisbon. During his residence in Portugal, he sailed in several expeditions to the African islands and the coast of Guinea. As it was the grand object of the Portuguese to find a passage to the Indies by *water*, Columbus was persuaded, from his knowledge of the spherical shape of the earth, that, instead of sailing round by the southern extremity of Africa, he could find an easier route by sailing westward across the Atlantic Ocean. He supposed that the eastern coast of India, and the western shores of Europe and Africa, were separated by an ocean of moderate extent. Several facts tended to confirm him in this belief. Pieces of carved wood, reeds of an enormous

---

273. Where was Columbus born? What were Columbus' opinions respecting a passage to India? What facts confirmed him in this belief?

16*

size, and above all, a canoe with the bodies of two men in it, differing in their appearance from any known race of people, had been driven by the westerly winds upon the Azores, or Western Islands.

274. *Columbus' application for Assistance.* Columbus having established his theory, he now began to think of the means necessary in order to make a voyage of discovery. Believing it too important an enterprise to be undertaken by a private individual, he deemed it necessary to apply to some sovereign power. In 1484, he applied to John II., of Portugal, but instead of receiving assistance, experienced contempt and injury. Columbus next laid his plans before the government of Genoa, but that republic was embarrassed with wars, and was in a decline; they were also unable to form correct opinions respecting the truth of his theory, and considered his proposed voyage as useless and visionary. He next applied to Ferdinand and Isabella, king and queen of Spain. They listened to his views with attention, and gave him some faint hopes of assistance. He was however kept several years in suspense, and was obliged to struggle with many difficulties, thrown in his way by ignorant and malicious persons. At length, by the influence of Queen Isabella, three small ships, and 120 men, were fitted out and placed under his command.

275. *First Voyage and Discovery of Columbus* On the third of August, 1492, Columbus set sail from the port of Palos, in Spain, and steered for the Canary Islands, where he refitted his vessels and took in fresh provisions. On the 6th of September, he steered directly west, into the unknown ocean before him. Three days after losing sight of land, many of the seamen on board wept bitterly, from the apprehension that they should never see it again. After sailing some days, the needle of the compass varied from its direct course, towards the

---

274. Who did Columbus apply to for assistance to make a voyage of discovery? How did he succeed?

275. Where did Columbus sail from? Give an account of the voyage. What land was first discovered, and at what time? Give an account of the landing.

north. At this the people, and even Columbus, became alarmed. To add to his perplexity, his seamen became mutinous, and even threatened to throw him overboard if he would not return. Columbus, after trying various ways to pacify them, promised that if land did not appear in three days, he would return. On the third day,

Landing of Columbus.

land, to their great joy, was discovered; it proved to be an island, which was afterwards named St. Salvador, now called Cat Island, one of the Bahamas. On the 12th of October, 1492, Columbus went first on shore, and was followed by his men. They all knelt, kissed the ground with tears of joy, and returned thanks to God for their successful voyage. Columbus, now drawing his sword, planted the royal standard, and took formal possession of the country, in the name of the king and queen of Spain.

PERIOD VII.

DISTINGUISHED FOR THE REFORMATION BY LUTHER

The Bible presented to the common people.

FROM THE DISCOVERY OF AMERICA TO THE SETTLEMENT OF JAMESTOWN.

(115 YEARS.)

276. *Columbus' Return from his first Voyage.* After his first landing in the new world, Columbus proceeded southward, and discovered Cuba and Hispaniola, (now Hayti,) on which he landed, and left a number of his men to form a colony. He also discovered a number of other islands in the vicinity, which he supposed to be near India. In consequence of this belief, he called the natives *Indians*, and this name was afterwards given to the natives of the western continent, and is still retained. As Columbus reached these islands by a *western* passage, he named them *West Indies*. Having obtained a quantity of gold, and other productions of the new world, with a number of the natives, he set sail for Spain. On his voyage a violent storm arose, which threatened their destruction. Columbus, in order to give

---

276. What islands did Columbus discover? Why did he call his discoveries the West Indies? Give an account of his return to Spain. What did he do when in a storm?

the world some chance to know his discoveries, wrote a short account of his voyage, on two skins of parchmen:, which he wrapped in an oiled cloth covered with wax, and having inclosed them in two separate casks, he threw them into the sea, in hopes that they would be discovered by some navigator, or be cast ashore. But the storm abated, and Columbus arrived in Spain, where he was received with wonder and acclamation by the multitude, and with great respect and admiration at court.

277. *Fate of Columbus.* Columbus, after his first voyage, made three others to the new world, and on the 1st of August, 1498, he discovered the continent, near the mouth of the Oronoko, in South America. His successes and honors excited a spirit of envy and intrigue against him, in the court of Spain. In consequence of false accusations, he was deprived of his command as governor of Hispaniola, and sent home in chains. Though declared innocent, and apparently restored to the favor of the court, he never received the reward due to his merits. His shameful and unjust treatment preyed upon his spirits, and through the whole of his after-life he carried his chains with him, as a memorial of the ingratitude which he had experienced. He hung them up in his chamber, and gave orders that they should be buried with him. Worn down with anxieties, fatigues, and disappointment, Columbus died at Valadolid, in 1506. His funeral, by order of Philip, who had recently ascended the throne, was extremely magnificent, and the following inscription was engraved on his tomb: " To Castile and Leon, Columbus has given a new world."

278. *Of Vespucius, Cabot, and other Discoverers.* The discoveries of Columbus produced a great excitement in Spain and Portugal, and several persons fitted out ships at their own expense, and crossed the ocean in hope of

---

277. When did Columbus discover the continent. and where? Why was he sent home in chains? What effect did the treatment have upon him ?
278. What effect did the discoveries of Columbus have ? Who was Americus Vespucius? Why was America named

obtaining wealth and honors. Among the earliest of these adventures was *Ojeda*, an enterprising officer, who accompanied Columbus in his first expedition. He sailed in 1499, and made some discoveries at the mouth of the Oronoko. He was accompanied by one *Americus Vespucius*, a native of Florence. This person, on his return, published an account of the voyage, in which he made it appear that he was the first discoverer of the continent of the new world. His publication was circulated rapidly, and was read with admiration; and by this means, in honor of the supposed discoverer, the name *America* was given to the new continent.

John Cabot, a Venetian by birth, but an inhabitant of England, received a commission from the English king, and sailed in 1497, on a voyage of discovery. He was accompanied by his son, *Sebastian Cabot*, and one or both of them discovered the continent of North America. The first land discovered by them, is supposed to have been *Newfoundland*. They proceeded farther to the north, in search of a passage to India, but not succeeding, they turned about, and sailed as far south as Florida. They erected crosses along on the coast, and took a formal possession of the country, in behalf of the crown of England. This was the foundation of the English claim to North America, though no settlements were made till many years afterwards.

In 1497, *Vasco de Gama*, a Portuguese, first sailed round, or doubled the Cape of Good Hope, and made a voyage to India. In 1520, *Magellan*, a Portuguese, in the service of Spain, passed through the straits which bear his name, and entered into a vast ocean, which he named the *Pacific*, on account of the stillness of its waters. He lost his life at one of the Philippine islands, but his officers proceeded on the voyage, and effected the *first circumnavigation* of the globe.

---

after him? Who was John Cabot, and in whose service was he employed? What discoveries did he and his son, Sebastian, make? What is said of Vasco de Gama? What of Magellan? Who effected the first circumnavigation of the globe?

MODERN HISTORY. 191

279. *Invasion of Mexico.* After the discovery of Columbus, the Spaniards flocked in considerable numbers to the new world and commenced settlements at *Jamaica, Porto Rico, Darien,* and *Cuba.* These new countries were supposed to contain vast quantities of gold and silver; hence the eagerness of the Spaniards to explore and conquer these countries, in order to obtain possession of the precious metals. Under the pretence of religion and policy, they were guilty of the most shocking inhumanity to the natives. The most forcible means were employed to convert them to Christianity: they were hunted down like wild beasts, and were sometimes burnt alive. Hispaniola, at the time of its discovery, contained three millions of inhabitants, and Cuba upwards of 600,000; but the Spaniards caused such destruction of human life, that in a very few years scarcely any of the natives remained. In 1519, the governor of Cuba fitted out an armament of eleven small vessels and 617 men, under the command of *Fernando Cortez,* for the invasion of Mexico. At this period, firearms were not in general use: only thirteen of his men had muskets, the rest being armed with cross-bows, swords, and spears. Cortez had, however, ten small field pieces and sixteen horses—the first of these animals ever seen in that country.

280. *Advance of Cortez to the city of Mexico.* Landing at Vera Cruz, Cortez advanced, though with a brave opposition, into the very heart of the country; he could, however, have made but little impression on the empire of Mexico, which contained many millions of people, had he not been joined by the people of some of the disaffected provinces, who wished to throw off the Mexican yoke. On the approach of the Spaniards to the

279. What made the Spaniards eager to explore and conquer the new countries? What is said of their treatment of the natives? What is said of Fernando Cortez, and how were his men armed?
280. By what means was Cortez enabled to advance into Mexico? How did Montezuma receive him? What did Cortez do to Montezuma?

capital, the terror of their name prepared the way for an easy conquest. *Montezuma*, the Mexican monarch, received the Spaniards with great hospitality, and he regarded them with the reverence due to superior beings. Cortez was very desirous of having Montezuma under his power: a pretext for this purpose soon took place. Some difficulty between his soldiers and the natives having taken place, Cortez, with fifty of his men, marched to the palace of Montezuma, where, seizing him, he put him in irons, and carried him off prisoner to his camp.

Fall of Montezuma.

281. *Death of Montezuma.* The seizure of the emperor by the Spaniards, aroused the Mexicans to arms Such was the fury of their attacks, that the situation of Cortez became desperate: he entrusted Montezuma, who was still a prisoner in his camp, to speak to his subjects, in order to make them desist from their attacks. Montezuma consented, and accordingly, addressed the people from a terrace, and requested them to cease from

---

281. What effect did the seizure of Montezuma have upon his subjects? What did Cortez entreat of Montezuma? Relate the manner of his death, and the flight of the Spaniards

hostilities, in order that the Spaniards might leave the city. While he was speaking, his people ceased their attacks; but on the conclusion of his speech, a shower of stones and arrows fell about the place where he stood, some of which struck him, and caused his death. On the death of their monarch, the fury of the Mexicans increased. The Spaniards in a dark rainy night attempted to affect their retreat from the city; they were discovered by the Mexicans, who attacked them with such numbers, that the greater part of the Spaniards were killed before they could effect their escape from the city. Many of the soldiers so loaded themselves with gold, that in their flight they were easily overtaken and killed by the enemy.

282. *Conquest of Mexico.* After this defeat, Cortez was reinforced by European soldiers, who flocked to him as volunteers, in order to receive a share of the spoils of Mexico: besides these, the *Tlascalans*, his allies, offered to assist him with 50,000 of their best troops, if he would again march against the Mexicans. Cortez being thus encouraged, laid siege to the city of Mexico, which was now governed by *Guatimozin*, a brave prince, who showed great skill, courage, and heroism, in defending his country. For more than three months the Spaniards and their allies were almost daily fighting the Mexicans, in order to obtain possession of the city. All their attempts were in vain, and Cortez must have raised the siege, had not an Indian, fatally for his country, advised him to blockade the city on the water. The Spaniards built several vessels, with which they surrounded the city, which was built on a number of small islands in a salt lake. By this means Mexico was cut off from all supplies, and a most dreadful famine followed. Guatimozin fled from the city, but was taken prisoner. Refusing to discover his treasures, Cortez stretched him naked on burning

---

282. By whom was Cortez assisted to make another attack upon the Spaniards? By what means did Cortez finally conquer Mexico?

17

coals. Afterwards, on the discovery of a conspiracy against the Spaniards, he was hung on a gibbet, with the princes of his blood, and Cortez thus became master of the empire.

283. *Invasion of Peru.* In 1518, the Spaniards formed a settlement at Panama, on the west side of the isthmus of Darien. From this place a number of attempts were made to explore the regions of South America. In 1625, *Pizarro* and a number of other adventurers sailed as far as *Peru*, and discovered that rich and flourishing country. Two years afterwards, Pizarro having received a commission from the king of Spain, landed in Peru: he was afterwards joined by *Almagro*, with a small reinforcement. The whole force with which these adventurers attempted to conquer one of the finest kingdoms in America, consisted of but 250 foot, 60 horse, and 12 small pieces of cannon. As was the case with Mexico, the empire was weakened by internal divisions, and by this means the Peruvians fell an easy prey to the Spaniards. Pizarro having marched to the residence of the *Inca*, or king, *Atahualpa* invited him to a friendly interview, and attempted to persuade him to adopt the Christian religion. This proposal being misunderstood, or received with hesitation, Pizarro seized the monarch as his prisoner, while his troops massacred 4,000 of his people on the spot.

284. *Conquest of Peru.* Finding the ruling passion of the Spaniards was the love of gold, Atahualpa offered, if they would release him, to fill the room in which he was confined, which was twenty-two feet by sixteen, with vessels of gold and silver as high as he could reach. This offer was accepted, and gold was collected from all parts of the empire, and was divided among the conquerors. But the perfidious Pizarro still

---

283. Who discovered and invaded Peru? How large a force did he have? What did Pizarro do to the Inca?

284. How much silver and gold did Atahualpa offer for his release? What did Pizarro do? What became of Pizarro and Almagro? What effect did the finding of so much gold and silver have?

held the Inca a prisoner, and being suspected of concealing a part of his treasures, was brought to trial as a criminal, and on a charge of being an usurper and an idolater, was strangled at a stake. The Peruvian government being destroyed, all parts of the empire were subdued, and became a province of Spain. The Spanish chiefs having divided the country among themselves, soon began to quarrel with each other, and both Pizarro and Almagro were put to death in the civil wars which followed. The great quantities of gold and silver found in Spanish America, greatly increased the quantity of specie, and much reduced the value of money all over the civilized world.

285. *Civilization of the Mexicans and Peruvians.* At the time of the invasion of the Spaniards, the Peruvians and Mexicans had made advances in civilization to a much greater extent than any of the other Indian tribes or nations of America. They understood the arts of architecture, sculpture, mining, and working the precious metals : they cultivated their lands, and had a regular system of government, and a code of civil and religious laws. The Peruvians had the superiority in architecture, and possessed some splendid palaces and temples. They had no knowledge of letters ; the Mexicans, however, had a system of recording events, by means of paintings, or figures, by which they represented facts with great certainty. These historical paintings were preserved with the greatest care by the Mexicans, and such of them as escaped destruction, at the time of the conquest of the Spaniards, are the source from which the history of the country is derived. The Spaniards at first, supposing them to be connected with their idolatrous worship, destroyed all they could find.

286. *Religion.* The Mexicans believed in a Supreme Being, although their ideas concerning him were very imperfect. They believed also like the Greeks and

---

285. What is said of the civilization of the Mexicans and Peruvians ? What of the paintings of the Mexicans ?

Romans, in numerous inferior deities, who presided over the air, fire, earth, water, &c., and they also believed in evil spirits. They believed in the doctrine of *transmigration*, and that the souls of mankind after death pass into other animals, as cattle, birds, fishes, &c. They had images of their inferior deities made of wood, stone, and some of gold, and other metals: these they worshiped with prayers, fasting, and many severe rites and ceremonies. To these idols they often sacrificed slaves and prisoners of war, with many circumstances of shocking barbarity. The Peruvians worshiped the sun, as the Supreme deity, and their religious rites were much less bloody than those of the Mexicans.

287. *Religious State of Christendom.* The religious state of the Christian nations of Europe, at the commencement of the sixteenth century, is represented by almost all historians, as being exceedingly deplorable. The nations of Christendom were all under subjection to the papal power. The Roman pontiffs not only gave law in all religious matters, but even in civil affairs; and kings and kingdoms were subjected by their will. The clergy possessed immense wealth, and in general, awfully neglected their spiritual duties, and employed their treasures in gratifying their corrupt desires and passions. The great body of the people were kept in ignorance, and were taught the efficacy of relics and utility of indulgences; but of the genuine precepts and spirit of true Christianity, they knew but little. At this period, the art of printing was discovered, and the human mind began to be awakened from the long sleep of ages, by means of this important discovery.

288. *Reformation by Luther.* The Reformation of religion in Germany, by *Martin Luther* and others, was the commencement of an important era in the religious

---

286. What was the religious belief of the Mexicans? What is said of their worship and sacrifices? What of the worship of the Peruvians?

287. What is said of the religious state of Europe at the commencement of the 16th century? What of the Roman pontiffs, the clergy, and common people?

and civil history of the world. This event is dated
A. D. 1517, when *Tetzel,* an agent of Pope *Leo X.,*
began to publish indulgences, and brought them into
Germany and offered them for sale. Leo X. was a
man of pleasure and ambition, who exhausted the papal
treasury, and took this method to raise money; but
the scandalous manner in which these pardons for all
sins, past, present, and to come, were disposed of,
together with the gross immorality of Tetzel and his
associates, gave offense to many religious persons. Luther at this time was a professor of divinity at *Wittenburg,* and when Tetzel came into the vicinity, he boldly
and eloquently protested against the iniquity of these
indulgences and other main doctrines, and the vices
of the monks. He also published his sentiments, which
spread over Germany with great rapidity, and were read
with the greatest eagerness. Leo and his agents,
alarmed by the progress of Luther's sentiments among
all classes of people, excommunicated him as a heretic,
and would have probably put him to death, had he not
been befriended by some of the princes of Germany,
who were friendly to the new doctrines he set forth.
In 1520, the pope issued a bull, or proclamation, threatening him with destruction as an excommunicated heretic, unless he should within sixty days publicly recant
his errors, and burn his own books. Amid a vast assemblage of people at Wittenburg, Luther threw the
papal bull, with the volumes of the canon law, into the
flames, renounced the authority of the pope, exhorted
the princes of Europe to shake off the oppressive yoke
which they had so long borne, and offered thanks to
Almighty God that he was selected as the advocate of
true religion, and a friend to the liberties of mankind.

289. *Progress of the Reformation.* The new opinions set forth by Luther, found friends in almost every

---

288. When did the Reformation by Luther commence?
What is said of Leo X. and Tetzel? Who was Luther, and
what did he do? What did Leo do respecting Luther? What
did Luther do with the pope's bull?

17*

country in Europe. In Switzerland, *Zuinglius* attacked indulgences with the courage not inferior to Luther himself; and the Reformation was established in Geneva, and in a number of the Swiss cantons, by the celebrated *Calvin*. It also found friends in France, the Netherlands, Spain, Hungary, and Bohemia Henry VIII., of England, having quarreled with the pope, on account of his divorce, renounced the papal authority, and by the prudent management of *Cranmer*, the re formed doctrines were effectually established in that kingdom. Scotland was emancipated from the papal power, by the unwearied and intrepid labors of *John Knox*. Luther translated the Bible into the German language, in order that the common people might read it; he also wrote many works, labored with great zeal in propagating the doctrines of the Reformation, and before he died had the measure of seeing vast numbers of people throughout Europe adopting his sentiments.

290. *Overthrow of the Papal power in England.* Henry VIII., king of England, was a man of distinguished abilities, though notorious for his beastly vices. At the beginning of the Reformation, he was opposed to it, and even wrote a book against Luther, which so pleased the pope, that he bestowed on him the title of *Defender of the Faith.* The wife of Henry, at this time, was *Catharine of Arragon,* widow of his brother. After having lived with her for about 18 years, he professed to have conscientious scruples about his marriage, on account of her having been the wife of his brother; and wishing to marry the beautiful and accomplished *Anne Boleyn,* he applied to the pope for a di-

---

289. What is said of Zuinglius and Calvin? Of Henry VIII. of England. Cranmer, and John Knox? Why did Luther translate the Bible?
290. What is said of Henry VIII.? What title did he have bestowed upon him? Why did he wish for a divorce, and why did the pope delay to give a decision? Why did Henry abolish the papal authority of England? What did he do with the monasteries? What is said respecting the introduction of Protestantism into England?

vorce. Catharine was the aunt of the emperor, Charles V., of Germany. The pope found that if he granted the divorce, he should affront the emperor, and if he did not, he should offend Henry: he accordingly delayed giving a decision. Henry, however, would not be defeated in the accomplishment of his wishes. The opinion of various universities having been obtained in favor of the divorce, *Cranmer*, archbishop of Canterbury, annulled his marriage with Catharine, and Anne was soon after crowned queen.

Pope Clement, wishing to keep well with the emperor, condemned the proceedings of Cranmer. Henry immediately abolished the papal authority in England, and proclaimed himself Head of the English church, in 1534. He proceeded to abolish the monasteries, which at this time were very numerous, and possessed immense wealth. The immoralities of the monks were now fully exposed, and the forgery of relics, false miracles, &c., were held up to the popular scorn and indignation. Henry, though a reformer, was far from being a Protestant; and he condemned to death both Catholics and Protestants, who ventured to maintain opinions contrary to his own. Though a most unworthy instrument, Henry, by his opposition to the pope, was the means of introducing the Protestant religion into England, which may be considered as the main source of the prosperity and superiority of that kingdom over most of the kingdoms of Europe.

291. *Reformation in Scotland.* About the year 1526, the doctrines of the German reformers were introduced into Scotland, by Patrick Hamilton, a youth of noble descent. For his efforts against the popish religion, he was put to death. Many excellent men in Scotland suffered death in the same cause. This, however, only served to increase the number of the reformed. The person who most distinguished himself, to extend the

---

291. By whom were the doctrines of the Reformers introduced into Scotland? Who is called the apostle of Scotland? What is said of him?

Reformation in Scotland was *John Knox*, who, for his uncommon zeal and piety, is called "the apostle of Scotland." Having embraced the tenets of the Protestants, he spread them abroad at the hazard of his life. He was ardent, bold, and persevering, and commanded the respect even of his enemies. He died in 1572, after having lived to see the Reformation fully established. The regent of Scotland pronounced his eulogium, as his body was laid in the grave : *There lies he who never feared the face of man.* Knox adopted the *Presbyterian* form of church government, which is now the form established by law in Scotland.

292. *Of the Jesuits.* The Jesuits, or the *Society of Jesus*, was instituted by *Ignatius Loyola*, a Spanish knight, about the year 1535. One of the vows which the Jesuits took upon themselves was, that they would go wherever the pope should command them, without any aid from him for their support. At this period, the papal power had received such a shock, by the progress of the Reformation, that the acquisition of such a body of men as the Jesuits, was to the pope of much importance. Pope Paul, therefore, confirmed the order, and granted them many privileges. The Jesuits are peculiar in their operations. Instead of retiring from the world, like most other religious orders, they considered themselves as formed for action. They attended to all the transactions of the world, on account of the influence they might have upon religion. They were directed to study the dispositions of persons of rank, gain their friendship, and become their spiritual guides and confessors. To have the management of the education of youth, they considered one of the most important parts of their system.

293. *Progress of the Jesuits.* Before the close of the sixteenth century, the Jesuits had obtained the chief direction of the education of youth in every Catholic

---

292. By whom was the order of Jesuits instituted ? What was one of their vows ? State the peculiar operations of the Jesuits.

MODERN HISTORY. 201

country in Europe. They had become the confessors of all its monarchs,—a function of great importance. They had, at different periods, the direction of the most considerable courts in Europe, and took part in every intrigue and revolution. In order to support themselves and their minions, they engaged in extensive and profitable commerce, both in the East and West Indies, and had their warehouses in different parts of Europe. Not satisfied with trade alone, they acquired possession of large and fertile provinces. In *Paraguay*, in South America, the Jesuits civilized the natives, and trained them to arts and manufactures. Such was their influence, that a few of their number presided over some hundred thousand Indians. But at length their power became so formidable, that they were expelled by most of the nations of Europe, and the order was suppressed by Pope Clement in 1773. In 1814, however, the order of the Jesuits was re-established by the papal authority.

294. *Massacre of St. Bartholomew's*. In 1572, during the reign of Charles IX. of France, 70,000 Protestants were murdered in that kingdom. At this period, the Protestant religion had spread extensively in France, and was professed by some men of great influence at the court. Previous to the massacre, a civil war had raged between the Catholics and Protestants, which was ended by granting toleration to the Protestants. In order to put down the reformed religion, Charles and his court had recourse to stratagem and treachery. The Protestants were treated with the greatest marks of favor, and their principal leaders were allured to the court. Every thing being arranged, on *St. Bartholomew's day*, a horrid massacre took place in Paris and throughout France.

---

293. State the progress of the Jesuits before the close of the 16th century. What did they in Paraguay? When were they suppressed, and when restored?

294. How many Protestants were murdered in France? What is said of the Catholics and Protestants previous to this time? During the massacre, what did Charles, the French king, do?

Charles, the savage monarch, from the windows of his palace, encouraged the furious populace to murder his Protestant subjects, by crying out "Kill! kill!" Of this atrocious massacre, a French historian observes: "No example of equal barbarity is to be found in all antiquity, or in the annals of the world."

295. *Reign of Queen Mary.* Mary was the daughter of *Catharine* of *Arragon*, one of the wives of Henry VIII., king of England. She was educated a Catholic, and endeavored to establish that religion again in England. She is often called the *bloody Queen Mary*, on account of the bloody persecution in England during her reign. In this persecution, upwards of 270 persons were burnt, among whom were five bishops and twenty-one clergymen. The men who had been the most forward in establishing the Protestant religion were singled out for punishment; and among the most eminent martyrs who were burnt at Smithfield, were *Cranmer, Latimer, Ridley, Hooper*, and *Rogers*. The excellent character of the sufferers, and the firmness which they exhibited, produced a strong feeling in their favor. Instead of overthrowing the Protestant religion, by burning its advocates, it caused it to be more firmly established.

296. *Queen Elizabeth's Reign.* After the death of Mary, in 1558, *Elizabeth*, another daughter of Henry VIII., ascended the throne of England. During her reign, which continued 44 years, tranquillity was maintained in her dominions, the Protestant religion was restored, and the *Church of England* was established in its present form. The nation attained a higher state of prosperity than it had ever known before, and, from being a secondary kingdom, rose to a level with the first states in Europe. The character of Elizabeth, however, has received a stain, from her treatment of her cousin, *Mary, Queen of Scots.* This beautiful, accomplished,

---

295. Who is called the bloody Queen Mary, and why so called? How many persons were burnt during her reign, and who were the most eminent? What effect did it have?

296. What is said of the reign of Queen Elizabeth? What of Mary, Queen of Scots?

and unfortunate woman, was, after Elizabeth, the next heir to the crown. Her friends contended that she was the lawful heir, and that Elizabeth had no right to the throne. Being educated a Catholic, and being guilty of many imprudences, she was obliged to flee from her Scottish subjects, and take refuge in England. Elizabeth kept her in prison for 18 years, when she was condemned for a conspiracy, and beheaded in prison.

297. *Spanish Armada.* At the period of Queen Elizabeth's reign, England and Spain were the two most powerful nations in Europe. Elizabeth was considered the leader of the Protestants, and Philip, king of Spain, of the Catholics. Elizabeth having assisted some of the Protestant powers with whom he was at war, he determined upon the conquest of England. Philip spent three years in making preparations for a mighty effort. His fleet consisted of 130 ships of war, carrying 30,000 troops and seamen, and was the most formidable which Europe had ever before witnessed, and was named the *Invincible Armada.* Troops from Italy, Germany, Flanders, and Spain, were embarked, or ordered to places from whence they might be sent over to England. The fleet entered the English channel in the form of a crescent, extending to the distance ot seven miles. It was met by the English fleet consisting of 108 ships, commanded by *Howard, Drake, Hawkins*, and other distinguished commanders. The Spanish fleet, being gradually weakened, and finally overtaken by storms, suffered an entire defeat, and only 50 vessels, with 6,000 men, returned to Spain.

298. *Gunpowder Plot.* In order to crush the power of the Catholics in England, King James I. enforced those laws which were enacted against them by his predecessors. Under the Jesuits in England, a con-

---

297. During Elizabeth's reign, what two nations were the most powerful? Who determined to conquer England? What is said of the Armada?

298. By whom was the gunpowder plot formed, and for what purpose? How was it discovered?

spiracy was formed, called the *gunpowder plot*, the object of which was, to blow up the parliament house, while the king, queen, and parliament, were assembled in it. One of the conspirators hired a coal-cellar, in which he deposited thirty-six barrels of gunpowder, which was to be fired at the time the king was delivering his speech. The secret, which had been in the keeping of at least twenty persons, was discovered by means of a letter, written to prevent Lord Monteagle, a Catholic nobleman, from entering the house on that day. The letter was shown to the king, who caused a search to be made in the cellar, the evening previous to the meeting of parliament. *Guy Fawkes*, one of the conspirators, was found in the cellar, with matches in his pocket, for firing the train. The other conspirators were discovered, and all suffered for their crime, in 1605.

299. *French Settlements in North America.* By the discovery of a new world, a spirit of enterprise was awakened in all the commercial nations of Europe. In 1524, the French king sent out navigators, who explored a great part of the coast of North America. Ten years afterwards, one *Cartier* was sent on another voyage of discovery. He sailed up the St. Lawrence, as far as Montreal, took possession of the country in the name of the French king, and called it *New France*. This name was afterwards changed to *Canada*. In 1540, Cartier, with a colony of 200 persons, began the first settlement in Canada, near the present city of Quebec. The first French settlement in *Acadie*, now Nova Scotia, appears to have been effected in the year 1604. During the religious wars in France, *Ribault*, a French Protestant, was sent to make a settlement in America, as a retreat from persecution. He landed near Edisto river, in South Carolina, built a fort, which he called *Carolina*, and leaving a garrison of twenty men, he re-

---

299. In what year did the French navigators explore the coast of North America? What is said of Cartier? Where did Ribault attempt to make a settlement, and what became of his men?

turned to France. The men who were left, soon aftei mutinied, killed their commander, and put to sea. Having been out several weeks, and provisions failing, they fed on human flesh, and at last were taken up by an English ship and carried to England.

300. *First English Settlement.* In 1584, Queen Elizabeth granted to *Walter Raleigh* authority to discover, occupy, and govern, "remote heathen and barbarous countries," not previously possessed by any Christian prince or people. Raleigh immediately sent over two ships to America, the commanders of which landed at *Roanoke*, and took possession of the country. On their return, they gave such a splendid description of the beauty and fertility of the country, that Elizabeth named it *Virginia*, because the discovery was made during the reign of a virgin queen. After many unsuccessful attempts to establish a permanent settlement, Capt. *Newport* was sent with 100 adventurers to settle the island of Roanoke. By stress of weather, they were driven north of their place of destination, and entered Chesapeake bay. They sailed up the *Powhatan*, or *James River*, and in May, 1607, commenced the settlement of *Jamestown*, so named in honor of king *James*. This was the first permanent English settlement in North America.

---

300. What is said of Walter Raleigh? Who named Virginia? What is said respecting the settlement of Jamestown?

PERIOD VIII.

DISTINGUISHED FOR THE SETTLEMENT OF THE ENGLISH NORTH AMERICAN COLONIES.

Commencing a Settlement.

FROM THE SETTLEMENT AT JAMESTOWN TO THE AMERICAN REVOLUTION.

(168 YEARS.)

301. *Of the Virginia Settlers.* During the first year, the colonists at Jamestown suffered severely from the scarcity and badness of their provisions; disease soon made its appearance, which in a few months swept off more than half their number. But as new settlers were arriving, the colonists amounted to 200 at the end of the year. Many of the settlers were very imprudent in their conduct towards the natives, and provoked them to hostility A party of 30 men was killed, and by a waste of their provisions a most distressing famine prevailed, long known afterwards by the name of the *starving time.* So dreadful was its effects, that the colonists were reduced from 500 to 60. So disheartened were those that were left, that they embarked for England;

---

301. What is said of the colonists during their first year at Jamestown? What is said of the starving time?

but meeting with *Lord Delaware*, with 150 men and a large supply of provisions, they consented to return.

302. *Pocahontas, the Indian Princess.* The most brave and enterprising of the Virginia settlers, was *Capt. John Smith*. Under a pretext of commerce, he was drawn into an ambush of a large body of Indians, who made him prisoner, and carried him to *Powhatan*, their king, who sentenced him to death. Capt. Smith was led out, and his head placed upon a large stone, ready for the fatal blow. At this moment, *Pocahontas*, the youngest and darling daughter of Powhatan, rushed to the spot where Capt. Smith lay, threw her arms about his neck, and placed her head on his, and declared that if the sentence was executed, the first blow should fall on her. The king was moved, and consented to spare his victim upon the condition of a ransom. The ransom was paid, and Capt. Smith returned safe to Jamestown.

About three years after the above event, Capt. Smith's life was again saved by Pocahontas. Powhatan planned a horrid scheme, for the entire destruction of the colony at Jamestown. His plan was to attack and murder them in time of peace. In a dark and stormy night, Pocahontas, like an angel of mercy, went alone to Jamestown, and disclosed the inhuman plot of her father. Pocahontas after this was married to an Englishman named *Rolfe*, with whom she went to England. She embraced the Christian religion, and after residing there several years, she died as she was about to embark for America.

303. *Indian Massacre in Virginia.* In 1622, the Indians in Virginia entered into a conspiracy for the purpose of murdering all the inhabitants of the English settlement. The plan was matured with the utmost secrecy. While

---

302. Who was the most enterprising of the Virginia settlers? Who took him prisoner, and how was his life preserved? How did Pocahontas save the colony from destruction? What farther is said of Pocahontas?

303. What plot did the Indians form against the English? Describe the manner of its execution. During the war, how much were the settlements and colonists reduced?

engaged in the plot, they visited and traded with the English, and bought their arms of them, that they might accomplish their design. On the evening before the massacre, they brought the colonists presents of game, and visited them the next morning as usual; suddenly at noon, when least expected, they fell upon the settlers, and murdered 347 men, women, and children. The destruction would have been more extensive, had not an Indian residing in one of the towns revealed the plot to his master. Information was given to part of the nearest settlements, and they were saved from the fate which fell upon others. The English were aroused to vengeance; an exterminating war succeeded; many of the enemy were destroyed, and the rest were driven far into the wilderness. During the war the settlements of the whites were reduced from eighty to eight. In 1624, out of 9,000 persons who were sent from England, but 1800 existed in the colony.

304. *Of the Native Indians.* It has long been a question among the learned, how America was first peopled. The opinion best supported is, that tribes of men passed over to this continent from the northern part of Tartary to the northwestern coast of America, as the two continents at this point are separated by straits only about 18 miles wide. The Indians in the northern parts of America were divided into many small tribes, governed by their sachems, or kings, and were often at war with each other. At the time of the arrival of the Europeans, the whole territory now embraced within the limits of the United States and British America, was almost an unbroken wilderness. It has been estimated, that at this period there were but about 150,000 Indians within the compass of the thirteen original states. A very mortal sickness is supposed to have prevailed among them, and swept off great num-

---

304. How is it supposed that America was first settled? What is said of the Indians, and how many is it estimated they were in numbers, in the limits of the United States and British America?

bers, a few years previous to the first settlement of the Europeans.

305. *Manners, Customs, &c., of the Indians.* The chief occupation of all the northern tribes of Indians, was hunting, fishing, and war. Their women were compelled to till the ground, and perform all the drudgery of their domestic affairs. Their clothing in summer was a slight covering about the waist; in winter they clothed themselves with the skin of wild animals. Their habitations, which were called *wigwams*, were made by erecting a strong pole for the center, around which other poles were placed and fixed to the center pole at the top, and then covered with mats, or barks of trees. Their warlike and domestic instruments were few and simple,—a *tomahawk* or hatchet of stone, bows and arrows, sharp stones and shells for knives and hoes. For money, they used small beads, wrought from shells and strung on belts, or in chains, called *wampum*. The Indians believed in the existence of a number of gods; one, however, they considered greater than all the rest, and him they called the *Great Spirit*, who was the creator of all things; their priests, or *powows*, who were also their physicians, had great influence over their minds.

306. *Of the Puritans.* About the period of the first English settlement in America, a respectable body of Protestants in England were dissatisfied with the religious state of things in that country. Queen Elizabeth, though a Protestant, was rather arbitrary in some parts of her conduct; she took violent measures to enforce uniformity in church discipline and service. Many of her subjects, though holding to the same doctrines as the established church, did not think it their duty to practice all its rites and ceremonies. They believed

---

305. What was the chief occupation of the Indians? What is said of their women? How were they clothed? Describe their wigwams, their warlike and domestic instruments, money, and their religious opinions.

306. What is said of Queen Elizabeth? Who received the name of puritans?

the English church retained too many of the popish forms and ceremonies, and manifested uncommon zeal in preserving the *purity* of divine worship; hence they received the name of *Puritans.*

307. *Persecution of the Puritans.* All those who would not conform to the established forms of worship, were subjected to severe penalties; they were compelled to collect for worship in private places, with great secrecy. Hundreds of puritan ministers were silenced, or deprived of their livings, and many were imprisoned while their families were starving. These persecutions were continued with little abatement, for about fifty years. The puritans, or *dissenters*, as they are sometimes called, were at first very unwilling to separate from the established church, and made many efforts to obtain toleration; but the queen and most of the bishops refused to grant the free exercise of their religious worship. In consequence of their persecutions, many of the puritans left their native country, passed over to Holland and formed distinct churches; there they remained till the most of them emigrated to America.

308. *Plymouth Settlers.* The colony at Plymouth was planted principally for the sake of the free enjoyment of civil and religious liberty. Mr. *Robinson* and his congregation, who left England in 1608, and removed to Holland, may be considered as the founders of the colony. Finding that the morals of their children would be corrupted by a residence in Holland, they resolved to emigrate to America. The first colony consisted of a part only of Mr. Robinson's congregation, who purchased two small ships, and repaired to Plymouth, in England. One of their ships proving leaky, the passengers were all crowded into one ship,

---

307. What is said of those who refused to conform to the established worship? How long did their persecutions continue? To what place did the puritans go when they left their native country?

308. For what purpose was the colony at Plymouth planted? Who were the first colonists? What is said of their voyage? When did they land, and at what time?

and after a furious storm, arrived at Cape Cod, November 10th. Before the landing, they formed themselves into a "body politic," and chose Mr. John Carver their

Landing at Plymouth, 1620.

governor, for one year. After much suffering from the severity of the weather, they selected a place for a settlement, which they named *Plymouth.* They landed at this place on the 22d of December, 1620. The anniversary of their landing is still celebrated by the decendants of the *Pilgrim Fathers,* as a religious festival.

309. *Sufferings of the Plymouth Colonists.* The whole company that landed at Plymouth consisted of 101 persons. Their situation and prospects were truly dismal and discouraging. The nearest European settlement was 500 miles distant, and from it no relief could be obtained, in case of famine or sickness. Sterile sands and gloomy forests were the principal objects that met their view; they were worn down by excessive fatigue, they suffered from the severity of the weather, and were without comfortable provisions or habitations.

---

309. How many landed at Plymouth? Give an account of their sufferings.

Disease prevailed among them, and in three months forty-five of their number died. The sickness was so general that at times there were only six or seven well persons in the whole company. Amid all their trials and privations, they bore their hardships with that patience, calmness, and resignation, which true Christianity alone can give.

310. *Dutch Settlements.* In 1609, *Henry Hudson*, an Englishman, in the service of the Dutch, discovered Hudson river, and ascended it about 160 miles. Four years afterwards, several Dutch merchants erected a fort, near Albany, which they named *Fort Orange*, and a few trading-houses where the city of New York now stands. This place they named *New Amsterdam;* the island on which the city is built was called, by the Indians, *Manhattan*. The country on both sides of the Hudson river was called, by the Dutch, *New Netherlands*. The Dutch also, in 1623, erected a fort on the Delaware, and ten years afterwards, one in Connecticut, where Hartford now stands. They remained in possession of these places till a war broke out between England and Holland, and in 1664 they were surrendered to the English forces. Charles II. granted the New Netherlands to his brother, the duke of *York* and *Albany;* and in honor of the duke, the name of Manhattan was changed to New York, and that of Orange to Albany.

311. *Destruction of the Pequots.* One of the most haughty and warlike tribes of Indians in New England, were the *Pequots*, who inhabited the southeastern part of Connecticut. In 1637, two years after the settlers arrived in this state, the Pequots having murdered a number of persons, a force of 90 men, under *Capt. Mason*,

---

310. Who discovered Hudson river, and at what time? Where did the Dutch merchants erect a fort and trading-houses? What name did they give these places and the country? What year were they surrendered to the English? Who gave the names New York and Albany?

311. Where did the Pequots reside, and what did they do? Give an account of their destruction.

was sent against them. In this expedition they were assisted by the *Mohegans*, a friendly tribe, and by the Narragansetts. Capt. Mason, marching by night, attacked their fort by surprise: the conflict was desperate ; the wigwams in the fort were set on fire ; the roar of the flames, the yells of the savages, and the discharge of musketry, presented an awful and terrific scene. The victory was complete. Out of five or six hundred Pequots who were in the fort, only seven or eight escaped ; the remainder were shot, or perished in the flames.

312. *King Philip's War.* In 1675, *Philip*, an Indian sachem, who resided at *Mount Hope*, in Rhode Island, began the most general and destructive war ever sustained by the infant colonies. Philip, for a long time previous to the war, was jealous of the whites. His object appears to have been, to unite all the Indian tribes to make a combined effort to exterminate the colonists, and thus preserve their hunting-grounds and their independence. A Christian Indian, having made known to the colonists the plot against them, Philip caused him to be murdered. The murderers were tried and executed by the English. Philip, to avenge their deaths, commenced hostilities, and, by his influence, drew into the war most of the tribes in New England.

The Indians at this period had acquired to some extent the use of firearms, and the war soon became general. The savages hovered about the frontier settlements, burnt and ravaged several towns, and killed many of the inhabitants. In December, about 1000 men, under the command of Gov. *Winslow*, marched through a deep snow to the Indian fortress in the Narragansett country, in Rhode Island. The conflict was bloody. Six captains and eighty men were killed, and 150 wounded ; but the success of the English was complete. About 500 wigwams were burnt, and it is supposed that

---

312. Who was Philip, and where did he reside ? Give an account of the origin of his war, of the swamp fight, and of the loss of the English. How many Indians perished ? What became of Philip ?

about 1000 of the Indians perished. From this blow, called the *swamp fight*, they never recovered. The war, however, continued, till the August following when Philip was shot by a friendly Indian, in the vicinity of Mount Hope. Thus closed a most distressing war, in

Death of King Philip.

which the English lost 600 men, the flower of their strength: 12 or 13 towns were destroyed, and 600 dwelling-houses consumed.

313. *William Penn.* The territory of Pennsylvania was granted to *William Penn*, from whom it derives its name. This grant was made by King Charles II. of England, in 1681, for services rendered to the crown by the father of Penn, who was an Admiral in the English navy. In October, 1682, William Penn arrived in the Delaware, with his colony of *Friends* or *Quakers*. He purchased of the natives the land for a city, which he called *Philadelphia*. He paid the natives for all the land he obtained, and at the same time gave them good counsel and advice, which proved of much service to

---

313. To whom was Pennsylvania granted? What is said of Penn and his colony of Friends? How long did Penn's treaty continue? Did the natives respect Penn and his followers?

them, and increased their affection for him. He concluded a treaty of peace with the natives, which lasted more than seventy years. He parceled out his lands at moderate rents, enacted mild and just laws, and gave free toleration to all religious sects. The respect and love which the natives had for Penn and his followers were so great, that it is related as a fact, that in all their wars with the whites they never killed a Quaker, knowing him to be such.

314. *Salem Witchcraft.* The year 1692 is memorable in New England for the convulsion produced in Salem and its vicinity by the supposed prevalence of *witchcraft.* Many were supposed to be *bewitched,* and would complain of being bitten, pinched, pricked with pins, &c.; some declared that they beheld a spectral representation of the person whom they said was the cause of their affliction. Some were struck dumb, others had their limbs distorted in a shocking manner, sometimes running on their hands and feet, creeping through holes, and under chairs, tables, &c.; barking like a dog, with other actions equally strange and unaccountable. Upon the accusation and testimony of persons thus afflicted, many were imprisoned, and nineteen were executed for *practising witchcraft,* most of whom died professing their innocence. The evil became awfully alarming; the most respectable persons in the country were accused; but the magistrates finally acquitted those who were accused, and the menacing storm blew over, to the great joy of the inhabitants.

At this period many learned and eminent men, both in England and America, fully believed in the existence of witchcraft. Sir *Matthew Hale,* of England, one of the greatest and best judges that ever sat in a court of justice, repeatedly tried and condemned persons as criminals, who were brought before him charged with this crime.

---

314 How were persons affected who were supposed to be bewitched? How many were executed for practising witchcraft? What is said of Matthew Hale and others?

315. *Account of the Bucaneers.* Between the years 1630 and 1700, the seas and some of the West India islands were infested by a set of pirates and freebooters, called *bucaneers.* They originated from some French vagabonds who had commenced a plantation at St. Kitt's, one of the West India islands. They were driven from it by the Spaniards, and fled to Hispaniola, now Hayti. There they subsisted for a time by hunting swine and cattle. They acquired the name of bucaneers from the practice of drying their meat, called in French "*boucaner.*" Having lived some time in this way, some of them became pirates, and others cultivated the soil. Many of them established themselves upon the isle of *Tortuga,* and there fortified themselves. They had a mortal hatred to the Spaniards, and often plundered their ships and put all their crews to death. They were the terror of every trader to the shores of America. When loaded with booty, they returned and divided it, and spent their time in all kinds of debauchery, until it was expended.

The bucaneers had all things in common; and when their plunder was gone, they were completely destitute. Their numbers increased so rapidly from Europe, that they became terrible to all Spanish America. With an army of 1200 men they attacked several Spanish towns, murdering the people and plundering the houses. Among these towns was *Carthagena,* which they plundered of its effects to the amount of seven or eight millions of dollars. But, while on their return, they fell in with a fleet of Dutch and English ships, which defeated them, and took and destroyed a number of their vessels. From this check they never recovered. They were hunted down by the nations of Europe till they were destroyed.

316. *Sovereigns of the House of Stuart.* On the death of Queen Elizabeth, *James,* the sixth king of

---

315. At what time were the West Indies infested by the bucaneers? How did they originate, and what is said of them? What town did they plunder of seven or eight millions of dollars? How were they defeated and destroyed?

Scotland, of that name, ascended the throne of England. He was the son of Mary, queen of Scots, the nearest relative of Elizabeth, and the rightful heir by descent. He was of the *Stuart family,*—a race of sovereigns distinguished for a succession of misfortunes, and their love of arbitrary power. By the accession of James, the crowns of England and Scotland became united, and eventually made the two kingdoms one. As James was educated a Presbyterian, the puritans hoped that they would enjoy the toleration of their religious worship. But they were greatly disappointed, and many fled and commenced settlements in New England. James was an arbitrary monarch, and held to the divine right of kings to govern their subjects without control. He was succeeded by *Charles I.,* who inherited the same principles with his father. Charles married a daughter of the French king, who was a zealous papist, and whose influence over the king is regarded as one of the principal causes of his calamities.

317. *Tyranny of Charles I.* Charles, soon after he ascended the throne, was offended with the parliament for refusing to grant him sufficient supplies to carry on a war with Spain. He then proceeded to raise money without their authority. One of these methods was by a tax called *ship-money.* Charles claimed the right to command his subjects to provide and furnish ships, together with men, victuals, and ammunition, in such numbers, and at whatever time he should think proper; a claim contrary to the *magna charta* of English liberty. A noble stand was taken against this tax by *John Hampden,* a man of great talents and patriotism, and had the effect of rousing the nation to sustain their liberties. Charles also created great discontent by his endeavoring to regulate the religious affairs of the nation: by

---

316. Who ascended the English throne after Elizabeth? What is said of the Stuart family? What is said of James, and Charles I., his ancestors?

317. How did Charles proceed to raise money? Who withstood this tax? In what other way did Charles create discontent?

the advice of *Laud,* archbishop of Canterbury, he introduced new ceremonies in the church, and endeavored to introduce Episcopacy into Scotland. The last attempt was most violently opposed by the Scots.

318. *War between Charles and the Parliament.* Charles, by his despotic acts, particularly his imprisoning and impeaching a number of the members of parliament, kindled the flame of civil war. In 1642, both parties resolved to terminate the contest by the sword. The cause of the king was supported by the greater part of the nobility and gentry, and by the Catholics; that of the parliament by the common people of the country, the merchants and tradesmen of the towns, and the opponents of Episcopacy. The supporters of the king were styled *Cavaliers;* those of the parliament, *Roundheads,*—a name given to them by their adversaries, because they cropped their hair. The war raged, with various success, for nearly five years; but at length the royalists were overcome, and Charles fell into the hands of his enemies.

319. *Execution of Charles I.* The parliament, now under the influence of the army, instituted a high court, consisting of 133 members, to try Charles as a tyrant, traitor, and murderer. Charles denied their authority to try him, and would not make any defense. He was, however, condemned to suffer death, by being beheaded. The unfortunate king submitted to his fate with fortitude and composure. Having laid his head on the block, one of the masked executioners severed it from his body by a single blow: the other holding it up, exclaimed, " Behold the head of a traitor." Charles, though unwise, imprudent, and unfaithful in his promises as a king, had nevertheless many virtues in private life ; and it is said of him, " He would have made a much better

---

318. What caused the civil war? By whom was the cause of the king supported? Who supported that of the parliament, and what names were given to each party?

319. By whom was Charles tried? Relate the manner of his death. What is said of his character?

figure in private life than he did upon a throne." He was executed on the 30th of January, 1649, in the 49th year of his age.

Execution of Charles the First.

320. *Oliver Cromwell.* The army of the parliament during the war against the royalists, was commanded by able officers, of whom *Oliver Cromwell* was the most distinguished. Without the aid of birth, wealth, or influential connections, he rose to be the head of three powerful kingdoms. On the death of Charles I., monarchy and the House of Lords were both abolished by the Commons, and a republican government established. The parliament at first was under the influence of the *Presbyterians*; next the *Independents* gained the ascendancy; then the power passed into the hands of the army of whom Cromwell had the management. Previous to his taking the sovereign power, Cromwell forcibly dissolved the *Long Parliament*, so called from its having been in session 12 years. This body having become jealous of Cromwell, determined to reduce the army, and thus diminish his power. Cromwell

---

320. Who was Oliver Cromwell? What was done on the death of Charles? What is said of the Long Parliament? Of Barebone's Parliament? What title did Cromwell receive?

perceiving their object, went with 300 of his soldiers to the parliament, turned the members out of the house, and locked the door. A new parliament was formed, often called *Barebone's Parliament*, from a leading member of that name, who was a leather dresser. After this body was dissolved, Cromwell was declared *Protector*, and became in every respect a king, except the name.

321. *The Commonwealth. Character of Cromwell.* The commonwealth of England is dated from the death of Charles I. to the restoration of monarchy under his son, Charles II., a period of about eleven years. During this period, when under the government of Cromwell, the nation arrived to a great degree of prosperity, and became the most powerful in Europe. The protector granted religious toleration, caused justice to be faithfully administered, and his officers of government were generally men of moral and religious principles, and vice was discountenanced at his court. He defeated with ease his enemies at home and abroad, and his power was everywhere respected, and the short period of the protectorate was the most brilliant found in English history. Cromwell died in the 69th year of his age, and was succeeded by his son, Richard, who soon resigned the office of protector, and retired to private life. Cromwell, in his private life, was exemplary,—though somewhat of an enthusiast, yet he appeared to be deeply impressed with religious feelings. His army, also, in a remarkable manner, partook of the same spirit. By many writers, Cromwell has been represented as a religious hypocrite; but, (as it has been well observed,) this supposition is contradicted by the whole course of his life.

322. *Of Russia. Peter the Great.* Russia was raised from a state of barbarism and ignorance by *Peter the Great*, who reigned from 1696 to 1725. Previous to

---

321. How long did the Commonwealth continue? What was the state of the nation under Cromwell? Who succeeded him? What is said of Cromwell's character?

this time, the history of Russia is obscure and unimportant. It is said to have received the light of Christianity in the tenth century. The Russian sovereigns receive the title of *Czar,* a word which signifies king. Peter, after ascending the throne, wishing to form a navy and to gain knowledge personally, disguised himself and went to Holland, where he engaged himself as a workman in one of the dock-yards. There he labored with his own hands, and was fed and clad like the rest of the workmen. He also attended lectures on various subjects while in Holland. From Holland he went to England, where he perfected himself in the art of ship-building. Having returned to Russia, he laid the foundation of a northern capital, which was named after himself, *St. Petersburg.* He endeavored, by every means, to introduce among his people a taste for the arts and sciences. Though defeated a number of times by the *Swedes,* he gained a great victory over them at *Pultowa,* by which means he extended the bounds of his kingdom.

321. *Of Sweden and its Sovereigns.* This country, with Norway, was the original seat of the Goths and Vandals, and was the *Scandinavia* of the ancients. In the early part of the 16th century, *Gustavus Vasa,* a descendant from the ancient kings, delivered his country f.o n the oppression of Christian II., of Denmark. He introduced the Protestant religion, and promoted the welfare of his subjects. *Gustavus Adolphus,* surnamed the Great, is ranked among the greatest commanders of modern times, and took the part of the Protestants in Germany. He was killed in the battle of *Lutzen.*

Charles XII. was one of the most remarkable men of his time. His ruling passion was the love of glory. He succeeded to the throne at the age of 15 years, and when only a boy of 17, he defeated the Russians, Poles

322. Who raised Russia from a state of barbarism? What did Peter do after he ascended the throne? What capital did he found?
323. What was Sweden originally? What is said of Gustavus Vasa? Gustavus Adolphus? What of Charles XII.?

and Danes, who had attacked his dominions on three sides. After a course of victories, he was signally defeated by the Czar Peter, at Pultowa. Charles now fled into Turkey, where he raised the Turks against the Russians. While in this country, he conducted like a madman, and was ordered to leave it. After his return to Sweden, he was killed by a cannon ball, while besieging a Norwegian fortress; and his death gave repose to the country.

324. *Of Prussia and the two Fredericks.* Prussia has existed as a kingdom from the year 1700. Modern Prussia is a kingdom formed from several small states, united by marriage or conquests. *Frederick William*, the father of Frederick the Great, was of singular habits; he was economical in the extreme, and hardly expended any thing except on his soldiers. He raised a regiment of men, whom he called his giants. He collected them from all parts of Europe, not one of whom was less than seven feet high. He was rough and savage in his manners, and brutal in his conduct towards his own family. He would knock down, with his fists, the princes and princesses, his own children, and at times they would be half famished.

Frederick II., the Great, ascended the throne in 1740, and, having the best army in Europe, was ambitious of military glory and conquest. He conquered Silesia, and published a declaration of war against *Maria Theresa*, empress of Germany, who was aided by the French and Russians. The contest was carried on for *seven years;* more than half a million of men perished on the field of battle. Frederick, notwithstanding the great superiority of numbers against him, maintained his ground, and acquired the name of the greatest commander of the age. The state of parties, at the end of the war, remained nearly the same as at the commencement. Frederick, besides being a military hero, aimed

324. How long has Prussia existed as a kingdom? What is said of Frederick William? What is said of the military transactions? What was his character?

at the reputation of being a philosopher and poet, and was the author of a number of works in prose and verse. He appeared to have no moral or religious principles, and was addicted to various kinds of vice. Atheists and libertines were his companions, particularly the infidel French philosopher, *Voltaire.*

325. *Of Holland.* The *Netherlands*, in which Holland is included, during the early period of their history, comprised various small states, governed by counts and earls. These states at different periods belonged to the various powers in Europe. In 1555 they were transferred to *Philip II.*, king of Spain. The Reformation at this period had made considerable progress in the Netherlands. Philip, with a view to repress it, established the Inquisition, and committed other oppressive acts; and to enforce them, sent an army under the duke of *Alva.* Seven of the provinces revolted. *William*, *prince of Orange*, raised an army, and effected the independence of the *Seven United Provinces*, or *Holland*, in 1579. The remaining ten were called *Flanders.* After the *Dutch* provinces were free from Spain, they rose by industry and enterprise to a great degree of prosperity, and became one of the most formidable naval powers in the world, particularly at the time of the Commonwealth of England.

326. *Of Germany.* In the ninth century, Charlemagne divided the empire of the West among his successors, into three monarchies, France, Germany, and Italy; Germany, however, was called, by way of eminence, *the empire.* Before the time of Charlemagne, Germany appears to have been divided into a number of small independent states, who frequently united in defence of their common liberties; they were not, how-

---

325. What is said of the early history of the Netherlands? What caused the revolt of the Seven United Provinces? What were the remainder called? What is said of the Dutch provinces, when freed from Spain?

326. Into what monarchies was the western empire divided? What is said of Germany? Of Charles? Of Austria? Who assisted the Protestants?

ever, considered of much importance till the time of Charlemagne, who is to be considered, in some respects, as the founder of the German empire. It has had a long line of distinguished sovereigns, among whom *Charles V.* presented the novel spectacle of voluntarily resigning his dominions and retiring to a monastery, after reigning 40 years.

During the reign of Ferdinand I., *Austria*, one of the most powerful of the German states, made an effort to extinguish the Protestant religion in the empire. In 1626, the Protestant princes, at the head of whom was Gustavus, of Sweden, united against the emperor, and the war of *thirty years* ensued, which ended by securing an equal establishment of the Protestant and Catholic religions. In this war, the Protestants were assisted by the Catholics of France, who took this method to humble the growing Austrian power.

327. *French and Indian Wars.* From the earliest settlement of the English colonies to the treaty of Paris, in 1763, they were often harassed by frequent wars with the French and Indians. The French had settled in Canada, on the north, and in Louisiana, on the south of the colonies; they had also explored the country along the Ohio and Mississippi rivers, and pretended the English had no claim to the territory west of the Alleghany mountains. In order to strengthen their possessions, they attempted to establish a chain of forts from Canada to Florida, back of the English settlements. They also used much art to gain over the various tribes to their interest, in which they were generally successful. The Indians, instigated, and sometimes accompanied by the French, came down upon the English, destroyed their settlements, and murdered or carried away captive the inhabitants. These and other injuries were soon succeeded by open war.

328. *King William's and Queen Anne's Wars.* The war during the reign of William and Mary, in England,

---

327. How long were the English colonies harassed by the French and Indian wars? Relate the proceedings of the French.

commonly called "*King William's war,*" commenced in 1690, and continued about seven years. In the depth of winter, *Count Frontenac,* governor of Canada, fitted out three expeditions against the colonies—one against New York, a second against New Hampshire, and a third against the province of Maine. The party destined against New York fell upon Schenectady in the dead of night, burnt the place, and massacred the inhabitants. The second party, who went to New Hampshire, burned Salmon Falls, and killed 30 men. The third party proceeding from Quebec, destroyed Casco, in Maine, and killed and captured 100 people. The colony of Massachusetts, roused by these proceedings, fitted out an expedition under Sir *William Phips,* who took possession of Nova Scotia. Another expedition was fitted out by New York, Connecticut, and Massachusetts, to take Montreal and Quebec, but this was unsuccessful.

Queen Anne's war commenced in 1702, and continued about ten years, and many places in New England were ravaged by the French and Indians, from Canada. The colonies fitted out a number of expeditions against Canada, but were generally unsuccessful. They, however, took Port Royal, in Nova Scotia, and in honor of Queen Anne, named it *Annapolis.*

329. *Indian War in Carolina.* In 1715, the *Yamasees,* a powerful tribe of Indians, inhabiting the southern border of South Carolina, formed a general conspiracy of all the neighboring tribes, to destroy the English settlements. Upwards of 6,000 warriors were engaged in the plot. They commenced by murdering 90 persons, who were in Pocataligo and around Port Royal. The inhabitants of Port Royal escaped by embarking on

---

328. How long did King William's war continue! What expeditions did Count Frontenac fit out, and what is said of them? What did the colonies do? What is said of Queen Anne's War?

329. What tribe formed a conspiracy in South Carolina? How did it succeed? Who defeated the Indians in their camp, and where did they flee to?

board a vessel and sailing to Charleston. On a plantation by Goose Creek, there were 70 whites and 40 faithful blacks, who were protected by a parapet, and they
determined to keep their post. Their courage failed
them on the first attack, and they surrendered; but the
moment they were in the hands of the enemy, they were
all massacred. The Indians now advanced still nearer
Charleston, but were repulsed by the militia. Governor
Craven, with 1200 men, marched against the ravagers
and found them in their great camp, at a place called
Saltcatchers. After a severe and bloody battle, he de
feated and drove them from the province. The greatest
part of them fled to Florida, and were received by the
Spaniards.

330. *Capture of Louisburg.* In March, 1744, war
having again broke out between Great Britain and
France, the legislature of Massachusetts planned a daring
but successful enterprise against *Louisburg.* This
place was on the island of Cape Breton, and was considered one of the strongest places in America. The
fortifications had been twenty-five years in building, and
had cost the French five millions and a half of dollars.
About 4,000 men from Massachusetts, New Hampshire,
and Connecticut, under the command of Gen. *Pepperell,*
sailed from Boston for the conquest of this place. Having the assistance of four ships of war, under Commodore Warren, the troops arrived at Louisburg about the
1st of May, 1745, and commenced the siege. For fourteen nights successively, the New England troops,
sinking to their knees in mud, drew their cannons and
mortars through a swamp two miles in length. By this
means the siege was pushed with so much vigor, that
the garrison surrendered on the 15th of June, to his
Britannic majesty.

331. *Braddock's Defeat.* The French continuing

---

330. Who planned the expedition against Louisburg? What
is said of its fortifications? How many troops went from the
colonies in this expedition? What is said of the exertions of
the New England troops?

ir encroachments on the back settlements, the British ministry took measures to drive them from the country. To effect this, they sent Gen. *Braddock* with an army, who arrived in Virginia in April, 1755. He was joined by Colonel (afterwards General) Washington, with a body of Virginia troops ; the whole force consisted of two thousand men, which marched for the French fort on the Ohio. General Braddock, with 1200 of his troops, on the 9th of July, arrived within seven miles of *Du Quesne*, a French fortress, which stood where Pittsburg is now built. The troops advanced in heavy columns, and passing through a narrow defile, they fell into an ambush of French and Indians, who poured in a deadly fire upon them. The British troops fired at random, as they could not see their foe. The slaughter at this time was dreadful among the officers : Washington was the only one on horseback, who was not either killed or wounded. He had two horses shot under him, and four bullets passed through his coat. After Braddock had received a mortal wound, his troops fled in confusion. The Virginians under Washington covered the retreat of the regulars, and saved them from entire destruction.

332. *Progress of the War.* The British generals who were sent over during the campaigns of 1756 and 1757, were unsuccessful and unpopular in the colonies. A change in the British ministry took place, and *William Pitt* (afterwards Lord Chatham) was placed at the head of the administration. This caused a change in the military operations. Fifty thousand men were raised, of which 20,000 were raised in America. Three expeditions were planned. The first against *Louisburg*, which had been given up to the French, the second against *Ticonderoga*, and the third against Fort *Du*

---

331. Who was sent to drive the French from Ohio? By whom was Braddock joined? Relate the circumstances of his defeat.

332. What is said of William Pitt? How many men were raised, what expeditions were planned, and with what success?

Quesne. Gen. *Amherst* subdued Louisburg, after considerable resistance, and took nearly 6,000 men prisoners. In the attack on Ticonderoga, Gen. *Abercrombie* was defeated, with the loss of 2,000 men. Fort Du Quesne was taken by Gen. Forbes, who changed its name, and called it, in honor of Wm. Pitt, *Pittsburg.*

333. *Capture of Quebec.* The command of the expedition against Quebec, was given to Gen. *Wolfe*, a young officer, who had distinguished himself at the capture of Louisburg. With an army of 8000 men, he landed in June, 1759, near Quebec, on the island of Orleans, just below the city. Quebec was a place of immense strength, and was at this time strongly garrisoned, by a force under *Montcalm*, an officer of distinguished merit. Failing in a number of attempts to make an impression on the city, Gen. Wolfe formed the bold design to ascend a steep craggy cliff, to an elevated plain called the *Plains of Abraham*, which commanded the city. This he effected under the cover of night, and before sunrise his whole army were arrayed on the plain in order of battle. A bloody action ensued. Wolfe and Montcalm were both mortally wounded, the French were defeated, and the city surrendered. Wolfe died in the moment of victory. As he lay fainting in death, hearing the cry, "they fly," asked, "who fly?" "The French," was the reply. "Then," said he, "I die happy," and expired. Montcalm, who was carried into the city, when told he could not live but a few hours, replied, "so much the better; I shall not live to see the surrender of Quebec." By the capture of Quebec, Canada came into the possession of Great Britain. This put a period to the French and Indian wars in America.

334. *Causes of the American Revolution.* Soon after the termination of the French and Indian wars, troubles assailed the colonies from a new quarter. The mother country began to assert her dominion over them, and in-

---

333. What did Gen. Wolfe do, in order to take Quebec? Relate the dying words of Wolfe and Montcalm. What followed the capture of Quebec?

terfered in their civil concerns, in a manner that created serious alarm for their liberties. Great Britain had, by her laws of trade and navigation, confined the trade of her colonies almost wholly to herself, and, in some cases, had even prohibited the establishment of manufactories in America. The colonies were treated as a distinct and lower class of subjects, and the British ministry, under the pretext of obtaining payment for the expense they had been at for defending them, claimed the right to raise money from them by taxation. The colonists, on the other hand, contended that as they had no representatives in the parliament, they could not be taxed without their consent, without violating their rights as British subjects. The claim of this right, on the one hand, and the denial of it on the other, may be considered as the cause of the American revolution.

335. *Stamp Act.* The British parliament, in the year 1765, passed the famous *Stamp Act,* for the purpose of raising a revenue from the colonies. This *act* required, that all paper and parchment which was used in the transaction of business, should be stamped, and a tax paid for it to the government. The act also declared that all writings on unstamped materials, should be null and void. When the news of this reached America, it excited the indignation of the people, and they determined to resist its execution. The day on which this act was to take place, Nov. 1st, 1765, the bells were muffled and tolled, and the shops were shut. In Boston, the effigies of the royalists were carried about and torn in pieces. At Portsmouth, a coffin was made on which was inscribed, *Liberty, aged* 145, and a procession followed it to the grave. In New York, the Stamp Act was cried about the streets, under the title of *the folly of England, and the ruin of America.* Many of

---

334. Relate the treatment of Great Britain towards her colonies. On what ground did the colonies contend against the mother country? What may be considered as the cause of the revolution?

235. Give an account of the Stamp Act. How was it received in America? What took place in Portsmouth? In New York?

the citizens assembled in the evening, broke open the governor's stable, and took out his coach and carried it about the city, suspended his effigy on a gallows, with a stamp bill in one hand and the figure of the devil in the other. After this, the gallows, the effigy, and the coach, were consumed in a bonfire, amid the shouts of the spectators. Simi.ar proceedings took place in many parts of the country, and the obnoxious act was soon after repealed.

336. *Destruction of Tea at Boston.* The British ministry still persisting in their right to tax the colonies, had, for this purpose, given permission to the East India Company to ship a large quantity of teas to America, charged with duty. The Americans, fixed in their opposition to the principle of taxation in any shape, opposed the landing of the tea. In New York, and in Philadelphia, the cargoes sent out were returned without being entered at the custom-houses. In Boston, the tea being consigned to the royal governor, (Hutchinson,) the populace, " clad like the aborigines of the wilderness," with tomahawks in their hands, and clubs on their shoulders, without the least molestation, marched through the streets with silent solemnity, amidst innumerable spectators, and proceeded to the wharves, boarded the ships, demanded the keys, and without much deliberation, knocked open the chests, and emptied several thousand weight of the finest teas into the ocean.

Intelligence of this transaction reached the British ministry, and in 1774, they passed an act to restrain all intercourse by water with the town of Boston by closing the port. They also removed the government and public offices to Salem.

---

336. Give an account of the destruction of tea in Boston. What did the British ministry do with regard to Boston?

PERIOD IX.

DISTINGUISHED FOR REVOLUTIONS.

FROM THE AMERICAN REVOLUTION TO THE PRESENT TIME.

337. *Continental Congress.* In September, 1774, delegates from all the colonies except Georgia, assembled in Philadelphia. This body was composed of 55 members, and is generally called the *First Continental Congress.* Their first act was an approval of the conduct of the people of Massachusetts, in resisting the arbitrary proceedings of the British government. They insisted on their rights as British subjects, and resolved to break off all trade with Great Britain, till their rights were acknowledged. They also drew up a petition to the king, and addresses to the people of Great Britain and the colonies. After a session of eight weeks, the congress dissolved themselves, after recommending that another should be held the next year. Although the *resolutions* of congress possessed no legal force, yet they were more faithfully observed than the laws of the best regulated state. The Americans now began to train themselves to the use of arms, and made vigorous exertions to sustain themselves in the coming conflict.

---

337. What is said of the First Continental Congress? What did they do? Were their resolutions observed? What did Great Britain do, on the news of these proceedings?

When the news of these proceedings reached Great Britain, Mr. Pitt (Lord Chatham) advocated the American cause in the British parliament, and endeavored to effect a reconciliation; but his efforts were in vain—parliament declared a *rebellion* existed in Massachusetts. In the beginning of 1775, the army in Boston was increased to 10,000 men, which number was deemed sufficient to reduce the colonies to submission.

British troops firing on the Americans, at Lexington.

338. *Skirmish at Lexington.* The Americans having deposited a considerable quantity of stores at Concord, about 18 miles from Boston, General *Gage*, who commanded the British forces at Boston, sent a force of 800 men in order to destroy them. On the evening of the 18th of April, at 10 o'clock, the British troops with great secrecy commenced their march for Concord. They were, however, discovered, and the alarm was rapidly spread by church bells and signal guns. When the British troops arrived at Lexington, they found about 70 of the militia assembled near the meeting-house. Major *Pitcairn*, of the British troops, rode up to them and called

---

338. What is said respecting the American stores at Concord? Relate what took place at Lexington.

out, "*Disperse you rebels; throw down your arms and disperse.*" Not being obeyed he discharged his pistol, and ordered his men to fire. Eight of the Americans were killed, and a number wounded. This was the first blood shed in the revolution. The British effected their purpose in destroying their stores; but on their return to Boston were severely harassed by the Americans.

339. *Battle of Bunker's Hill.* A considerable army was collected near Boston, by the Americans, for the purpose of dislodging the British from that place. To accomplish this, 1000 men were ordered, on the night of the 16th of June, 1775, to throw up a breast-work on *Bunker's Hill;* but in consequence of a mistake they took possession of *Breed's Hill,* which is nearer Boston. Before the return of light they had nearly finished a strong redoubt. As soon as the fortifications of the Americans were discovered, a severe cannonade was commenced from the ships, to destroy the progress of the works. The roaring of the cannon alarmed the inhabitants of Boston and the surrounding towns, and soon the steeples, the roofs of the houses, and the adjacent hills, were covered with spectators, to witness the scene. As nothing was accomplished by the cannonade, a body of 3000 men, commanded by General Howe, was landed, and advanced to the attack. As the British troops were advancing, orders were given to set *Charlestown* on fire, and the place, containing 400 houses, was laid in ashes. The Americans allowed the enemy to approach within a short distance, and then discharged a shower of musket balls into their ranks, which did such execution as caused them to retreat. They rallied a second time; again the Americans suffered them to approach, and again they poured in upon them a fire which effected such carnage that it caused them to retreat to the banks

---

339. What did the Americans do, in order to dislodge the British from Boston? How were the American works first attacked? What place was burnt on their advance? Describe the battle. What is said of General Clinton? What was the loss on each side?

of the river. At this time General Clinton, who had observed the battle from Boston, crossed over with a reinforcement, to assist his countrymen. By his exertions the troops were again rallied, and marched up to the entrenchments with fixed bayonets. The Americans, having expended their ammunition, and having no bayonets, were forced to retreat. The loss of the British was over 1000 men, while the Americans had only 100 killed, and 300 wounded; among the killed, however, was General Warren, a brave officer and firm patriot.

340. *Arnold's March through the Wilderness.* The Americans, wishing to get Canada into their possession, sent Colonel *Arnold*, with a detachment of the army, by a new and unexplored route. Arnold ascended to Kennebec, and after crossing the mountains which divide Canada from Maine, he descended the Chaudiere to the St. Lawrence. The army encountered great difficulties in their march of 300 miles, through an uninhabited country, abounding with swamps, woods, and craggy mountains, which so opposed their progress, that for a part of the time they only went four or five miles a day. One third of their number were obliged to return: provisions were so scanty, that some of the men ate their dogs, leather, small clothes, and shoes. Still they proceeded with unabated fortitude, and on the third of November, after thirty-one days spent in traversing a tedious desert, they reached the inhabited parts of Canada, to the astonishment of the inhabitants.

341. *Assault on Quebec, and Death of General Montgomery.* In 1775, General *Montgomery*, a native of Ireland, but ardently attached to the American cause, was entrusted with the command of the expedition against Canada. After taking *Montreal*, he joined the force

---

340. What route did Arnold take to get into Canada? What difficulties and sufferings were encountered?

341. What is said of General Montgomery? Describe the assault on Quebec. What is said of the appearance of the bodies of the soldiers who were killed?

which Arnold had led through the wilderness, and advanced to the siege of Quebec. On the last day of the year, 1775, General Montgomery, under the cover of night, and during a snow storm, made an assault on the city. In passing a barrier, a gun from a battery was discharged, which killed him and his two aids. The division commanded by Arnold took a battery, but he, being wounded, was compelled to leave the field. His men fought bravely; but being bewildered and benumbed amidst the darkness and snow, and being unable to retreat, surrendered. A shocking spectacle was presented in the morning after the assault, by the appearance of the bodies of the soldiers who were killed: they were frozen stiff in the various distortions produced by the agonies of death.

342. *Declaration of Independence.* Notwithstanding the active war now carried on by the colonies, they still considered themselves subjects of the British king, contending for constitutional liberty. But the determined hostility of the British government induced them to dissolve their connection with the mother country. A pamphlet entitled *Common Sense,* written by *Thomas Paine,* in which the excellencies of a republican government were described, and the monarchical system ridiculed, produced a great effect on the public mind. On the 7th of June, a motion was made in congress by *Richard Henry Lee,* of Virginia, and seconded by *John Adams,* of Massachusetts, for declaring the colonies *free and independent.* A committee, consisting of *Jefferson, Adams, Franklin, Sherman,* and *Livingston,* were appointed to prepare a Declaration of Independence. The Declaration, written by Mr. Jefferson, was adopted by congress, by almost an *unanimous vote,* on the 4*th of July,* 1776, by which the thirteen *United States of America* were declared free and independent.

---

342. How did the colonies at first consider themselves? What is said of the pamphlet entitled "Common Sense?" Who made the motion in congress for a Declaration of Independence? Who were the committee appointed to prepare a Declaration, and by whom was it written?

343. *Battle on Long Island.* In June, 1776, the British fleet arrived at Sandy Hook, having on board 35,000 troops, including a body of Hessians, from Germany, a body of cavalry, and warlike apparatus of every kind. Washington's force consisted of only 17,000 men, most of whom were inexperienced, and weakened by sickness. While in this state they erected fortifications on Long Island, and prepared to resist the enemy. Before hostilities commenced, General Howe, the commander of the British forces, sent one of his officers to Washington, and proposed conditions of peace, which amounted to little more than the offer of pardon. Washington observed, that as the Americans had not committed any crime, they wished for no pardon. The officer returned, and both parties prepared for action. On the 22d of August, the British troops landed on the southwest side of the island, and gained the rear of the American army. On the 27th the attack began; but the Americans being exposed to the fire of the Hessians in front, and the British regulars in the rear, were defeated, with a loss of 1200 men. After this defeat, General Washington commenced a silent retreat on the night of the 29th, which was effected with complete success. An army of 9000 men, with all their cannon, tents, and baggage, were transported to New York, over a difficult ferry of a mile in breadth, without being discovered by the enemy.

344. *Death of Captain Hale.* After the retreat from Long Island, Washington was very desirous of gaining some knowledge of the future designs of the enemy. For this purpose, General Washington applied to Colonel Knowlton, who communicated this request to Captain *Nathan Hale*, of Connecticut, who at once nobly

---

343. What number of British troops arrived in 1776? What is said of Washington's force? What of the proposals of peace? What was the result of the battle on Long Island, and of Washington's retreat?

344. For what service did Capt. Hale offer himself? Relate the circumstances of his execution.

offered himself for this hazardous service. He passed in disguise to Long Island, examined every part of the British army, and obtained the desired information respecting their situation and future operations. While on his way back, he was arrested and carried before Sir William Howe. The proof of his object was so clear, that he acknowledged it; and he was ordered to be executed next morning. Before he was executed, he requested a clergyman and a Bible. Both were refused; and the letters which he wrote to his mother and friends were destroyed. The only reason given for this unfeeling conduct was, "That the rebels should not know that they had a man in their army who could die with so much firmness." This patriot was a young man of amiable character, and he died lamenting that he had but one life to lose for his country.

345. *Retreat of Washington and Battle of Trenton.* General Washington, after a series of disasters, was obliged to retreat from New York towards Pennsylvania, being pursued by the enemy. This retreat was attended with circumstances of a painful and trying nature. The army, which had consisted of 30,000 men, was diminished down to scarcely 3000, and these were without provisions, without pay, and many of them very poorly clothed. Their footsteps were stained with blood as they fled before the enemy. Such was the desperate condition of the American cause, that many who had been most confident of its success, began to despond and give up all as lost.

In this season of general gloom, the American congress recommended to each of the states to observe " a day of solemn fasting and humiliation before God." Washington felt it important to make a desperate effort in behalf of his country. On the night of the 25th of December, 1776, the American army re-crossed the Delaware, and marched to attack the Hessians, who had

---

345. Relate the circumstances of Washington's retreat through New Jersey. Give an account of the battle of Trenton. How many of the enemy were captured?

advanced to Trenton. The sun had just risen as the tents of the enemy appeared in sight. Washington, rising on his stirrups, waved his sword and exclaimed, "There, my brave friends, are the enemies of your country; and now all I have to ask is, to remember what you are about to fight for. March!" The troops, thus animated by their commander, pressed on to the charge. The Hessians were taken by surprise, about 1000 of them made prisoners, and 40 killed, among whom was their commander.

346. *Expedition of General Burgoyne.* In 1777, it was determined in England to invade the states through Canada. An army was to be sent by the way of Lake Champlain to Hudson River, and effect a communicaion with their forces at New York; and by having the command of the Hudson, they expected to cut off the communication between New England and the other states. For this purpose, Gen. *Burgoyne*, with a chosen army of 7000 men, besides Canadians and Indians, moved down from Canada towards Albany. Having obtained possession of Ticonderoga, he led his army to Fort Edward, on the Hudson. The militia of New England and New York were aroused to stop the progress of the invader, and beset him on every side.

Burgoyne, wishing to obtain provisions, sent Col. *Baum* to *Bennington*, in Vermont, to seize the American stores. They were signally defeated by Col. *Stark*, with the loss of 600 men. Burgoyne, collecting his forces, encamped at *Saratoga.* After a number of obstinate battles, Burgoyne finding his provisions nearly exhausted, his retreat cut off, and surrounded by a brave army, was forced to surrender to Gen. *Gates* his whole army consisting of 5,752 effective men, on the 17th of October, 1777. This event caused great joy among the Americans, and hastened their alliance with France, which was effected in February, 1778. On the 20th of

---

346. What was the plan of Burgoyne's invasion? H
far did he penetrate? Give an account of his defeat. Wl
effect did his surrender have?

March, the American Commissioners were received at the Court of France, as the representatives of a sister nation.

347. *Treason of Arnold.* In the year 1780, a plot of great danger to the American cause, was timely discovered. The author of the plot was General *Arnold*, who, being wounded, was appointed to a command in Philadelphia. For his extravagance and haughty conduct he was reproved by the American congress. This aroused his passions, and he determined to have revenge. General Washington still valued him for his bravery, and entrusted him with the command of the important post at West Point. This post he determined to deliver up to the enemy. To effect this he entered into a negociation with Sir Henry Clinton, through Major *Andre*, of the British army, who came in disguise to West Point, and concerted with Arnold upon the time and method of seizing the fort. Andre obtained a passport from Arnold, under a disguised name, and set out on his way to New York. He succeeded in passing all the outposts of the American army without suspicion. About 30 miles from New York, as he was entering the village of *Tarrytown*, three militia men who came that way, stopped him, and asked him *where he was bound*. He did not answer this question, but asked them *where they belonged*. They said, "*below.*" Mistaking them for men of his own party, he informed them that he was a British officer, and could not be detained. When arrested, he offered them a large reward if they would release him. But these men, though poor, were not to be bribed; and after examining his person, found evidence of his being a spy, in the papers which were hid in his boots. Andre was tried and executed as a spy, at Tappan, N. Y., October 2d. Arnold, hearing of the capture of Andre, made his escape to the British, and was made a brigadier general in their army.

348. *Sufferings of the American Army.* The American army often suffered extremely during the revolu-

---

347 What is said of Gen. Arnold? What did he attempt to do? Relate the circumstances of the capture of Andre.

tionary war, for the want of food and clothing. While they were encamped at *Morristown*, during the severe winter of 1780, their sufferings were unusually severe. Congress, having but little money or credit, were obliged to issue a paper currency, commonly called *continental money*, in order to carry on the war. This became so much reduced in value, that the four months' pay of a soldier would not procure a bushel of wheat, and the pay of a colonel would not procure oats sufficient for his horse. The necessities of the army were so great, that Gen. Washington was obliged to send out detachments to procure provisions at the point of the bayonet; and many a soldier, contending for American freedom, perished through hunger, cold, and disease.

349. *Arrival of the French Troops.* In July, 1780, M. de Ternay, with a French fleet, consisting of seven ships of the line, besides frigates, and 6000 land forces, commanded by *Count de Rochambeau*, arrived at Newport, in Rhode Island. The troops were landed, which gave new life to the American councils and arms. The fleet, however, suddenly returned to France, and, at that time, all hope of naval assistance vanished. The land forces remained, and rendered important assistance in bringing the war to a close. Before the treaty with France, the young *Marquis de Lafayette*, a French nobleman, ardent in the cause of liberty, hired a ship at his own expense, came over to America when nineteen years of age, and joined the army under Washington. He was appointed a major general, and by his services through the war, gained the affections and gratitude of the American people.

350. *War in the Southern States.* During the latter part of the period of the revolutionary war, the most important military operations were in the southern states. The British generals found it much easier to make an

---

348. Where did the American army encamp during the severe winter of 1780 ? What is said of the continental money, and the necessities of the army ?
349. How many French troops arrived in 1780, and by whom were they commanded ? What is said of Lafayette ?

impression here, as it was much less populous than at the north. *Savannah* and *Charleston* were both taken by the enemy, and a great part of the country was considered as conquered. Gen. Gates being appointed to the command of the southern American army, was routed by *Lord Cornwallis*. After this, Gen. *Green* carried on the war against the British forces, with vigor and success. Gen. *Morgan* and Gen. *Marion*, two veteran American commanders, greatly distinguished themselves in the war in this section of the country.

351. *Capture of Cornwallis*. Lord Cornwallis having collected a large army in Virginia, Washington resolved to concentrate his forces against him. The main body of the American army was at this time at *White Plains*, in the vicinity of New York. After making a show of attacking New York, in order to deceive the British commander, and prevent him from sending assistance to Cornwallis, Washington, with his army, suddenly left his camp at White Plains, crossed the Hudson, and passed rapidly on to Virginia. When he arrived there, a French fleet, under *Count de Grasse*, appeared in the Chesapeake, and a body of French troops were landed from the fleet, to assist the Americans.

The combined force of the Americans and French, under the command of Washington, 12 or 13,000 in number, besides the militia, closely invested the British at *Yorktown*. Cornwallis being closely blockaded by sea and land, and the besiegers regularly advancing upon him with a tremendous cannonade, he was obliged to surrender, with upwards of 7000 men, on the 19th of October, 1781.

352. *Conclusion of the War*. As the capture of Cornwallis was considered as deciding the war, the

---

350. Why did the British remove the seat of the war to the southern states? What places did they take, and what army did they defeat? What is said of Gen. Green and Marion?

351. Relate the proceedings of Washington before he went on to attack Cornwallis By whom was he assisted, and by what means was Cornwallis captured?

news was received by the American people with emotions of the greatest joy. Divine service was performed in their armies, and a day of thanksgiving was recommended and observed throughout the United States In Great Britain a new ministry was appointed, who advised the king to discontinue all farther efforts to subdue the Americans. On the 30th of November, 1782, provisional articles of peace were signed, by which the independence of the United States was acknowledged. The final treaty was concluded at *Versailles*, in France; in which the United Colonies were admitted to be " Free, Sovereign, and Independent States." Thus ended the revolutionary war, which cost Great Britain, in addition to the loss of her colonies, one hundred million pounds sterling, and about 50,000 subjects.

353. *Disbanding of the Army.* When the American army was about to be disbanded, serious difficulties arose with respect to the payment of their wages. The paper, or *continental* money, with which the soldiers had been paid, was worthless. Many of the officers and soldiers could not make a decent appearance in point of dress, and the families of others were suffering at home. Many of the officers had expended their private fortunes in the service of their country, and had the prospect of being dismissed in poverty, with no provision for their future support. In this state of things, addresses were privately circulated among the officers, designing to stir them up to violent measures to obtain their just rights. This was a most dangerous crisis. By the efforts and entreaties of Washington the rising tumults were quelled, and the army was disbanded in peace. Washington delivered to the president of congress his military commission, and retired to private life.

354. *Confederation of the States.* In 1778, a plan of confederation and perpetual union was formed by con-

---

352. What effect did the capture of Cornwallis have in the United States, and in Great Britain? When was the independence of the United States acknowledged?
353. What was the state of the American army when about to be disbanded? What took place at this time?

gress, and submitted for the consideration of the states, which was finally agreed to by all the state legislatures. The states were compelled, during the war, to act in concert, by the principle of common safety; and the resolutions of congress were generally carried into effect by the several state legislatures. When freed from external dangers, the weakness of the confederation began to appear. Congress had no power to levy taxes, to supply their treasury; the sums voted for the public service were apportioned to each state, which raised the money in a way they thought the most proper. The states soon became delinquent, and the national treasury was left unsupplied. Congress then attempted to raise a revenue by a duty on foreign goods; this was agreed to by all the states except Rhode Island and New York, and their opposition defeated the measure.

355. *Organization of the Federal Government.* The confederation being found utterly insufficient to accomplish the ends of a national union, delegates were assembled for the purpose of consulting on the formation of some general and efficient government. This body adjourned, and recommended that a *general convention* should be held the next year. Accordingly, in May, 1787, delegates from all the states except Rhode Island, assembled at Philadelphia, and appointed Gen. Washington their president. "After four months' deliberation, in which the clashing interests of the several states appeared in all their force," the convention agreed to a frame of government, which was finally agreed to by all the states. On the 30th of April, 1789, Gen. Washington was inaugurated the *first president* of the United States. The ceremony was performed in the open gallery of the Federal Hall in New York, and the oath was administered by *Chancellor Livingston*, in the pres-

---

354. What is said of the confederation? How were the laws of congress carried into effect? What is said of the attempt of congress to raise revenue?

355. By what means was the federal government organized? Who was inaugurated the first president, at what time, and where was the ceremony performed?

ence of a countless multitude of spectators. From this moment the American republic has steadily advanced in a tide of prosperity and growing power.

356. *Causes of the French Revolution.* The French revolution, which commenced in 1789, and convulsed the whole civilized world, was brought on by a variety of causes. Previous to this time, the French people were borne down by a load of taxation, to support the extravagance and profligacy of their monarchs. The nobility and clergy had many privileges which were not allowed to other subjects, especially their exemption from taxes. The common people were despised, yet they bore all the burdens and expenses of the state. The feelings of liberty were much excited by the American revolution, especially on the return of the French officers and army from the United States. The fearful horrors accompanying the revolution, may be ascribed to the general prevalence of *infidelity* throughout all classes of the French people. The atheistical writings of *Voltaire, Rousseau*, and other French philosophers, brought on a fearful state of public morals.

357. *Of the National Assembly.* The French monarch, Louis XVI., wishing to restore the disordered state of the finances to order, convoked the *notables*, a body selected from the higher orders. To this body it was proposed to lay a land tax, proportioned to property, without any exception of the nobility or clergy; this measure they refused to sanction. The assembly of the *states general* was now called, which was composed of three orders, the nobility, clergy, and the third estate, or *commons*. This body, which had not been assembled since 1614, was convened in 1789. Difficulties arose in this assembly how questions should be decided.

---

356. What was the state of the French people previous to the revolution of 1789? What is said of the nobility, clergy, common people, and of the effect of the American revolution? What is said of the prevalence of infidelity?

357. What did Louis XVI. do with regard to his finances? What assemblies were convened? What is said of the national assembly?

At length the commons, together with such of the nobility and clergy as would join them, seized upon the legislative authority, and constituted themselves the *national assembly*. After this body was formed, there remained nothing of the monarchy but the name.

358. *Progress of the Revolution.* As Louis showed some disposition to oppose the proceedings of the national assembly, the people were thrown into a state of violent commotion. The *bastile*, a huge state prison, long an engine of tyranny, was demolished by the populace. Other excesses were committed, in the city and elsewhere, by the furious rabble, and by mobs of women of the vilest character. The king and royal family were forced by the mob to remove from *Versailles* to Paris, and were protected from violence by the influence of *Lafayette*, who at this time commanded the national guard.

The progress of the revolution was rapid. The privileges of the nobles and clergy were abolished; religious liberty and the freedom of the press established; the church lands confiscated; the religious houses suppressed; and France was divided into 83 departments. After these measures were accomplished, the assembly next proceeded to form a constitution. The king, finding his situation perilous, escaped from Paris, with his family, but was stopped on the frontiers and brought back. A constitution, which established a limited monarchy, and the equality of all ranks, was accepted by the king.

The next assembly which met, was under the influence of the *Jacobin club*, so called from its place of meeting, in a suppressed convent of *Jacobin* monks. At this period the hostile armies of Austria and Prussia were ready to enter France, and the people imagined the king and the nobility were confederated with them.

---

358. How were the people thrown into commotion? What is said of the bastile? The royal family? Lafayette? What was done with regard to the nobles, clergy, and constitution? What is said of the Jacobins?

The prisons of Paris were filled with the nobility priests, and opulent citizens, and the Jacobins urged the necessity of destroying them before the enemy should reach the capital. Accordingly bands of ferocious assassins burst open the prisons and murdered 5000 persons.

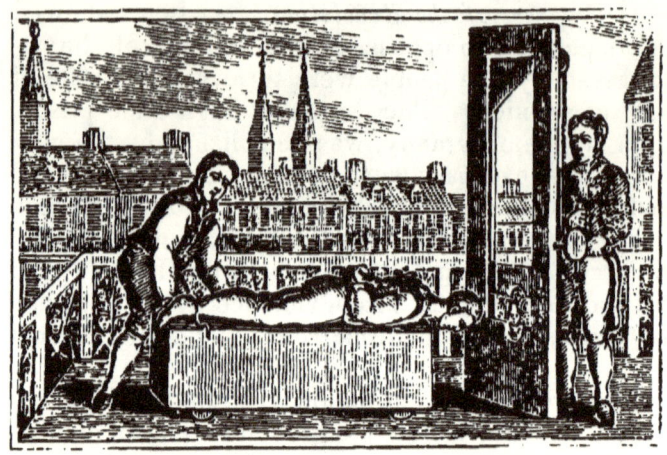

Execution of Louis XVI., by the Guillotine.

359. *Trial and Execution of Louis XVI.* In September, 1792, the *national convention* commenced their deliberations. They abolished the regal government, and declared France a *republic*. Louis was arraigned before their bar, to answer to various charges, which he answered with composure and dignity. His enemies being bent on his destruction, the convention decided that he was guilty of a conspiracy against the liberties of the nation, and the security of the state. By a majority of five voices only, out of 721 voters, he was condemned to suffer death by the *guillotine*. One of the most influential men in procuring the death of the king, was the *duke of Orleans*, one of his relatives, who was distinguished for his low and infamous vices.

---

359. What did the national convention do? What is said of the trial of Louis XVI.? Of the duke of Orleans? State the circumstances of the execution of Louis.

On the 21st of January, 1793, Louis was brought out for execution, and ascended the scaffold in the presence of a large concourse of spectators, with a firm step. He attempted to address the multitude, but was prevented by the beating of drums, and the executioner was ordered to perform his office. At this moment his confessor called to him from the foot of the scaffold, " Son of St. Louis, ascend to Heaven," and immediately the ax of the guillotine severed his head from his body.

360. *Triumph of Infidelity.* After the death of the king a revolutionary tribunal was erected under *Robespierre, Marat,* and their associates, monsters of depravity and cruelty. Their bloody domination is usually styled " *The Reign of Terror.*" It was during this period that the national convention suppressed the Christian religion, and declared that *death was an eternal sleep;* they abolished the Sabbath, and a respite from labor was allowed on every tenth day. They also passed a decree that the only French deities hereafter should be *Liberty, Equality,* and *Reason.* This last deity, represented by a naked prostitute, was drawn in triumph through the streets of Paris, and all the principal officers of the city and national government joined in the parade. The queen and sister of Louis XVI. were guillotined, and as each faction gained the ascendency, they put to death all who opposed them, and the blood of victims flowed in every part of France.

361. *Of the Directory and Napoleon Bonaparte.* After the fall of Robespierre and the Jacobins, the executive power was entrusted to a *directory* of five, and the legislative power in two councils. The sovereigns of Europe, from the commencement of the French revolution, were fearful that the disorganizing principles of the revolutionists would be extended to their dominions.

---

360. What is said of Robespierre and Marat? What did the national convention decree? What is said of the different factions?

361. What was the directory? What did the sovereigns of Europe do? What is said of Napoleon Bonaparte? What of his military operations in Egypt?

In order to stop them they formed *coalitions* against France, by which nearly all the European nations were drawn into war. France, however, sustained herself against all her enemies, and such was her energy, that she had at command, in 1794, *one million* of fighting men.

In 1796, *Napoleon Bonaparte*, a native of Corsica, in the 27th year of his age, was entrusted with the command of an army against Italy. He had commenced his military career as a lieutenant, and rose rapidly to distinction. Italy was soon conquered. In 1798, Gen. Bonaparte, with an army of 40,000 men, was sent to conquer Egypt. He took Alexandria by assault, after a great slaughter of the *Mamelukes* and Arabs. By the battle of the *Pyramids* he took possession of Cairo; but by the *battle of the Nile*, in which Lord *Nelson* destroyed the French fleet, Bonaparte was finally obliged to return to France.

362. *Bonaparte the First Consul and Emperor.* On the return of Bonaparte, he found that the ill conduct of the directory had brought the country to the brink of ruin. By the aid of some friends, and a military force, Bonaparte abolished the directory and caused himself to be elected *first consul*. From this period the affairs of the republic took a new turn. The military force was reorganized; Bonaparte by his energy put down all the various factions which had raged in the empire; corrected many abuses; restored order and tranquillity to the government, and commenced a career of victorious conquests, which have no parallel in modern history. He defeated the Austrians at the great battle of *Marengo*, in 1800, and was afterwards elected first consul for life, with supreme power. In 1804, Bonaparte was proclaimed *emperor of France*, and was crowned by the pope; and the next year he assumed the title of *king of Italy.*

---

362. To what office was Bonaparte elected after his return? What is said of the affairs of the republic after this period? In what year was Bonaparte proclaimed emperor of France? By whom crowned?

363. *Battle of Austerlitz.* Alarmed at the growing power of Napoleon, Austria and Russia formed a coalition against him. Napoleon, as usual, beforehand with his enemies, advanced rapidly into Austria, and became master of *Vienna,* the German capital. At *Austerlitz,* in December, 1805, he met the combined armies of Russia and Austria. The force on each side was nearly equal, and the *three emperors,* of France, Russia, and Austria, being present, gave great interest and energy to the contest. The French army advanced to the attack at sunrise, with shouts of "*long live the emperor.*" At one in the afternoon, after a severe battle, victory was decided in favor of the French, who took more than 30,000 prisoners, and 150 pieces of cannon. By this victory Austria was humbled, and submitted to humiliating conditions of peace.

364. *Other Victories of Napoleon.* Napoleon, in order to strengthen his power, united several German states into a union, called the "*Confederation of the Rhine,*" of which he was chosen protector. The great increase of power acquired by this alliance, was a cause of jealousy, and in 1806, another coalition was formed against him, by Prussia, Russia, Austria, Sweden, and England. Prussia, who began the war, was overthrown by a great battle at *Jena.* The following year he defeated the Russians, and with the Prussians forced them to agree to shut their ports against Great Britain, and gave their assistance in excluding British commerce from the continent. Napoleon, now triumphant, disposed of crowns and kingdoms at his will. His brother *Louis* was appointed king of Holland; the crown of Spain was conferred on his brother *Joseph;* *Jerome,* another brother, was made king of *Westphalia,*

---

363. What nations formed a coalition against Napoleon? Where did he defeat them, and what is said of the battle?
364. What formed the confederation of the Rhine? What coalition was now formed against Napoleon? Where were the Prussians overthrown? What crowns did Napoleon confer upon his relatives?

a new kingdom formed from Prussia, and *Murat*, who had married his sister, was raised to the throne of Naples.

Retreat of the French Army from Moscow.

365. *Napoleon's Campaign in Russia.* The Emperor *Alexander*, of Russia, refusing to concur with the French emperor in excluding British commerce from the continent, gave rise to a war which commenced in 1812. With an army of nearly half a million of men, collected from almost every nation in Europe, Napoleon advanced to the conquest of Russia. After the battle of *Borodino*, which terminated the lives of seventy-five thousand human beings, the French army entered *Moscow*, in September, 1812. The Russians, in order to deprive the French of winter quarters, destroyed their provisions, abandoned the city, set it on fire, and three fourths of this ancient capital was laid in ashes.

This unexpected sacrifice on the part of the Russians,

---

365. What gave rise to Napoleon's war against Russia? How many men in Napoleon's army, and what is said of the battle of Borodino? What caused the ruin of Napoleon? What did he offer, and what was he obliged to do? Describe the retreat of his army. How many survived to cross the frontier?

caused the ruin of Napoleon. Being without quarters, and short of provisions, he offered terms of peace. The Russians replied that they could listen to no terms, while an enemy remained in their country. No alternative was now left but to retreat towards the frontiers. One of the most distressing scenes on human record now followed. A Russian winter, unusually severe, now set in with all its horrors. The wretched soldiers, pursued by the Russians, overcome by hunger, cold, and fatigue, sunk down by thousands, and were left by their companions to perish amid the Russian snows. About 30,000 horses perished in one day, by the severity of the weather. It is stated that not more than 50,000 men, (being one man in ten,) survived to recross the Russian frontier.

366. *Defeat of Napoleon by the Allies.* Napoleon having effected his retreat to the Russian frontiers, with a remnant of his army, left it and fled in disguise to Paris. He resolved to hazard another campaign, and raised a fresh army of 350,000 men. As the Russians advanced in the pursuit of the French army, they were joined by the Prussians and Austrians. Napoleon met the allied armies in Germany, and gaining some advantages over them, was entirely routed at the great battle of *Leipsic*, in which more than 400,000 combatants were engaged : a greater number than has been engaged in any battle in modern times. The allies followed up their victory and entered Paris in April, 1815. Napoleon was now obliged to abdicate the throne of France, and retire to *Elba*, a small island near Italy. *Louis XVIII.* now ascended the throne of his ancestors.

367. *Napoleon's Return from Elba.* A general congress was assembled at Vienna, in order to arrange the affairs of Europe. While they were deliberating on these matters, Napoleon, dissatisfied with his situation at *Elba*, made an effort to regain the throne of France.

---

366. What did Napoleon do, after his defeat in Russia? What is said of the battle of Leipsic? What was Napoleon obliged to do?

He landed at *Frejus*, with a small force, without opposition. Wherever he appeared to the soldiers, even those who were sent to oppose his march, received him with the shout, "*long live the emperor!*" In 20 days from his landing at Frejus he found himself quietly seated on the throne, without having shed a drop of blood. Louis XVIII., on his approach to Paris, fled to the frontiers, and the allied powers immediately took measures to prosecute a war against Napoleon, whom now they pronounced to be a traitor and an outlaw.

368. *Battle of Waterloo*. Napoleon having collected an army of 150,000 men, suddenly passed into *Belgium*, and attacked the Prussian and British armies. The Prussians were commanded by *Blucher*, and the British by *Wellington*, who had distinguished himself in the war with the French forces in Spain. The French commenced a furious assault upon the Prussians, who retreated, leaving 15,000 of their number dead and wounded on the field of battle. The British troops, after bravely withstanding the French, fell back to the village of *Waterloo*. Here, on the 18th of June, 1815, a memorable battle was fought, in which the French were totally routed, with the loss of 40,000 in killed and wounded. Napoleon fled to Paris, abdicated the throne, and afterwards went on board of a British ship of war and surrendered himself to the hospitality of the British people. By direction of the allied sovereigns, he was sent a prisoner to the island of *St. Helena*, in October, 1815; and there died in May, 1821, in the 52d year of his age.

369. *War between the United States and Tripoli*. The cruisers of *Tripoli*, one of the Barbary states, having seized a number of the American merchantmen, and enslaved their crews, Commodore *Preble*, in 1803,

---

367. Where was the general congress assembled, and for what purpose? Give an account of Napoleon's return from Elba. What did Louis XVIII. and the allied powers do?

368. How large an army did Napoleon collect? Where did he go? Whom did he attack? What is said of the battle of Waterloo? What did Napoleon do after the battle of Waterloo, and what became of him?

was sent with a squadron to obtain redress. Preble repeatedly attacked and bombarded the city of Tripoli, although strongly defended, with such success that the haughty *bashaw* was chastised and humbled into a peace. Closely connected with the above is the celebrated expedition of Gen. *Eaton*, across the deserts of *Barca*. *Hamet*, who had a claim to the throne of Tripoli, was joined by Gen. Eaton in Egypt. They mustered a force of about 400 men, consisting of a few Americans and Greeks, the remainder principally Arabs. Eaton led this motley force from Egypt, through the sandy deserts of Barca, to *Derne*, through many adventures and sufferings. After attacking Derne a peace was effected with the Tripolitans.

370. *War between the United States and Great Britain.* During the war with Great Britain and France, the Americans wished to preserve a neutrality. Jealousies, however, arose between the contending powers respecting the conduct of the Americans, and both nations passed *decrees* and *orders* which injured the American commerce. The Americans had an additional cause of irritation from Great Britain, in her claiming the *right of search*, in order to find her subjects, and seize them, while in service on board American vessels. The British also *impressed* some thousands of American seamen into their service. In 1807, the American congress laid an *embargo* on all the shipping in the United States; in 1809, the embargo was removed, and *non-intercourse* with France and Great Britain was substituted. On the 18th of June, 1812, congress declared war against Great Britain.

371. *Progress of the War in* 1812. In July, Gen. Hull, with upwards of 2000 men, crossed over into

---

369. Who was sent against the Tripolitans? For what purpose? With what effect? State what is related concerning Gen. Eaton.
370. How was the American commerce injured? What additional cause of irritation from Great Britain? What was done by the American congress?

Canada, apparently for the purpose of attacking Malden. This place being reinforced, and a large body of British and Indians collecting, Hull retreated to Detroit, and being besieged, he surrendered his army and the territory of Michigan, to Gen. *Brock*. A second attempt to invade Canada was made by Gen. *Van Rensselaer*, who crossed the Niagara, with about 1000 men, and attacked the British at *Queenstown*. After an obstinate engagement he was forced to surrender.

While defeat and disgrace attended the attempts of the Americans to subdue Canada, brilliant success favored the American flag on the ocean. In August, Capt. *Hull*, who commanded the frigate *Constitution*, captured the *Guerriere*. In October, Capt. *Decatur*, commanding the frigate *United States*, captured the *Macedonian*. In November, Capt. *Jones*, commanding the *Wasp*, took the British sloop of war *Frolic*. In December, the *Constitution*, commanded by Capt. *Bainbridge*, captured the *Java*. In these four engagements the loss of the British in killed and wounded, was 423; that of the Americans only 73.

372. *The war in* 1813. In January, about 800 men, under Gen. *Winchester*, were surprised and defeated at Frenchtown, on the river Raisin, by the British and Indians under Gen. *Proctor*. Many of the Americans, after they had surrendered, were inhumanly murdered by the Indians. In May, a detachment of 1700 Americans, under Gen. *Pike*, took possession of *York*, in Canada. Gen Pike, with 100 of his men, was killed by the explosion of a mine. In May, 1000 British troops, under Sir *George Provost*, made an attack on *Sackett's Harbor*, but were repulsed by Gen. *Brown*.

---

371. What is said of Gen. Hull! What of the invasion of Gen. Van Rensselaer? What ships were taken by the Americans on the ocean? What was the loss of the British and Americans in these engagements?

372. What is said of the surprise of Gen. Winchester! How was Gen. Pike killed, and what place did his soldiers take? Give an account of the victory on Lake Erie. Where was Tecumseh killed, and what is said of him? What Amer-

The most brilliant affair in this year, on the side of the Americans, was the capture of the British fleet on *Lake Erie*, by Commodore *Perry*. The British fleet consisted of six vessels, carrying 63 guns; the Americans had nine vessels, and 56 guns. The conflict lasted for three hours; but the victory was complete. Perry announced his victory in the following laconic epistle· " We have met the enemy, and they are ours."

After this victory, Gen. *Harrison* embarked his army on board of the American fleet, landed in Canada, and defeated the British army under Gen. Proctor, near the river Thames. In this battle *Tecumseh*, the celebrated Indian chief, in alliance with the British, was killed. This chieftain was one of the greatest of Indian warriors, and was distinguished for his eloquence, dignity of manners, and nobleness of soul. During this year the British obtained some success on the ocean, the most important of which was the capture, by Capt. Broke, in the *Shannon*, of the frigate *Chesapeake*, commanded by Capt. *Lawrence*. This intrepid officer, being mortally wounded, was carried below, and became delirious, from excess of mental and bodily suffering. Whenever he was able to speak, he would exclaim " *Don't give up the ship*,"—an expression long to be remembered by his countrymen.

373. *The war in* 1814. This year was distinguished by severe fighting in Canada. In July the Americans, under Gen. *Brown*, crossed the Niagara, with 3000 men, and took possession of *Fort Erie*. A bloody action took place a few days after, at *Chippewa*, in which the Americans were victorious. In the same month, the American forces, under Generals *Brown* and *Scott*, and the British under Generals *Drummond* and *Riall*, fought a severe battle at *Bridgewater*. This battle began before sunset and continued till midnight. The

---

ican frigate did the British take in 1813? What were the dying words of Capt. Lawrence?

373. Who took fort Erie, and gained the victory at Chippewa? What commanders fought at the battle of Bridge-

action was fought near the cataract of Niagara, whose roar was silenced at times, by the thunder of cannon and the rattling of arms. The British were forced to leave the field, with the loss of about 900 in killed and wounded. The Americans were so much weakened that they fell back to Fort Erie, which the British afterwards attempted to storm, but were repulsed wtih great loss.

In September, Sir *George Provost*, with 14,000 men, advanced on *Plattsburgh*. The operations of this army were accompanied by a British fleet, on Lake *Champlain*, carrying 95 guns, and 1050 men, under Commodore *Downie*. This fleet was defeated by Commodore *Macdonough*, whose fleet carried 86 guns, and 826 men. Upon the loss of the British fleet, Sir George Provost, after having been repulsed by Gen. *Macomb*, retreated.

In August, a British fleet arrived in the Chesapeake, and landed an army of 5000 men, about 40 miles from Washington. Having defeated the militia at Bladensburg, they entered Washington, burnt the public buildings, and then retreated to their shipping. About a fortnight afterwards, nearly 7000 men, under Gen. *Ross*, and Admiral *Cockburn*, made an attack on *Baltimore*, but were defeated, and Gen. Ross was killed.

374. *Battle of New Orleans.* While negotiations for peace were in progress between the United States and Great Britain, a large force, under Sir *Edward Packenham*, landed for the attack of New Orleans. The defense of this place was intrusted to Gen. *Jackson*, whose force was about 6000 men, chiefly raw militia. On the morning of the 8th of January, 1815, the main body of the enemy, 7 or 8000 in number, marched to the assault of the American lines. The Americans, in security be-

---

water! Give an account of this battle. Who advanced on Plattsburgh? Who captured the British fleet on lake Champlain? What was the British loss in this expedition? What is said of the burning of Washington, and the attack on Baltimore?

374. Who commanded the expedition against New Orleans, and by whom was it defended? Give an account of the battle of the 8th of January. What was the loss of the British and

hind their breast-works of *cotton bales* and other materials, which no balls could penetrate, were formed in two ranks, those in the rear loading for those in front. By this they were enabled to fire without intermission As the British approached sufficiently near for shot to take effect, the rolling fire from the American lines resembled peals of thunder, and the plain before them was strewed with the dead and dying. After three brave attempts to force the American lines, in which Gen. Packenham and Gen. Gibbs, the second in command, were mortally wounded, the British troops retreated from the field of action. Their loss in killed, wounded, and captured, was 2600, while that of the Americans amounted to only six killed, and seven wounded.

Soon after this event, news arrived that a treaty of peace had been signed at *Ghent*, by the commissioners of the United States and Great Britain, on the 25th of December, 1814. This treaty was immediately ratified by the President and Senate.

375. *Revolution in Spanish America.* The jealous policy of Spain, with regard to her American colonies, led her, as much as possible, to cut off all intercourse between them and the rest of the world. Consequently, they were behind other civilized countries in the knowledge and improvements of the age. About the period of the usurpation of the throne of Spain by the Bonaparte family, the Spanish colonies began to take measures to assert their independence. In 1810, *Venezuela* declared herself independent. The fatal earthquake of 1812, which nearly destroyed the city of *Caraccas*, so operated on the ignorance and superstition of the people, that they again submitted to royal authority. The earthquake was represented by the priests of that coun-

---

Americans? Where was the treaty of peace signed, and at what time?

375. What was the policy of Spain with regard to her colonies? What was the effect? At what period did the Spanish colonies take measures for their independence? In what year did Venezuela declare herself independent? What effect did the earthquake at Caraccas have? By whom was Venezuela

try, who were hostile to liberty, as a token of the wrath of heaven, for daring to change their government.

Venezuela remained thus subject to Spain till 1813, when it was again emancipated by *Simon Bolivar*, who defeated the Spanish forces, and expelled them from his country. The revolution has extended to the Spanish provinces of *Colombia, Mexico, Peru, Buenos Ayres*, and *Chili*, all of whom have thrown off the yoke o. Spain, and established republican governments. Most of these governments, however, are republican only in name: they have been torn by domestic factions, and still appear to be in an unsettled state. Religion and public morals in the South American republics, are generally in a low state; and wherever these great sources of public and private happiness and prosperity are wanting, the blessings of civil and religious liberty cannot exist.

376. *Of Hayti*. The island of *Hispaniola*, or *St. Domingo*, is distinguished for being the place where the first European settlement was made, and the seat of the first independent empire, founded by the descendants of African slaves. It is now called *Hayti*, which is the ancient name given it by the natives. About the middle of the 17th century, a French colony was established on the west end of the island, and, before the revolution, its products were valuable, and its commerce was in a flourishing state. In 1792, the national assembly of France proclaimed the freedom of all French subjects, and the numerous African slaves in the French colony in St. Domingo were emancipated. Many of the planters were dissatisfied. They contended that the government had no right to grant freedom to their slaves, and therefore resisted the decrees of the national assembly, and appeared determined to retain the system

---

again emancipated? What other provinces established their independence? What is said of the state of these republics, their religion and public morals?

376. What is the island of St. Domingo, or Hayti, distinguished for! In what year was the freedom of all French subjects proclaimed? What was done by the planters? What is said of the contentions between the whites and blacks?

MODERN HISTORY. 259

ι slavery in the island. This the blacks resisted In th contentions which followed, both the whites and blacks were guilty of the most horrid atrocities upon each other, till, at last, all the French were either massacred or driven from the island.

377. *Of Touissant L'Ouverture.* In the confusion attendant on a state of revolution, the British government sent a body of troops to Hayti, in order to bring it under its own power. They landed and took possession of a number of places, from most of which they were driven by the celebrated *Touissant L'Ouverture,* a man of color, whom the French national government had appointed commander-in-chief of the troops in the island. The British troops, after an enormous loss of men by disease and the sword, evacuated the island in 1793. On the 1st of July, 1801, the independence of Hayti was proclaimed, and Touissant being placed at the head of the government, the island rapidly improved in wealth and prosperity under his wise administration.

In the latter part of 1801, Bonaparte, then first consul, dispatched an army of 25,000 men, under Gen. *Le Clerc,* to subdue the Haytians to their former state of slavery. After a campaign fought with varied success, a truce was concluded between the contending parties. Taking advantage of this, the French, with unexampled perfidy, seized upon the person of Touissant, and conveyed him to France, where he perished in a dungeon, in 1803. History records but few examples of military chieftains who will bear comparison with Touissant L'Ouverture, for greatness of mind, virtue, patriotism, and nobleness of soul.

378. *Progress of the Revolution in Hayti.* The outrage committed by the French upon Touissant, caused a renewal of the war, with greater animosity than ever.

---

377. What is said of the British invasion of Hayti, and of Touissant L'Ouverture? When was the independence of Hayti proclaimed? What general, and how many men, did Bonaparte send to subdue Hayti? Of what act of perfidy were the French guilty? What is said of the character of L'Ouverture?

The Haytians, under *Dessalines*, prosecuted the war with vigor and success. The yellow fever also swept off great numbers of the French troops, who were finally compelled to abandon the island in 1803. The next year Dessalines was appointed governor for life, with very extensive powers; and soon after he assumed the imperial title of Jacques I., emperor of Hayti. His ambition and tyranny were such, that he was killed in a conspiracy in 1806. *Christophe*, his second in command, them assumed the government; *Petion*, however, another chieftain, disputed his sovereignty. A long struggle ensued, in which Petion was defeated. In 1811, Christophe assumed the title of King Henry I. Petion retired to the southern part of the island; a republic was formed here, and Petion appointed president for life. He died, greatly regretted, in 1818. Christophe, who appears to have been an avaricious and cruel despot, was killed by his soldiers in 1820. After this event, the whole of the French part of Hayti was united under President *Boyer*, who is said to possess many virtues. In 1825, the French succeeded in inducing the Haytian government to agree to pay about £5,000,000 sterling, payable by installments, as a compensation for the plantations on the Island, formerly owned by the French inhabitants. .... President Boyer was .... compelled to leave Hayti, by a revolution in the government, the effect of which remains to be seen.

379. *Of Brazil and Portugal.* At the time of the French invasion of Portugal, in 1807, the royal family removed the seat of government to *Brazil*. Here they remained till 1820, when they returned to Portugal, excepting *Pedro*, the king's eldest son, who was left behind as regent. In 1823, Brazil was declared an independent empire under Pedro, who took the title of

---

378. In what year did the French abandon the island? What is said of Dessalines? Of Christophe? Of Petion? Of President Boyer? What sum did the Haytians agree to pay the French, as a compensation?

MODERN HISTORY. 261

emperor, and was acknowledged as such by Portugal In 1826, the king of Portugal died. Pedro, who laid a claim to the throne, resigned it in favor of his daughter, *Maria de Gloria*. Her right to the throne was contested by *Don Miguel*, (brother of Don Pedro,) who was aided by the nobility and the monks. Donna Maria was favored by the constitutionalists and patriots. In 1831, Don Pedro abdicated the crown of Brazil in favor of his infant son, Don Pedro II., and embarked with his daughter for Portugal. She has since been established upon the throne of that country.

380. *Revolution in Greece.* The modern Greeks, by a long course of degradation and slavery inflicted upon them by their Turkish masters, have generally, for a long period, been an ignorant and vicious people; they, however, bore the yoke of their oppressors with reluctance. Individuals among the Greeks, receiving an education in various countries in Europe, were awakened to a sense of their national degradation; and by their exertions, the Greeks were induced to enter on a struggle for liberty. It appears that the Greek leaders expected assistance from Russia; but, being disappointed, they resolved to rely on themselves and the justice of their cause. In 1820, war commenced between the Turks and the Pacha of Albania. This being considered a favorable opportunity, *Ypsilanti*, a Greek officer, who had been in the service of Russia, succeeded in rousing his countrymen to arms, and drove the Turks from the greater part of their country. The Turkish government, in order to strike terror into the Greeks, caused the Greek patriarch of Constantinople, who was venerated for his character, to be hung in his robes before his own cathedral. This atrocity, how-

---

379 In what year was the seat of government removed from Portugal to Brazil? When was Brazil declared independent? What is said of Don Pedro, Don Miguel, and Donna Maria?

380. What is said of the modern Greeks? How were they induced to enter into a struggle for liberty? What is said of Ypsilanti? What did the Turkish government do?

ever, instead of producing the intended effect, urged on the Greeks to acts of dreadful revenge.

381. *Massacre at Scio.* The island of *Scio*, containing about 130,000 inhabitants, having enjoyed many peculiar privileges, had arrived to a considerable degree of refinement and knowledge. In 1822, the Greeks from some of the other islands, landed in Scio, and induced the peasantry to join them against the Turks They marched to the city, and drove the Turks into the castle. The Turkish fleet, lately reinforced from Egypt, being in the neighboring seas, on learning these events, landed 15,000 men in Scio. These troops immediately entered the city, and began the massacre of men, women, and children, of whom 25,000 were murdered. The city was fired, and in four days the fire and sword of the Turks rendered the beautiful island of Scio a scene of blood and ashes. Of the whole population, not more than 1000 remained alive on the island. Upwards of 40,000 Sciots, mostly women and children, were sold into slavery. The inhuman *Capudan Pacha*, the Turkish commander, after this, while preparing to desolate other Greek islands, met with summary vengeance. The *Ipsariots*, with 70 small vessels and *fire-ships*, hovered round the Turkish fleet, and in the night rowed among them and attached their fire-ships to Capudan Pacha's vessel, which blew up with upwards of 2,200 men, and mortally wounded the Pacha.

382. *Progress of the War.* In 1822, an army of 25,000 Turks passed the celebrated straits of Thermopylæ, in order to lay waste the *Morea*, or Grecian peninsula. The Greek commanders afterwards occupied these straits, and cut off the communication and supplies of the Turkish army, who, in a desperate effort to break through the Greek defenses, in the night, were mostly destroyed. Many persons now took a deep in

---

381. What is said of the island of Scio? How many did the Turks land in Scio, and what did they do? How many remained on the island? What became of the Capudan Pacha?

terest in the affairs of the Greeks, among whom was Lord *Byron*, the celebrated British poet. He proceeded to Greece, and made considerable sacrifices in her cause: he, however, died soon after at *Missilonghi*, in April, 1824. The Turkish armies made but little progress in Greece till *Ibrahim Pacha*, of Egypt, was sent by the Sultan to manage the war. In 1825, he opened the campaign with energy, and ravaged the Morea. The Greeks, under the brave Admiral *Miaulis* and *Kanaris*, with their fire-ships, performed many gallant actions, and greatly harassed their enemies.

383. *Battle of Navarino.* In July, 1827, the ministers of Great Britain, France, and Russia, by a treaty at London, settled the affairs of Greece, and gave notice to the Turkish government, that " Greece must thereafter govern herself." The Turks rejected the interference of the three powers, and Ibrahim, with the Turkish-Egyptian fleet, entered the bay of *Navarino*, in September. Soon after, the combined squadrons of British, French, and Russian ships, arrived, and informed Ibrahim Pacha of their determination to establish an armistice between the Turks and Greeks. Ibrahim being prevented from sailing from Navarino, commenced his ravages by burning houses, and killing women and children. In consequence of this the combined fleet entered the harbor of Navarino, to compel Ibrahim to desist from these brutal outrages. The Turkish force, consisting of 110 ships, were found drawn up in order of battle, and as the allied fleet approached, a deadly conflict ensued. The Turks fought with desperation, till their whole fleet was burnt, sunk, or disabled. Hostilities now ceased, and the sultan soon after agreed to the treaty of London. A monarchial gov-

382. How many Turks passed the straits of Thermopylæ, and what became of them ! What is said of Lord Byron? What of Ibrahim Pacha ! What of Miaulis and Kanaris?

383. What three powers, by a treaty at London, settled the affairs of Greece! What notice did they give to the Turkish government? What did the combined squadrons do? What is said of the battle? What of the government of Greece?

ernment is now established for the Greeks; also the religion of the ancient Greek church. Schools are encouraged, and commerce and agriculture begin to revive.

384. *French Revolution of* 1830. The immediate cause of the revolution in Paris, in July, 1830, was the attempt of the ministers of Charles X., to enforce a number of ordinances, or acts, signed by the king, in violation of the charter confirmed to the French people, after the downfall of Napoleon. The most odious of these ordinances, was against the liberty of the press, so that nothing could be printed without being inspected and authorized by the government. One of the ordinances interfered with the law of election, and another illegally dissolved the chamber of deputies, or representatives of the people. As the journalists were the first called upon to obey these ordinances, they assembled and drew up, in great haste, an address to their countrymen, which displayed a noble example of courage and patriotism, and as the ordinances were contrary to the charter, they expressed their determination to disobey them. Such was the alarm excited by these proceedings, that the bankers suspended discounts; many of the manufacturers discharged their workmen; crowds assembled in various parts, and were addressed by fearless orators, and their speeches were received with clapping of hands, and cries of " down with the ministers,"—" the charter forever."

385. *Progress of the Revolution.* The revolution in France, in 1830, has been often termed the " revolution of three days," from the circumstance of its being accomplished in that time. On the morning of *July* 27, many of the public journals appeared in opposition to the ordinances. The offices of those journals which dared to appear were broken into, and their presses seized by an armed police. The crowds in the streets

---

384. What was the immediate cause of the revolution in Paris? Which was the most odious of these ordinances? Who were first called upon to obey, and what did they do? What was the effect of these proceedings?

increased, and the military, in attempting to clear them, were assailed by stones and other missiles, thrown from

Conflict in the streets of Paris, 1830.

the houses. During the evening of this day the people armed themselves, and many of the streets were barricaded with timbers, stones, &c., to arrest the course of the cavalry. *July 28th.* On the morning of this day the whole population of Paris were in motion, and there was regular fighting in all quarters of the city during the day, between the king's troops and the armed citizens; the barricades were increased, and Paris was put into a state of defense. *July 29th.* At break of day, the whole population were in arms. Some of the adherents of Charles X. entreated *Polignac*, his principal minister, to resign his office, and the king to repeal his ordinances. Polignac refused to listen to any proposition, and the struggle continued. For two days the people were seen fighting without a chief but on this day two generals, *Dubourg* and *Gerard*, put themselves at their head. A desperate conflict was maintained by

---

385. What is the French revolution of 1830 often called? What was done on July 27th, what on the 28th, and what on the 29th?

the *Swiss* guards, and other troops of the king, at the *Thuilleries* and *Louvre*, but before the day had closed the people were in possession of all parts of Paris. Thus ended this memorable conflict of *three days*, in which more than 2000 were killed, and 5000 wounded.

386. *Accession of Louis Philippe to the Throne.* On the 30th of July, a great number of the French deputies assembled at their usual place of meeting and temporarily filled the offices of state. The venerable Gen. *Lafayette* was appointed commander-in-chief of the National Guards, and Louis Philippe, *duke of Orleans*, was appointed lieutenant-general of the kingdom Charles X., being deserted by the greater part of the army and ministers, abdicated the throne, and was suffered to depart, with his family, to England. The throne of France being declared vacant by the chamber of deputies, the duke of Orleans was, by a vote of that body, invited to become king of the French. He accepted the crown, under the title of Louis Philippe I., and took the oath to support the new charter. The rights of the French people now became better defined; hereditary nobility was abolished, and many new privileges granted to the people.

387. *Revolution in Belgium.* The French revolution of 1830 was immediately followed by that of *Belgium*. The Belgic people were principally Catholics, and were French in their language, intercourse, and feelings. They had been united to Holland without their consent, by the congress of Vienna, in 1814. The Dutch were mostly Protestants, and no cordial union existed between them and the Belgians. An insurrection broke out in Brussels, in August, and on the 4th of October, 1830, the Belgians made a formal declaration of their independence. In 1831, the Belgium congress elected *Leopold*, prince of Saxe Cobourg, and son-in-law of George IV.,

---

386. What body met on the 30th of July, and what did they do? What is said of Charles X.? Who was invited to become king of the French? What is said of the rights granted to the people?

of England, as their king, which choice has been sanctioned by the leading powers of Europe. Leopold is now united in marriage with the daughter of Louis Philippe, king of the French, and his kingdom may be considered as firmly established.

388. *Revolution in Poland.* From the infamous partition of the Polish kingdom, in 1795, by Russia, Austria, and Prussia, to the revolution of 1830, the spirit of Poland had never been entirely crushed, and many of her patriots lived in the hope, that their country would be restored to the rank of an independent nation. They expected much from Napoleon, and many of her patriots shed their blood in his service, but shed it in vain. The success of the revolutions in France and Belgium, inspired the Polish patriots with the hope, that the time for the deliverance of their country was come. On the 29th of November, 1830, a young Polish officer entered the military school at Warsaw, and called the cadets to arms. The cadets instantly took up their line of march, and being joined by the students of the university, proceeded to the residence of the Arch-Duke *Constantine*, the viceroy of Poland. This tyrant of the Polish people, however, escaped by a private passage. The insurrection immediately became general; 40,000 Polish troops and citizens, having seized the public arsenal, armed themselves, and expelled the Russian troops from Warsaw. A Polish diet, or assembly, was immediately convened, and independence declared.

389. *Progress of the Revolution.* The Emperor Nicholas, having denounced the Poles as rebels, sent an army of 200,000 men against Poland, which could raise but about 50,000. On the 25th of February, 1831, the Russians, 150,000 in number, under Count *Diebitsch*, advanced upon Warsaw. The Poles, under

---

387. What is said of the Belgic people? At what time did they declare their independence? Who did they elect as their king? To whom is he married?

388. What is said of Poland since 1795? What effect did the revolutions in France and Belgium have? At what time, and how did the revolution commence? State what was done.

the command of *Skrzynecki* and other generals, were but 40,000 in number; but they fought with such fury, that the Russians were driven back, with the loss of 15,000 in killed and wounded. The Poles displayed great bravery in many actions, but every victory weakened their strength. On the 6th of September, 1831 a Russian army of 100,000 men, with 300 pieces o cannon under the command of Field Marshal *Paskewitsch*, advanced to storm Warsaw. After two days hard fighting, in which 20,000 Russians were killed and wounded, Warsaw was taken, her brave defenders imprisoned, or exiled to Siberia, and Poland was incorporated into the Russian empire.

390. *Of India.* The great and populous country known by the name of India, has thus far made but little figure in history. Like most other Asiatic countries, it has been often and easily conquered, without effecting much change in its government, or in the manners and customs of the people. *Herodotus*, who lived about a century before Alexander the Great, gives the earliest account of the inhabitants of India. The character which he gives of the people, is said to be exactly the same as that of the Hindoos at the present day. The Mahometans, as early as A. D. 1000, had begun to establish an empire in India. In 1222, Genghis Khan conquered the country, and is said to have given the the name *Mogul* to India. A century afterwards Tamerlane took possession, and allowed the petty princes, *Rajahs* or *Nabobs*, to retain their territories, of which some of their descendants are now in possession. In 1738, *Kouli Khan*, after having usurped the Persian throne, overran a great part of the Mogul empire, and

---

389. What was done by the Emperor Nicholas? What is said of the battle of Count Diebitsch and Skrzynecki? What is said of the storming of Warsaw, and what of Poland?

390. What is said of India, and of the account of its inhabitants by Herodotus? At what time did the Mahometans begin to establish an empire in India? What is said of Genghis Khan, Tamerlane, and Kouli Khan? How were the Europeans able to extend their influence?

weakened the power of Tamerlane's descendants. The frequent wars between the petty princes of India, led them to seek the aid of Europeans to conquer each other. By this means the Europeans were able to maintain and extend their settlements and influence in India.

391. *British East India Company.* In 1600, Queen Elizabeth gave to the merchants of London an exclusive right to the commerce of India for 15 years. This appears to have been the origin of the East India Company, which was established by an act of parliament, in 1708. The local affairs of the company were entrusted to the three councils of *Madras, Bombay,* and *Calcutta,* while the general direction was retained in England. The political power of the British in India may be said to have commenced in 1748. As the European troops were but few in number, the company adopted the plan of disciplining the native Indian troops, called *Seapoys,* according to the European method. By this means the company were able to have a large and efficient military force at command. By the naval superiority of the mother country, the establishments of other European countries were broken up, and the British are now the ruling nation in India. The company having become powerful, have been in many instances arbitrary and tyrannical in their conduct towards the natives. The whole number of Europeans residing in India does not probably exceed 40 or 50,000; but such is their influence over the inhabitants of India, they are able to sustain a dominion over an *hundred millions* of people.

392. *Of China.* China is one of the most ancient empires in the world, and is noted for its pride of antiquity. Their records extend back to upwards of 2000 years before the Christian era, and it is supposed by some, that the empire was founded by one of the colo-

---

391. What was the origin of the East India Company, and when was it established? By what means did the East India Company become powerful? What is said of their conduct towards the natives? How many Europeans are there in India, and how many people over whom they hold dominion?

nies formed at the dispersion of Noah's posterity. The Chinese differ from all other people in their government, manners, customs and religion, and while every other nation and people have changed, they have existed, a great and flourishing nation, remaining nearly in the same state four thousand years. The Chinese having suffered much from the inroads of the northern Tartars, built a wall upwards of 1200 miles in length, from east to west; this astonishing work is still in existence. This wall secured the peace of China for several centuries; but the Tartars, after repeated assaults, succeeded in breaking over the wall, and in subduing the empire, in 1635, and a Tartar dynasty is now on the throne.

China was first visited by the Portuguese, in their voyages of discovery in the Indian ocean, in 1586, when they obtained a grant of the Island of *Macao*, at the entrance of the harbor of Canton. Since that period various nations have carried on commerce with China, by the way of the Cape of Good Hope. In August, 1841, commercial difficulties having arisen with the Chinese, a British force took possession of the fortress of Amoy, and afterwards forced the Chinese government to consent to a treaty, by which the island of Hong Kong was ceded to the British Crown and several important ports opened to commerce. In 1851, a formidable insurrection broke out under a leader named *Tien-teh*, who appears to have obtained some knowledge of the principles of Christianity. He announced himself as the second son of God, a restorer of the true worship, and demanded universal submission. At first the insurgents were very successful, but of late most of the places taken by them have been recaptured, but the country still remains unsettled.

392. What is said respecting the ancient history of China? For what purpose did they build a wall, and what was its length? What is said of the Tartars? When was China visited by the Portuguese? At what time did the insurrection break out? Under what leader, and what is said of him?

393. *Condition of France in* 1847. After Louis Philippe ascended the throne, the government was conducted with ability, and the state of France, in many of its interests, appeared much improved. The French monarch, however, made himself unpopular with his subjects on account of his restraining the liberty of the press, laying heavy taxes, &c. This, with the neglect of his poorer subjects, his disposition to aggrandize his family, and the restriction of the right of suffrage, or voting, to the higher classes, caused much dissatisfaction. During a commercial derangement in 1847, the French people began to hold *reform banquets* for the purpose of discussing the subject of their grievances. These meetings were numerously attended. A banquet was appointed to be held in Paris on February 20th, 1848, which was prohibited by the authorities as a seditious meeting. The people deeming this illegal, postponed the banquet till February 22d.

394. *French Revolution of* 1848. On the day appointed, vast crowds of citizens assembled in the streets of Paris. They soon found themselves engaged with a military force of eighty thousand men which had been ordered into the city. The people took arms from shops and houses, raised barricades, attacked the Chamber of Deputies and the residence of Guizot, the Prime Minister. The insurrection became so general that the National Guard refused to fire on the people. Louis Philippe being defeated, abdicated in favor of his young grandson, the Count of Paris, and then fled in disguise to England. Lamartine, one of the principal leaders of the people, now proclaimed " *The French Republic, Liberty, Equlity and Fraternity.*" A provisional government was organized, every citizen was made an elector, and all slaves on French territory were declared free.

---

393. What made Louis Philippe unpopular with his subjects? What is said of Reform Banquets?
394. How did the French citizens accomplish the revolution of 1848? What became of Louis Philippe? What was the result of the revolution?

395. *Louis Napoleon, President and Emperor.* In December, 1848, Napoleon Bonaparte, nephew of the great Napoleon, having received five millions out of seven millions of votes, was elected President. His most important act while in this office, was the suppression, in 1849, of the Italian Republic at Rome, by military force. In 1851, as his term of office drew near its close, Louis Napoleon endeavored to have the clause of the Constitution which forbid his re-election repealed. Failing in this, he dissolved the Assembly, imprisoned some of its members, and suppressed the newspapers opposed to his views. He then called upon the French people to vote by universal suffrage, *yes* or *no*, on the question whether he should be President for ten years, with dictatorial powers. The people, by an immense majority, decided in his favor. In Nov., 1852, the Senate, in compliance with the will of the President, by a vote of 86 out of 87, adopted a measure to re-establish an imperial government. This was adopted by the people by a vote of 7,864,189 out of 8,180,660. Accordingly Louis Napoleon was declared "Emperor of the French," under the title of *Napoleon III.*, and the hereditary title secured in his family.

396. *The Roman Republic.* The success of the French revolution of 1848 emboldened the people of several European states to make efforts for their more perfect freedom. A strong party in the Italian states endeavored to secure union, and constitutional freedom. In Rome, the revolution was begun by the murder of Count Rossi, an able, but tyrannical minister. A general insurrection now broke out. The mob proceeded to the Pope's palace, attacked his guards, and would have taken

---

395. Who was Louis Napoleon? How did he become President? What did he while in this office? How came he to be Emperor?

396. How did the modern Roman Republic originate? What became of the Pope? Who were the Italian leaders? How was the Republic overthrown?

the edifice, had he not yielded and granted a popular ministry. He, however, soon fled to Naples in disguise. A "*Roman Republic*" was now formed, and Joseph Mazzini placed at its head. Louis Napoleon, contrary to his professed principles, sent an army to Rome, and attacked the city soldiery under Gen. Garibaldi. After a brave resistance, the French entered the city, (July 3d, 1848,) put down resistance and caused the Pope to be reinstated in his authority.

397. *Hungarian Revolution.* Hungary, a large country in the Austrian Empire, had for a long period a Diet, or government of its own. When the French Revolution of 1848 occurred, Kossuth, an active leader of the *Magyars*, or Hungarians, headed a deputation to Vienna to obtain a guarantee against the violation of their rights. He was able to obtain a new ministry for Hungary, of which Count Batthyanzi and himself were constituted chief members. They immediately commenced the work of reform by emancipating the peasantry and extending the right of suffrage. This displeased the Austrian government, and they instigated the *Croats*, a neighboring people, to invade Hungary. Görgey being entrusted with the command of the troops, with great valor drove the Croats back. On April 14th, 1848, the National Assembly of Hungary issued a Declaration of Independence.

398. *Subjugation of the Hungarians.* The Austrian government fearing the final success of the Hungarians, applied to the Russians for aid. Nicholas, the Czar of Russia, willingly lent his aid. He accordingly sent Prince Paskiewitz with an army of 130,000 men across his frontier into Hungary. At this period some elements of discord began to appear among the Hungarians, and

---

397. Where is Hungary? What is said of Kossuth? Of the Croats? Of Görgey? Of the National Assembly?
398. What is said of the Austrian government? Of Nicholas the Czar of Russia? What of the Hungarians and Görgey? What became of Kossuth and the Hungarian officers?

even Görgey, their principal commander, was suspected of treachery. The Magyars everywhere made a brave defense, but they were overwhelmed by the combined forces of Austria and Russia. Komorn, the principal fortress, surrendered Sept. 17th, 1849. Kossuth and some of his officers escaped into Turkey, where the Sultan generously gave them protection. The Austrian commander, Baron Haynau, infamous for his cruelty, executed thirteen Hungarian Generals and staff officers. The noble Kossuth finally reached Great Britain and the United States, where he was received with enthusiasm for his brave though unsuccessful struggle for the freedom of his country.

399. *Origin of the Crimean War.* This war originated from the jealously of Great Britain, France, and some other European powers against the encroachments of Russia. This formidable power, for a long period, had been very desirous of adding Turkey to her already vast extent of country. Should this be effected, it was feared it would destroy the balance of power among European governments. In May, 1853, Russia demanded the perpetual protectorate of twelve millions of Greek Christians in the limits of the Sultan's dominions. As this comprised nearly one half of his subjects, it was rejected with great spirit. Great Britain, France, Austria, and Prussia approved the stand taken by Turkey. Russia to enforce her claims took possession of the provinces of Moldavia and Wallachia; in consequence of which, Turkey declared war against Russia.

400. *Allied movements against Russia.* The allied fleets of Great Britain and France, upon the Sultan's declaration of war, entered the Dardanelles. After the Russians had destroyed the Turkish fleet lying in the harbor of Sinope, the allied fleet entered the Black Sea

---

399. How did the Crimean war originate? What did Russia demand of the Turkish government? How was the demand received?

while that of the Russians retired to the harbor of Sebastopol, at the southern extremity of the peninsula of *Crimea*. In Feb., 1854, France and Great Britain dispatched an ultimatum to Russia, that she should within six days after it was received, pledge herself that she would evacuate the Turkish provinces before the 1st of April. If she declined to do this, they would consider it equivalent to a declaration of war. The Russian court making no answer, war was formally declared. After several conflicts, the combined fleet, consisting of nearly four hundred vessels, arrived at the Crimea, and landed about thirty miles north of Sebastopol, a force of 60,000 men, consisting of 27,000 British, 25,000 French, and 8,000 Turks.

401. *Battles of the Crimea.* The first important conflict between the allies and the Russians, was on the banks of the Alma, where a Russian force of about 45,000 men were strongly entrenched. The British, 26,000 strong, under Lord Raglan, and the French under Marshal St. Arnaud, boldly advanced up the heights under a tremendous fire; the Russians were driven from their position utterly routed, with the loss of between four and five thousand men. The *Battle of Balaklava*, (Oct. 25th, 1854,) was commenced by 20,000 Russian infantry, supported by masses of cavalry, against the British troops. They captured the Turkish redoubts, but were defeated by the Highlanders. The most daring exploit of the war was the charge made by the famous "six hundred" British light cavalry, who rode through the Russian ranks and returned after losing two-thirds of their number. The *Battle of Inkerman*, (Nov. 5th,) between the allies and Russians, in which the latter endeavored to force them to raise the siege of

---

400. Who allied themselves against Russia? Where were their fleets sent? What was the ultimatum sent to Russia? What followed?

401. What was the first important conflict on the Crimea? What is said of the battle of Balaklava and Inkerman?

Sebastopol, was a sanguinary conflict of eight hours, in which the Russians were defeated with the loss of nearly 15,000 men.

402. *Capture of the Malakhoff—Fall of Sebastopol.* After a siege of *eleven months*, it was arranged that on Sept. 8th, 1855, at 12 o'clock at noon, the French should attack the strong tower of the Malakhoff, while at the same time the British should attack the Redan, another strong fortress near by. At the signal gun, the drums and trumpets sounded the charge; thirty thousand Frenchmen headed by Zouaves, sprang from their trenches,—dashed like the waves of the sea against the defenses of the Malakhoff—swarmed up the steep embankments until they covered the whole parapet. Soon the French tri-color floated over the Malakhoff. Again and again, the Russians brought up reinforcements, but were driven back by the irresistible fury of the French. The contest and carnage was horrible; men fought hand to hand, and dashed out each other's brains with their muskets. At last the Russian General, weary of the frightful slaughter of his men, sullenly withdrew.

About eight in the evening of this eventful day, the Russians under cover of darkness withdrew from the town. After midnight, fires broke out in various parts of Sebastopol, the batteries were blown up, ships in the harbor were sunk, and in the morning the town was a mass of burning ruins. The contest was now decided; and in March, 1856, a treaty of peace was signed at Paris by the plenipotentiaries of Great Britain, France, Austria, Sardinia, Turkey and Russia.

403. *Of Texas.* This extensive tract was originally comprised in the limits of Mexico. In 1821, Moses Austin, of Connecticut, obtained permission from the

---

402. How long did the siege of Sebastopol continue? How was the capture of the Malakhoff effected? What is said of Sebastopol? By whom was the treaty of peace signed?

Mexican authorities to introduce an American colony into Texas Mexico having abolished slavery within her limits, the American settlers being mostly southern planters, felt themselves so aggrieved that they established a provisional government, and declared on March 2d, 1835, the independence of Texas. In 1836, Santa Anna, the President of Mexico, moved a large force forward, threatening to exterminate the Americans, or drive them from the country. At the Alamo, the garrison, consisting of about one hundred and seventy-five men, were all slain, among whom were Cols. Travis, David Crockett and Bowie. A few days afterwards, 330 of the American garrison at Goliad, under Colonel Fanning, were treacherously murdered in cold blood, after they had surrendered themselves as prisoners of war.

Santa Anna having driven the Americans nearly out of Texas, came upon the American force near the San Jacinto, under Gen. Houston, now reduced to about 800 men. Houston now resolved upon the desperate measure of attacking the Mexicans in their camp, although double in number to his own men. The charge was ordered; and the war cry, *Remember the Alamo!* was wildly shouted by Texans, who, with their double-barrelled guns, pistols and knives, rushed through and over the Mexican ranks with such terrible effect, that their whole force was either killed, wounded or taken prisoners; among the latter was Santa Anna This secured the Independence of Texas.

404. *War with Mexico.* Texas was received into the Union, by a joint resolution of Congress, Feb. 28th, 1845. This caused an immediate rupture with Mexico. In consequence of her hostile movements, Gen. Taylor in July, was sent with several military companies to

---

403. What is said of Texas,—of Moses Austin—and of the American settlers? Who was Santa Anna? What of the Alamo? What is said of Gen. Houston and of the battle of San Jacinto?

404. When was Texas received into the Union? What is said of Gen. Taylor and others? Of the battle of Luena Vista?

Corpus Christi Bay, near the Mexican border. He aferwards took a position on the Rio Grande, opposite Matamoras. While marching to this place, he was attacked by the Mexicans; the battles of *Palo Alto* and *Resaca de la Palma* ensued, which proved victorious to the Americans. On Sept 21st, Gen. Taylor attacked Monterey, which soon surrendered. About the same time, divisions under Gens. Wool, Kearney, Fremont and others, penetrated New Mexico and *California*, and took possession of some of the principal towns. On Feb. 22d, 1847, Gen. Taylor gained a decisive victory at *Buena s Vista*. over the Mexican army under Santa Anna. The American force in this bloody conflict, consisted only of about 5,000, while that of the Mexican consisted of 20,000 men.

405. *Operations of Gen. Scott.* In Jan., 1847, Gen. Winfield Scott, who was appointed to the chief command, reached Mexico, and commenced the investment of Vera Cruz, where was situated the strong Castle of San Juan d' Ulloa. On March 29th, the city and Castle surrendered, with 5,000 prisoners and 500 cannon. At least 1,000 Mexicans were killed, and a great number wounded. The American loss in killed and wounded was about 80 men. Gen. Scott now proceeded against the capital. At *Cerro Gordo*, he was met by Santa Anna, the President of the Mexican Republic, with a force of 12,000 men. The action took place at a difficult mountain-pass which was strongly fortified. With about 8,000 troops Gen. Scott attacked the Mexicans and drove them from their strong position, with a loss of 4,000 in killed, wounded and prisoners, while that of the Americans was but 431. Santa Anna narrowly escaped capture by fleeing on a mule taken from his carriage. The strong Castle of *Perote* was next taken without opposition, as was *Puebla*, the second city of Mexico, with 80,000 inhabitants, May 15th, 1847.

---

405. When did Gen. Scott reach Mexico? What is said of Vera Cruz? Of Cerro Gordo and Puebla?

406. *Capture of Mexico.* Gen. Scott remained in Puebla till August, when being reinforced, he advanced towards the capital at the head of 10,700 men The fortified camp of *Contreras*, near the heights of *Cherebusco*, was attacked, and after a sanguinary contest, the Americans were victorious, capturing 3,000 prisoners. Cherubusco was also taken after a heavy loss had been inflicted on the Mexicans. Sept. 8th, about 4,000 Americans attacked 14,000 Mexicans at *El Molinos del Rey*, near Chepultepec. They were at first repulsed with severe loss, but afterwards drove the Mexicans from their position. *Chepultepec*, on a lofty hill, the last fortress outside of the capital, was taken by storm. The Mexicans fled to the city, which was abandoned by Sana Anna and the officers of government. Sept. 14th, 1847, Gen. Scott entered the city of Mexico in triumph. This closed the war. It is estimated that *thirty thousand* American lives were lost, and *seventy-five millions* of dollars expended in this war. California and New Mexico were ceded to the United States for fifteen millions of dollars.

407. *War in British India.* Although India has been long held in subjection under the British Government, yet there has been several revolts against its authority. The most dangerous of these outbreaks commenced in May, 1857, and continued till near the close of the next year. The outbreak commenced at Meerut, about 32 miles from Delhi, the principal city in the northwestern part of India. The *Sepoys*, at this place, in the service of the British Government, felt themselves aggrieved by the introduction of cartridges which had been greased with the fat of a sacred animal. It was also privately circulated among the *Bramin Sepoys*,

---

406. With how many men did Gen. Scott advance towards Mexico? What is said of Contreras, El Milinos del Rey. Chepultepec and Mexico? What were the number of lives lost, and money expended? What of California and New Mexico?

407. When and where did the last revolt commence in British India? What is said of the Sepoys, and their grievances?

that the Government meant to deprive them of the privileges of *caste*, by having the bones of bullocks ground and mixed up with their flour, so that the Hindoo might inadvertently partake of it. By this they would be polluted and become outcasts, and thus be compelled to embrace Christianity. Most of the troops refused to touch the greased cartridges. A Colonel was killed, and a massacre of the Europeans followed.

408. *Progress of the War in India.* After the massacre at Meerut, the insurgents passed on to Delhi. Here they were joined by the native troops. They proceeded to the palace of the native king, and induced him to ascend the throne. The foreign residences and buildings were plundered and burnt, and a general massacre of the Europeans was commenced. The mutiny soon became widely extended. At Lucknow, Sir Henry Lawrence was besieged by a large force; he bravely held out till he was mortally wounded, and his heroic little band compelled to retire into an inner fort. At Cawnpore, Sir Hugh Wheeler entrenched himself with less than 300 men, who had with them upwards of 500 women and children. The insurgents were commanded by *Nana Sahib*, who offered them a safe passage to Allahabad if they would give up their guns and treasure. They accepted the terms, and were marched to the boats to descend the river. Suddenly a masked battery was opened and many were shot dead, others drowned, 150 were taken prisoners. The men were instantly put to death, and the women and children were spared a few days longer. Gen. Havelock marched to the relief of Cawnpore, but the day before his arrival, the women and children were barbarously murdered and thrown into the well of the court yard. Gen. Havelock forcing his way through all obstacles entered Lucknow, and relieved the heroic garrison. About this time Delhi was taken, and the Rebellion was crushed. In 1858 the govern-

---

408. What is said respecting Delhi? What was done at Lucknow? at Cawnpore? of Nana Sahib? of Gen. Havelock? of the East India Company?

ment of the country was transferred from the East India Company to the British Crown.

409. *Causes of the Secession War.* For a long period it seems to have been the design of certain leading men at the South, either to obtain the control of the National Government, or to establish a new one in the Southern States, whereby their domestic institutions should be better protected and established, than they could be while they remained in the Union. According to their construction of the Constitution, each State had a right to withdraw from the Union whenever the National Government should manifest a disposition to impair or abridge what they believed to be their Constitutional rights. The election of Abraham Lincoln as President, (who was opposed to the further extension of slavery,) caused the Secessionists to take immediate steps to accomplish their purposes. At this period, several of their number held important offices in the Federal Government, by whose means the national army and navy were scattered to distant points; 115,000 arms, of the most approved patterns, were transferred from the Northern to the Southern arsenals. A vast amount of cannon, mortars, balls, powder, &c., were also sent in the same direction.

410. *Commencement of the War.* The 20th of Dec, 1860, the ordinance of Secession was unanimously adopted by the South Carolina Convention, assembled at Charleston, and four days afterwards, their delegation withdrew from the U. S. Congress. On Dec. 26th, Major Anderson, with a garrison of about 80 men, withdrew from Fort Moultrie to Fort Sumter. Jan. 9th, 1861, the "Star of the West," an unarmed steam-

---

409. What is supposed to have been the designs of the Secessionists? What was done by them when in the U. S. Government?

410. Where was the secession ordinance first adopted? What is said of Maj. Anderson and Star of the West? Where was the Confederate government formed? What is said of the attack on Ft. Sumter?

er, with a reinforcement of 250 men, and supplies for the beleaguered garrison, was fired on, and forced to re-

Attack on Fort Sumter.

tire. This roused the indignation of the people in the loyal States; but owing to the treachery of some of the leading officers of the Government, the Nation was comparatively helpless. Feb. 4th, forty-two Secessionists, from five of the more Southern States, met at Montgomery, Ala., and formed a Constitution of Government. *Jefferson Davis* was chosen President, and *A. H. Stephens* Vice-President of the *Confederate States of America*. On the morning of April 12th, 1861, a terrific fire was commenced upon Fort Sumter, garrisoned with less than 100 men. After enduring a bombardment for 48 hours, Major Anderson was forced to surrender. Thus opened the most tremendous conflict affecting human rights known in history—a conflict which cost the lives of more than *half a million* of men.

411. *Uprising of the People.* When the news of the insult on the national flag by the attack on Ft. Sumter arrived, and that a defiant war was thus made on the United States, every loyal heart was moved with indignation. All party distinctions, for a time, seemed forgotten. Such an uprising in cities, towns and villages throughout

---

411. What is said of the uprising of the people, and how many volunteers?

the loyal States was never before known. Apparently but two parties remained, that of Secession, with its sympathizers, and that of the friends of the Union. On Monday, April 15th, President Lincoln issued a call for 75,000 volunteers for three months. This call was met with the utmost enthusiasm. Immense Union meetings were held in almost every city in the loyal States, and immediately *three hundred and fifty thousand volunteers* offered their services to sustain the Union cause.

412. *Battle of Bull Run.* The first important conflict between the Union and Confederate forces took place on the Bull Run, a small stream about thirty miles from Washington. The Union troops under Gen. McDowell, 32,500 strong, left their camp near Washington, on their march towards Richmond. July 21st they attacked the Confederates near the Manassas Junction, on the right bank of the Bull Run. They were found strongly entrenched, with masked batteries on commanding heights concealed by bushes and trees. The Union troops fought skillfully, and bravely drove the Confederates from part of their works. Victory seemed to appear on the Union side, till a heavy reinforcement of Confederates under Gen. Johnson arrived on the ground. This decided the contest. The Unionists began to fall back, and owing to a misunderstanding of orders, confusion prevailed. A panic seized the troops, which ended in a disorderly and disgraceful retreat.

413. *Capture of Hilton Head, S. C.* A land force of 15,000 men under Gen. W. T. Sherman, in conjunction with a squadron of eighteen men of-war and thirty eight transports under Com. Dupont, sailed for the invasion of South Carolina. They arrived before the two forts at Hilton Head, at the Port Royal entrance, Nov. 7th, 1861. The ships, fifteen in number, formed in a

---

412. How many Union troops at the battle of Bull Run? What caused their defeat?

413. What force was sent to Hilton Head? In what manner did the fleet attack the fort? What was the result?

line, steamed round in a circular manner between the forts, delivering their fire as they passed. When the whole fleet was in operation in this fiery circle, *fifty* of the most terrible projectiles, round shot and shells, fell into and upon the forts *every minute.* The effect was so terrible that the garrisons fled out of their forts, which they had deemed impregnable, in such haste that they left everything behind. The triumph was complete. Beaufort, near by, the summer resort of the first people of the State, one of the best harbors and military stations on the coast secured and taken, and the Union flag firmly planted on the richest soil in South Carolina.

414. *Capture of Forts Henry and Donelson.* Feb. 3d, 1861, a combined naval and land expedition set out to reduce Fort Henry, a strong fortress on the Tennessee river, garrisoned with 7,000 men. Admiral Foote, with seven gunboats, three of which were ironclads, proceeded up the Tennessee. On the 6th he came in range of the guns of Fort Henry, when a heavy fire was opened upon him. He however pressed steadily forward, keeping up an incessant fire, till he approached within 300 yards of the ramparts. Every shot was now terribly effective—the garrison could stand it no longer, they abandoned everything in a moment, and fled, a terror-stricken rabble.——*Fort Donelson*, on the Cumberland river, surrendered to the Union troops Feb. 16th, 1862. Its defenses were far more formidable than those of Fort Henry, being a cluster of forts surrounding a vast central fortress. On Feb. 14th, Admiral Foote made an attack on the fort, but two of his gunboats being crippled, and himself wounded, he was forced to retire. Gen. Grant, having invested the place, made a general attack, and carried several of the outworks by storm. Gen. Buckner, with nearly 15,000 men, was forced to an

---

414. How was Ft. Henry reduced? How was Ft. Donelson captured?

unconditional surrender. This victory opened the way to Nashville, which soon after was taken.

Conflict between the Monitor and Merrimac.

415. *The Merrimac and Monitor.* One of the most important events in naval history is the conflict between the iron clad Confederate steamer Merrimac, and the U. S. iron clad boat Monitor, at the mouth of James River, Virginia, March 9th, 1862. The Monitor was built under peculiar circumstances. Washington was blockaded—a Confederate fleet threatened it, and the Confederate iron clad Merrimac was almost ready to ruin our wooden men-of-war, towards the close of 1861. To meet this formidable ship, a kind of raft boat was constructed by Capt. Ericsson, in which the crew were below the water line except those who worked the two guns placed in the revolving turret, placed on the iron clad deck which appeared a few inches above the water.

The Merrimac commenced her work of destruction by sinking the frigate Cumberland, and burning the Congress; she then proceeded to destroy the Minnesota. At

---

415. Where was the conflict between the Monitor and Merrimac? By whom was the Monitor constructed, and how? What is said of the Monitor and Merrimac?

this critical time, when all hearts were filled with dismay, the Monitor arrived from New York, and by a few well directed shots forced her to retire. This was considered by many as a special interposition of Providence, as the Merrimac never afterwards committed any depredations, and was finally destroyed to prevent her from falling into the hands of the Unionists.

416. *Gen. Burnside's Expedition.* Jan. 12th, a fleet of one hundred and twenty five vessels under Com. Goldsborough, with a land force of 14,000 men, under Gen. Burnside, sailed for North Carolina. After a detention of nearly three weeks by severe storms, in the vicinity of Cape Hatteras, the fleet arrived at Roanoke Island after a loss of several vessels. The troops were landed, and after a march of two hours, through miry swamps and a dense growth of underwood, came upon the central fort of the enemy. Gen Foster having given the order to storm the battery, Hawkins' Zouaves rushed forward, raising their war cry *Zou, Zou, Zou!* Their onset was so impetuous, that the enemy, surprised, staggered, and bewildered, immediately fled. Six forts, 2,500 prisoners, 42 heavy guns, and a large quantity of military stores were captured. After taking several places on the inland waters of the State, *Newbern*, the former capital, was taken. This place was strongly fortified by forts, earth works, &c., in the vicinity. Most of these were carried by storm, and by the assistance of gun-boats the victory was complete.

417. *Battle of Shiloh, or Pittsburg Landing.* In order to stop the advance of the Union troops southward, Gen. Beauregard made a stand at Corinth about 20 miles south from Pittsburg Landing, on the Tennessee river. Part of Gen Grant's force having arrived at this point, 70,000 Confederate troops left Corinth April 6th, 1862, and attacked the Unionists with such

---

416. Who were sent against North Carolina? What is said of the battle of Roanoke Island, of the Zouaves, of Newbern?
417. What commanders were at the battle of Shiloh? What result of the action?

force, that they were driven from their camps almost into the river. At this critical moment, 8 000 Union troops under Gen. Buell appeared on the opposite side of the river. Two gun-boats now arrived, and threw bomb-shells with great effect into the ranks of the enemy. Night closed upon the combatants: in the morning the contest was renewed; but the Confederates were finally driven back to their fortifications at Corinth. The Union loss in killed, wounded and missing, in this, one of the hardest fought battles of the war, was 13,508 men. The loss of the Confederates is supposed to have been greater.

418. *Capture of New Orleans.* To regain this important place, a fleet of 46 vessels (ships and gun-boats) under Admiral Farragut, was sent to the mouth of the Mississippi river to reduce the two strong fortresses of St. Philip and Ft. Jackson. Gen. Butler, with 18,000 men, were sent to take possession of the city. Every precaution was taken to prevent the passage of vessels up the river to New Orleans. An iron cable was stretched across the river; 18 iron mailed gun boats, with steam rams, floating batteries and fire rafts, were stationed along the river to repel any attempt to pass by the forts. April 18th, 1862, Admiral Farragut commenced his attack and kept up a terrific bombardment on the forts for more than a week. He now resolved upon the desperate expedient of forcing his way up the river. After being under a furious fire for one hour and twenty minutes, the fleet passed the forts. Seven of the Confederate gunboats were destroyed; three of the National vessels were disabled and drifted down the river. The Admiral appeared before New Orleans April 26th, when it was formally surrendered to the United States authorities.

---

418. What commanders were sent against New Orleans? Their force? What is said of the defenses of Forts St. Philip and Jackson? What was the result of the attack?

419. *Gen. McClellan—Military Operations, &c.* On Nov. 1st, 1861, Gen. Scott, being about 75 years of age, resigned his office, and Geo. B. McClellan was appointed his successor, as commander of the armies of the United States. He was a young officer who had acquired distinction for military services in West Virginia, and had secured in a remarkable degree the confidence and affection of his soldiers. He took the command of the Army of the Potomac, March 11th, 1862. On the 14th of the same month, he issued an address to his army from his headquarters at Fairfax Court House, complimenting his men for their discipline and patience during the long delay incident to the work of preparation. On the 5th of April, he arrived at Yorktown, and began to entrench himself before that place. May 3d, the enemy evacuated the place and fled towards Richmond. They were followed by the Union troops, and skirmishes and conflicts took place with varied success till McClellan reached the vicinity of Richmond. June 1st, the battle of Fair Oaks resulted in the repulse of the Confederates; the Union loss was 890 killed, and 4,844 wounded.

The "six days' fight" before Richmond, commenced June 26th. The Union right wing was attacked, and the day closed, leaving the battle undecided. On the next day, the contest was renewed. The Union troops were driven back, and the White House was evacuated. Incessant fighting continued all the next day; the enemy were repulsed, but in the evening the Union troops were ordered to fall back. On the 29th, the battle before Richmond was renewed by an attack on the Union forces at Peach Orchard; the contest continued until nine at night. The Union wounded troops fell into the hands of the enemy. The 30th of June was distinguish-

---

419. What is said of Gen. Scott and Gen. McClellan? What respecting Yorktown? Of Fair Oaks? Of the "six days' fight" before Richmond? What was the Union loss, and what of the result of the expedition?

ed by the battle of White Oak Swamp. The loss was heavy on both sides, and Gen. McClellan continued to fall back towards James River. The last of these battles before Richmond was on July 1st, and the Confederates were repulsed at every point. Gen. McClellan, however, fell back, and securely stationed his army on James River, where he was defended by the gun-boats. The Union loss during the six days' conflict was 1,561 killed, 7,701 wounded, and 5,958 missing. The result of the expedition was a serious check to the Union arms, and the President called for 300,000 additional volunteers. Gen. McClellan was recalled from Virginia; and on Sept. 2d, was appointed to command the troops for the defense of Washington.

420. *Battle of Antietam.* Gen. Lee being emboldened by the retreat of the Union forces from before Richmond, marched on to Maryland. On his entrance into that State, he called on the people by a Proclamation to throw off the U. S. Government, and join the Confederacy. September 14th, 1862, the Confederates were defeated at South Mountain; on the 15th, Harper's Ferry and 12,500 men surrendered to the Confederates; on the 17th, Gen. McClellan's forces overtook Lee at Antietam Creek, when a general engagement took place. All the available forces of each army, each consisting of about 100,000 men, were on the field with their best commanders. The contest was severe, and continued all day. At night the Confederates fell back to the Potomac, which they crossed into Virginia, having been in Maryland two weeks. The total Union loss at South Mountain and Antietam, was 14,794; that of the Confederates was estimated at upwards of 25,000.

421. *Proclamation of Emancipation.* After the Confederates had taken up arms to sustain secession, it was

---

420. Who were the opposing commanders at the battle of Antietam? What is said of the battle, the numbers engaged, the losses on each side?

evident that no lasting peace or union could be expected unless slavery was destroyed. As this element of discord had been left to the control of the several States where it existed, President Lincoln at first declined to take any steps for its suppression. At length the rebellion became so formidable, threatening the dismemberment of the country, that the President, in order to preserve the Union, was compelled to issue his Proclamation of Emancipation. At the conclusion of this instrument he says: "And upon this act, believing it to be an act of justice warranted by the Constitution, upon military necessity, I invoke the considerate judgment of mankind and the gracious favor of Almighty God!" This great act of the nineteenth century, by which *four millions* of the human race eventually became free, went into effect on Jan. 1st, 1863.

422. *Battle of Gettysburg.* The beginning of July, 1864, was distinguished by several important Union victories. In the latter part of June, Gen. Lee, with the Confederate forces, crossed the Potomac, and directed his march towards Harrisburg, Penn. July 1st he was attacked near Gettysburg by the Union troops, under Gen. Meade. After a series of severe contests, the issue of which seemed doubtful, the Confederates, July 3d, opened an artillery fire of 125 guns on the center and left of the Union forces, which they followed up with an assault by a heavy column of infantry. The opposing forces were about equal in numbers, and both fought with desperate courage. The attack was successfully repulsed with a terrible loss to the Confederates, who retired from the field, and soon after retreated over the Potomac into Virginia. The Union loss in killed, wounded and missing during these contests was upwards

---

421. At what time did the Emancipation proclamation go into effect? What were President Lincoln's reasons for this act? How many were emancipated?

422. When did Gen. Lee cross the Potomac? What is said of the battle of Gettysburg? What loss on both sides?

of 23,000; that of the[Confederates is estimated to have been 33,000.

423. *Capture of Vicksburg, &c.* The free navigation of the Mississippi being obstructed by the strong fortifications at Port Hudson and Vicksburg, efforts were made for their reduction. Gen. Grant, who commanded the Union forces, made great efforts to capture Vicksburg. After several unsuccessful attacks, its fortifications were found too strong to be taken by assault, without a great loss of life. A canal was opened in order to turn the course of the Mississippi from Vicksburg; Grant also made the attempt to approach by the Yazoo Pass and river. Both these attempts proved unsuccessful. He then moved his army down the west side of the river, and succeeded in the hazardous attempt to run his transports past the Confederate batteries at Vicksburg. This place was now approached from the south. The Confederates having been defeated in five battles outside, it was completely invested. After a siege of forty-seven days, Gen Pemberton was compelled to surrender Vicksburg and its garrison to Gen. Grant. The entire loss to the Confederates was 37,000 prisoners, 10,000 killed and wounded, and arms and munitions of war for 60,000 men. July 8th, Port Hudson was surrendered to Gen. Banks: 7,000 prisoners and 10,000 stand of small arms, besides numerous pieces of artillery.

424. *Operations near Chattanooga, Tenn.* In Jan., 1863. an important Union victory was gained at *Murfreesboro*, Tenn., by Gen. Rosecrans, over the Confederates under Gen. Bragg, after a conflict of three days. The Union loss in killed, wounded and prisoners, was about 10,500, that of the Confederates 15,500. On Sept. 4th the Union forces occupied Chattanooga, a

---

423. What forts obstructed the navigation of the Mississippi? What is said of Gen. Grant, and by what means did he capture Vicksburg? What was the loss of the Confederates?

424. What is said of the battle of Murfreesboro? of Chattanooga, of Missionary Ridge, of Gen. Hooker, and of the result?

strong position near the south line of Tennessee, on the borders of Georgia and Alabama. As this was a point of great importance, the Confederates made great exertions to retake it. For this purpose they took a strong position on Lookout Mountain, which commanded the Tennessee river, by which most of the Union troops derived their supplies. On Nov. 23d, Gen. Grant ordered Gen. Thomas to *Missionary Ridge,* an elevation of 500 feet, the extremity of which he seized. Gen. Hooker scaled the slopes of Lookout Mountain, drove out the enemy, captured 2,000 prisoners, and finally established himself on the peak of the mountain, in full view of Chattanooga. Much of this brilliant action was fought *above the clouds,* which hid the combatants from the view of those watching them below. Missionary Ridge was swept of all opposition. About 6,000 prisoners and 50 guns were captured, the siege was raised and Chattanooga was saved.

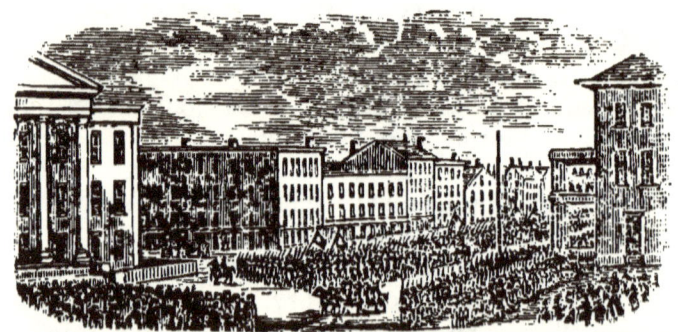

Sherman's army entering Savannah.

425. *Sherman's March through Georgia.* Gen. Sherman having made a victorious march southward from Chattanooga, occupied Atlanta, Ga., Sept. 2d, 1864. On Nov. 15th this place was evacuated and burnt. His

---

425. How far did Gen. Sherman march through Georgia? the number of his men? the manner of his march? With what results?

army, consisting of about 70,000 men, began the adventurous march towards the sea, about 300 miles distant. The army marched in two main columns, which, with its detachments, swept through a belt of country sixty miles wide. On Dec. 10th, Sherman arrived within five miles of Savannah, without the loss of a wagon. He brought with him a large number of emancipated slaves, horses and mules. On the 21st he entered Savannah, where he captured 800 prisoners, 150 guns, a large supply of ammunition and upwards of 30,000 bales of cotton.

426. *Capture of Fort Fisher.* The capture of Fort Fisher by a combined land and naval force, was one of the most brilliant victories of the Union troops. This fort guarded the entrance to Wilmington, the principal port through which the Confederacy obtained its supplies from abroad. The first attempt against it was made by a land force of 6,500 under Gen. Butler, in connection with a fleet under Admiral Porter. Owing to some misunderstanding, or from a want of harmony between the commanders, the expedition proved a failure. In the next attempt, Admiral Porter retained the command of the fleet, but the military command was assigned to Gen. Alfred H. Terry, a young but skillful and meritorious officer. Terry's force was the same as Butler's, with the addition of a brigade, which numbered about 1,000 men. In addition to these, Porter had over 1,000 marines available for an assault.

The fleet and transports arrived off Fort Fisher Jan. 12th, 1865. After a fearful bombardment from the fleet for two days, the assault was arranged by Gen. Terry and Admiral Porter. The assaulting party was formed in two separate columns, one consisting of the naval brigade 1,200 strong, under Com. Breese, the other 3,000

---

426. What is said of Fort Fisher? What of Gen. Butler's expedition? What is said of Admiral Porter, of Gen. Terry, and of the number of his men? Describe the attack on the fort, its capture, the fire of the fleet.

strong, under Gen. Ames. The naval brigade advanced against the fort, but its fire was so fatal that this column was forced back. While the attention of the enemy was directed to this point, the land force, upwards of 3,000 strong, under Gen. Ames, entered the fort on the east side almost by surprise. A fierce hand to hand conflict ensued, which lasted nearly eight hours. The Confederates were driven out of the fort and compelled to surrender. Of the garrison 1,900 men surrendered and 400 were either killed or wounded. The Union loss was 1,021. During the contest the fire from the fleet is described as terribly effective. The iron clads threw their immense shells into the fort at the rate of four per minute, and were joined in their fire by more than 300 guns from the wooden fleet, and it is estimated that for more than two hours four shots were fired every second. By sunset every gun in the fort was silenced.

427. *Capture of Richmond.* March 25th, 1865, Gen. Lee made a sudden and overwhelming attack on Gen. Grant's lines by capturing Fort Steadman. The Confederates, however, were soon driven out with a loss of 3,000 men. At this time, also, Gen. Grant made a fierce attack on the enemy at Hatcher's Run. April 1st, after several desperate struggles, Gen. Sheridan succeeded in driving the enemy from their entrenchments at Five Forks, and capturing 6,000 men. Gen. Grant now ordered an attack along the whole line in front of Petersburg. At 3 o'clock Sunday afternoon, Lee telegraphed to Davis, the Confederate President, that his army had been driven out of its entrenchments, and that he must abandon Petersburg—that Richmond also must be given up. Upon this Davis and the principal officers of government fled. Early Monday morning Gen. Weitzel, with his soldiers, chiefly colored troops, entered Richmond without opposition. Nearly 500 guns, 5,000 stand

---

427. What is said of the attacks by Gen. Lee? Of Grant and Sheridan? What of Davis? Who first entered Richmond?

of arms and 6,000 prisoners were captured. The Confederate fleet in James River was destroyed, and the city was fired by Gen. Ewell, before leaving, which caused much destruction. On April 4th President Lincoln, with a number of foreign ministers, entered Richmond, and was received with enthusiasm, particularly by the emancipated slaves.

428. *Surrender of Lee's Army.* Gen. Lee, after abandoning Petersburg and Richmond, struck westward, apparently with the design of reaching Lynchburg, 113 miles distant. April 5th, the main body of the Confederate army reached a point near Amelia Court House, 47 miles on its way. Sheridan, by this time, with his horsemen, had put themselves between Lee and Lynchburg. Gen. Meade, on the 6th, attacked the retreating army, and after a most severe encounter routed them completely, capturing several thousand prisoners, among whom were Generals Ewell, Kershaw, and Custis Lee. Lee's position was now desperate. His army, now reduced more than one-half, was fairly surrounded. Gen. Grant having now arrived, wrote to Gen. Lee, asking him to surrender his army, to save the further effusion of blood. An interview was held, and Gen. Grant's terms, " That the men surrendered shall be disqualified from taking up arms against the United States until properly exchanged," was accepted. Nearly 30,000 men were surrendered.

429. *Assassination of President Lincoln.* On the evening of April 14th, 1865, President Lincoln accompanied his wife to Ford's Theatre in Washington. Booth, a stage actor, (who, with other desperate characters, had formed a plot to assassinate the principal officers of the Government,) came into the Theatre by a private entrance, approached the President's box from behind, and

---

428. Which way went Lee after leaving Richmond? What is said of Sheridan, Mead and Grant? How many men were surrendered, and on what terms?

with a pistol shot him through the head. The assassin, having effectually accomplished his bloody work, leaped upon the stage, made his exit to the rear by passages with which he was familiar, and made his escape. This was all done before the spectators knew of what had occurred.——Just about the time the President was shot down, another assassin attacked Secretary Seward, who was lying sick at his house. After severely wounding him, his son, and two other attendants, he made his escape. Ten days afterwards Booth was shot in a barn in Maryland, where he was concealed with an accomplice.

Abraham Lincoln, having accomplished the work assigned him, was removed from sublunary scenes. He departed at the zenith of an unsullied fame. His kindness of heart, and unselfish patriotism, endeared him to his countrymen. His simplicity of character, his tender sympathy with down trodden and suffering humanity, joined to an iron determination to sustain the right, gave an exhibition of the strength of moral principle. His child-like trust and confidence in the Supreme Being, and finally his exit as a martyr, by ruffian hands, will embalm his memory in the annals of mankind.

---

429. When and where was President Lincoln assassinated? Who by, and in what manner? What became of the assassin? What is said of the character of Abraham Lincoln?

BIOGRAPHICAL SKETCHES

OF

DISTINGUISHED PERSONS.

Addison, Joseph, was an eminent English writer; he was educated at Oxford, where, by his application to study, and by the composition of Latin verses, he became one of the most correct and elegant of writers. His merits as a writer procured for him the office of Secretary of State. His most admired writings, are his essays in the *Spectator*, a publication which commenced in 1711 : his tragedy of *Cato* is also a celebrated composition. Late in life he married the countess dowager of Warwick, who, being vain of her superior rank, was a source of unhappiness to Addison, who died in 1719, aged forty-seven.

Angelo, Michael, was a painter, sculptor, and architect. In architecture he surpassed all the moderns, and was the greatest designer that ever lived. The most celebrated of his paintings is the *Last Judgment*, and his abilities as an architect are seen in the church of St. Peter's, at Rome, a building which he constructed. His style is that of grandeur and sublimity, united with simplicity and beauty. He died in 1563, at the age of 90 years.

Arminius, James, was a Professor of Divinity at Leyden, and founder of the sect of *Arminians*, whose tenets with regard to predestination, &c., are in opposition to those held by the Calvinists. He was born in Holland, and after receiving much opposition, died in 1609. His motto was, "a good conscience is paradise."

Boyle, Robert, was born in Ireland, in 1626, and was the son of the earl of Cork. He ranks, as a philosopher, with Bacon and Newton. After having traveled over many countries in Europe, he settled in England, and devoted himself to science, especially to natural philosophy and chemistry ; and to the close of life he persevered in his scientific pursuits, in which he made many important discoveries. He invented the air-pump, and founded the Royal Society. He showed his regard for religion by the purity of his life, his aversion to temporal honors, and his liberal benefactions in aid of benevolent and pious undertakings.

BIOGRAPHICAL SKETCHES.

Buynan, John, was born in England, in 1628; he was of humble origin, being the son of a traveling tinker, and in the early part of his life followed the occupation of his father. Having embraced religion, he became a preacher in a Baptist society in Bedford. Refusing to conform to the established religion, he was imprisoned nearly thirteen years. While in prison he wrote his celebrated allegory, " *The Pilgrim's Progress*, from this world to that which is to come," a work which ranks high among those of original genius, and will probably be read with admiration and profit in all ages to come.

Burke, Edmund, was born in Ireland, in 1730. In 1753, he came to London, where he entered himself a student of law; he, however, applied himself almost wholly to literature, and by his " Essay on the Sublime and Beautiful," he established his reputation as a man of genius, and a fine writer. Being a most eloquent speaker, he was introduced into parliament, and became one of the first orators of modern times. The American war he denounced with great vehemence and justice; he also opposed with great force the French revolution, and his celebrated speech against *Warren Hastings*, the governor general of India, is among the greatest efforts of genius.

Burns, Robert, was born at Ayr, in Scotland, in 1759. He was originally a ploughman, and has been called the greatest untaught poet since Shakspeare. His poems, which are principally in the Scotch dialect, are distinguished for their humor, pathos, vivid imagery, and energy. The publication of his poems introduced him into the higher ranks of society, which ultimately proved his ruin. Habits of intemperance were acquired, to which his constitution gave way, and he expired at the age of thirty-nine.

Bacon, Sir Francis, the son of Sir Nicholas Bacon, was born in England, in 1561. He has been called " the wisest, brightest, and *meanest* of mankind." His great faculties were early discovered, and when only a child he was favorably noticed by Queen Elizabeth. Bacon was perhaps one of the greatest and most universal geniuses, that any age or country has produced. His "*Novum Organum*," with his other works, has immortalized his name. He was the first who taught the proper method of studying the sciences, and the way in which we should proceed in order to arrive at the truth. Before his time, men generally formed their theories, and then sought for facts in order to have them substantiated; but Bacon first found out what the facts were, and from them formed his system of philosophy. Bacon, while holding the office of lord high chancellor, was accused in parliament of gross bribery and corruption; he plead guilty, and was fined, imprisoned, and removed from his office. It has been, however, believed, that it was the servants of Bacon who committed the crimes for which he was disgraced.

BIOGRAPHICAL SKETCHES.

Baxter, Richard, a celebrated non-conformist divine, was born in England, in 1615. He wrote 145 treatises, some of which were very popular, particularly " *The Saints' Rest.*" In his religious views he held a middle course between Calvinism and Arminianism.

Bartram, John, an eminent botanist, was born in Pennsylvania, in 1701. He was the first American who had a botanic garden, for the cultivation of American and other plants. He made such proficiency in this pursuit, that Linnæus pronounced him "the greatest natural botanist in the world."

Benezet, Anthony, was born in France, of Protestant parents, who came and settled in Philadelphia. He was a member of the society of Friends, or Quakers, and devoted himself to the education of youth. His whole life was spent in acts of benevolence, and he was one of the earliest opponents of the slave trade, and made great exertions for the benefit of the colored people. He died in 1784, universally regretted. A striking eulogium was passed upon him by an American officer, who attended his funeral. "I had rather be," said he, "Anthony Benezet, in that coffin, than the great Washington, with all his honors."

Butler, Joseph, bishop of Durham, a prelate of distinguished piety, was born in 1692. His deep learning and comprehensive mind appear in his writings, particularly in that celebrated work entitled, " *The Analogy of Religion*, natural and revealed, to the constitution and course of nature." This able work was first published in 1736.

Butler, Samuel, one of the wittiest of English poets, was born in 1612. He was the author of *Hudibras*, a satirical poem, intended to ridicule the adherents of Cromwell and others, which has since afforded a fertile source for ludicrous quotations.

Byron, Lord, was born in Dover, 1788, and was son of Capt. Byron, who was notorious for his dissipated conduct. Deserted by her husband, Mrs. Byron retired to Aberdeen. The youthful Byron was of delicate health, in consequence of which his studies were interrupted, and he was indulged to an improper extent. By the death of his uncle he succeeded to the family titles and estates. The first work he published was treated with great severity by the Edinburgh reviewers. Byron however, amply revenged himself in one of the keenest satires of the age, entitled, "English Bards and Scotch Reviewers." Byron coming of age, took his seat in the house of peers; he, however, soon left the political life, and visited Spain, Portugal, and Greece. After his return from this latter country, he published his " *Childe Harold's Pilgrimage,*" and other poems, which at once established his fame, and he became the poetic idol of the day. He died at Missolonghi, in Greece, in 1824. The poetry of Byron, though of a high order as regards genius and powers of description, is calculated to have an injurious effect, particularly that written in the latter period of his life. Such was the moral charac

BIOGRAPHICAL SKETCHES.

ter of Byron, and the tendency of his writings, that his remains were not allowed to be interred in Westminster Abbey.

Calvin, John, one of the first Protestant reformers, was born in France in 1509. On account of religious persecution he was obliged to retire to Basil, where he published his celebrated "*Institutions of the Christian Religion.*" He settled at Geneva, and greatly advanced the Protestant cause. He established the form of church government called Presbyterian, and was the founder of a numerous sect of Christians called Calvinists, distinguished for their peculiar views on the subject of predestination, decrees, &c.

Cervantes, Saavedra, was born at Madrid, in 1549. He was the author of *Don Quixote*, the hero of *La Mancha*, the master piece of Spanish literature. This celebrated work is a strong and pleasant satire on the books of knight errantry, which were then so fashionable in Spain. It met with universal approbation; and though written to ridicule the follies of a particular age, it is still read and admired in various languages, in every part of the civilized world.

Chesterfield, Philip Dormer Stanhope, earl of, was born in London, in 1694. He was a distinguished nobleman, a writer of celebrity, and an accomplished orator. He was adorned by all the graceful arts of high bred politeness, of which he has been considered the standard. The governing principle of Lord Chesterfield's life appears to have been the applause of the world. His fame as an author rests on the celebrated Letters written to his illegitimate son. These Letters are written in an elegant and popular style; but in wishing to form his son for the higher ranks of life, he has shown himself, in some instances, the advocate of hypocrisy, licentiousness, and infidelity.

Confucius, a Chinese philosopher, was born about 550 years before the Christian era. He was the most learned and virtuous man of his age, and rendered great service to his country by his moral maxims, in reforming the manners of his countrymen. His memory, and the works which he wrote, are held in the highest veneration by the Chinese.

Cook, James, an eminent navigator, was born in England, in 1728, of humble parentage. For his abilities as a mariner he was employed by the British government in making discoveries in the Pacific ocean. He was killed by the natives of the Sandwich Islands, in 1779.

Copernicus, Nicholas, a celebrated astronomer, was born in Prussia, in 1473. He went to Italy, where he was appointed professor of mathematics. After twenty years of laborious study, he adopted the present system of astronomy, in placing the sun in the centre of the universe, and the earth and other planets to revolve about it. This great discovery he kept concealed for more than thirty years, for fear of exciting against himself the persecuting spirit of bigotry. His friends finally prevailed upon him to have his work published. He expired in a few

BIOGRAPHICAL SKETCHES.

hours after the first copy was brought to him, in the 70th year of his age.

Cowper, William, an excellent English poet, was born in 1731. He was equally distinguished by his genius and his virtues. His poems are various; but the most celebrated of them is " *The Task.*" The general tendency of his writings is to enlarge the soul to every liberal sentiment, and to improve the heart. Cowper was of a delicate constitution, and extreme sensibility of feelings; he was subject at times to great depression of spirits, and at one time was insane. It is a curious fact, that his humorous ballad of *John Gilpin*, was written when he was a prey to the deepest melancholy.

Dante, Alighieri, the sublimest of Italian poets, was born at Florence, in 1265. He early displayed his poetic talents, but the ambition of being elevated among the ruling men of his own city, engaged him in all the troubles and miseries of violent faction. His party was defeated, and he sought safety in banishment to Ravenna. His literary works owe their origin to his misfortunes, and revengeful spirit against his enemies, whom he wished to pierce with his satires. His fame rests on the " *Divina Commedia,*" which consists of three parts, Hell, Purgatory, and Heaven. This poem displays wonderful powers of genius. For boundless and wild imagination, for gloomy grandeur, for terrific energy, it has no superior; while on the other hand, it charms by its sweetness, simplicity, and grace.

Davy, Sir Humphrey, one of the greatest of chemists, was born in England, in 1778, and died at Geneva, in 1829, whither he had gone for the benefit of his health. The discovery which has immortalized his name, is that of the *safety lamp*, which is used in coal mines, and has removed the dangers formerly experienced in working in mines.

Defoe, Daniel, was born in London, in 1661. He wrote on a great variety of subjects; but the work which stands as the most lasting monument of his literary fame, is his history of *Robinson Crusoe*, which for a work of the kind, has never been excelled. It is said that this popular novel was founded upon the adventures of *Alexander Selkirk*, a Scotchman, who lived more than four years upon the uninhabitable island of Juan Fernandez.

Dryden, John, gave early proof of poetic talents, and continued to write till his death, at the age of seventy, in 1701. He wrote much in poetry and prose, and with such rapidity that it sometimes prevented correctness. His most celebrated works are his translation of Virgil, his Fables, and his Ode on St. Cecilia's Day. Dryden has been represented as too accommodating in his religious views, to the spirit of the times in which he lived; but his poetry is of the first order for beauty of description, and for spirit, freedom, and melody of verse.

Edwards, Jonathan, is considered by many as the greatest of modern

BIOGRAPHICAL SKETCHES.

divines. He was born in Connecticut, in 1703. His uncommon genius discovered itself early, and while a boy, he read Locke on the Human Understanding, with a keen relish. He was a minister of the gospel about 24 years, and afterwards became president of Princeton College, in New Jersey. His treatise on the "*Freedom of the Will*," is considered by many of his admirers as one of the greatest efforts of the human mind.

Erasmus, Desiderius, was one of the greatest scholars of the age, and was born at Rotterdam, in 1467. In the great question of Protestantism and Papacy, he was claimed on both sides, though neither party were pleased with him. He lashed the vices of the Papists, while he seemed indifferent to the success, or jealous of the labors of the Reformers.

Euclid, an eminent mathematician, flourished in Alexandria about 300 years before the Christian era. He wrote on music, optics, and other subjects; but the work which has handed his name down to posterity, is his "*Elements of Geometry*." The celebrated reply, "There is no royal road to geometry," was made to King *Ptolemy*, who had asked him whether geometrical knowledge might not be acquired in some easier manner than was pointed out by the Elements.

Fenelon, archbishop of Cambay, was born in France, in 1651, and died in 1715. He was one of the ablest of the French writers, and was distinguished for his virtues. He wrote many works; but what has gained him the greatest reputation, is his "*Telemachus*." This publication roused the anger of Louis XIV., it being considered as a covert satire against the vices of this monarch and his courtiers. Such is the merit of this work, though in prose, that it ranks among the epic poems, and has been translated into all the languages of Europe

Franklin, Benjamin, was born in Boston, Mass., in 1706, and served an apprenticeship to the printing business. After his removal to Philadelphia, he began those inquiries respecting the nature of electricity, the result of which has placed him in the first rank among men of science. He invented the method of guarding buildings against lightning, by means of rods. In 1757, Franklin was sent by his country as an agent to England; in 1766, he was called to the bar of the house of commons, and underwent that famous interrogatory which has raised his name in the political world. He was a member of the first congress, a signer of the Declaration of Independence, and in various ways rendered important services to his country. His "Poor Richard's Almanac," containing valuable maxims in prudence and economy, was first published in 1732, and is considered as a kind of standard for the principles of true economy. Dr. Franklin died in 1790.

Fox, George, the founder of the society of the English *Friends*, or Quakers, was born in 1624. He received a religious education, and, being apprenticed to a grazier, was employed in keeping sheep, and in this business spent much of his time in contemplation. When about nineteen, he believed himself to have received a divine command to forsake all and preach the gospel. His labors were crowned with considerable success, and 1669 he came to America, where he spent two years. During his labors he endeavored to persuade men to regard the "divine light" implanted within, as being sufficient to lead to salvation. He was imprisoned no less than eight times. He appeared to be sincere in his religious tenets, and is represented to have been a meek, devout and pious man. He died in London, in 1690.

Fulton, Robert, a native of Pennsylvania, was born in 1765. He is distinguished for making the first successful application of steam for propelling boats. This was accomplished in 1807, at New York. Previous to this, in 1787, *John Fitch*, of Connecticut, succeeded in moving a boat by steam power at Philadelphia, but for want of assistance was not able to perfect his invention, to accomplish any useful purpose.

Galileo, an Italian astronomer, was born in 1564. Having constructed a telescope, he made such discoveries in the science of astronomy, that it convinced him of the truth of the Copernican system. At that period, a belief of this system was considered as heretical, and as contrary to the word of God. No sooner was it known that he had embraced this system than he was summoned before the Inquisition, and was twice confined in its terrible dungeons, where, in the whole, he spent three or four miserable years.

Gall, John Joseph, the founder of the science now called *Phrenology*, was born in 1758, in the duchy of Baden, in Germany. He was, for a considerable period, a physician in Vienna; but, in consequence of the Austrian government having prevented the exposition of his new doctrines there, he traveled through the north of Germany, delivering lectures. He settled at Paris, where he died in 1828. The system of Gall, which has since been developed by *Spurzheim*, assumes, that each faculty of the mind has a separate organ in the brain, and that these organs are marked externally by elevations on the cranium, or skull.

Genlis, Madame de, was born in France, in 1746, and is distinguished as one of the ablest of female writers. Being obnoxious to the prevailing faction at the head of government, she was obliged to quit France, in 1793. She was allowed, by Bonaparte, to return to her native country, and he settled a pension upon her. For the last thirty years of her life, she wrote a great variety of works, falling but a little short of an hundred volumes. She died at Paris, in 1830. Her productions are distinguished for fertility of imagination, and purity of style.

Goldsmith, Oliver, a celebrated poet and miscellaneous writer, was born in Ireland, in 1731. He was educated at the universities of Dublin, Edinburgh, and Leyden, with a view to his adopting the medical

BIOGRAPHICAL SKETCHES.

profession. He left Leyden, however, abruptly, and without money wandered over a considerable part of Europe, and returned impoverished to London. By his literary productions he was able to support himself in respectable style. His most celebrated compositions are the Traveler, Vicar of Wakefield, and The Deserted Village. As an author he stands high. His poetry, natural, melodious, affecting, and beautifully descriptive, finds an echo in every bosom; and his prose, often enlivened with humor, and always adorned with the graces of a pure style, is among the best in our language.

Gray, Thomas, an eminent British poet, was born in London, in 1716. As a scholar he was profound, elegant, and well informed, and possessed the most refined taste in painting, architecture, and gardening. His letters are correct, pleasing and instructive. His poems are few, but they are of the first order; particularly his celebrated "Elegy in a Country Church Yard."

Hale, Sir Matthew, an eminent and uncorruptible judge, was born in England, in 1609. He was bred to the profession of law, and was called to the bar about the time of the civil wars between the king and parliament. He conformed to the republican government, and became a lay member of the Westminster assembly of divines. In 1661, he became the chief justice of the king's bench. The seat of judgment was never more purely filled than by Sir Matthew Hale. No influence, no power could turn him aside from the path of uprightness. The knowledge of Hale was not confined to law, but extended to divinity, mathematics, and history, upon all which subjects he has written.

Haydn, Joseph, one of the most celebrated modern composers of music, was born in Austria, in 1732. At the age of eight, he was admitted as one of the choristers at the cathedral at Vienna. He twice visited England, and received the degree of music from the university of Oxford. His compositions amount to twelve or thirteen hundred. "His grand and sublime Oratorio on the Creation," says a modern musician of eminence, "and his picturesque and descriptive Seasons, if music were as intelligible and durable as the Greek, would live and be admired as long as the Iliad and Odyssey of Homer."

Hogarth, William, one of the most original of painters, was born in London, in 1697. He served an apprenticeship with a silver plate engraver, and afterwards designed and engraved a set of plates to illustrate Hudibras, a work which he was admirably fitted to perform, as his chief skill as a painter lay in his unrivaled capacity for drawing ludicrous and comic scenes.

Howard, John, the celebrated philanthropist, was born in England, about 1727. He was bound apprentice to a grocer by his guardians; but, being possessed of a fortune, he purchased his indentures, and traveled on the continent. Having been taken by a French privateer, he

BIOGRAPHICAL SKETCHES.

was confined in a prison, and by this means he seems to have been first excited to compassionate those " who are sick and in prison." He now commenced his career of benevolence, which closed only with life. Not only were all the prisons of his own country repeatedly visited, but he minutely explored those on the continent, "to remember (as Mr. Burke beautifully expresses it) the forgotten, to attend to the neglected, to visit the forsaken, and to compare and collate the distresses of all in all countries." His glorious career was terminated, in this life, at Cherson, in Russia, by a fever, which he caught in attending on the sick, in 1790.

Henry, Patrick, a native of Virginia, remarkable for his commanding eloquence, was the first man who proposed to the colonies hostile meas ures against Great Britain. He declined a number of appointments un der the government of the United States. He died in 1799.

Hopkins, Samuel, D. D., a distinguished divine, was born in Connecticut, in 1721. He maintained in his writings that holiness consists in disinterested benevolence, and that all sin consists in selfishness.

Hume, David, an historian and Philosopher, was born in Edinburgh, in 1711. Having made a brief attempt to reconcile himself to mercan tile pursuits, he gave himself up to a literary life. After having written on a number of subjects without much success, in 1754 he brought out the first volume of his History of England. This work, at first, was coldly received; but it gradually became popular. The sum which was paid for the copy right, together with a pension from government, made him independent in his circumstances. His History charms by the ease and spirit of its style, and its philosophical tone, but it is unfaith ful in some instances, and a leaning towards principles abhorrent to the friends of freedom. His principles on moral subjects should be read with caution, as they are calculated to undermine the foundations of religion and morality.

Irving, Washington, was born in the city of New York, about the year 1783. He is at present one of the most distinguished American authors. In 1810, he published " Knickerbocker's History of New York," which established his fame. He has since written the " Life of Columbus," the materials of which were obtained from original documents in possession of the government of Spain.

Jenner, Edward, the celebrated introducer of vaccine inoculation, was born in England, in 1749, and was bred a physician. About 1776, his attention was turned towards the cow-pox. For twenty years he pursued his investigation, and laid the foundation of that success which his important discovery at last obtained. Through much opposition, *vaccination* was introduced into London, in 1796. It is now extended into every part of the globe. For this important discovery the parliament of Great Britain voted him £20,000.

BIOGRAPHICAL SKETCHES.

Johnson, Samuel, one of the greatest of literary characters, was born in England, in 1709, and was the son of a bookseller. He was educated partly at Oxford, which he was obliged to leave, on account of his impoverished circumstances. He went to London, and, after struggling through difficulties, established his reputation as an author. He completed his celebrated *Dictionary* in about seven years; and while engaged in this work, wrote papers called *The Rambler*. His " Lives of the Poets," is a noble model of that description of writing, and contains some of the choicest criticism in the English language. Notwithstanding all the labors of this "literary giant," as he is sometimes called, his income was not adequate to his wants. In 1762, he was presented by the king with a pension of 300*l.* per annum, as the grant expresses it, for the moral tendency of his writings. He died in 1784. His life has been written by *Boswell* and others, who describe, with much minuteness, the particulars of his daily life and conversation.

Josephus, Flavius, the Jewish historian, was born at Jerusalem, A. D. 37, and died in 93. His History of the Jewish War, and the Destruction of Jerusalem, was composed at the command of Vespasian, and is uncommonly interesting and affecting, as the historian was an eye-witness of all he relates. His " Jewish Antiquities," in twenty books, written in Greek, is a work of great merit.

Kosciusko, Thaddeus, a celebrated Polish general, was partly educated at the military school at Warsaw, but completed his studies in France. When the American colonies threw off the yoke of the mother country, Kosciusko entered into the American service, and was made a colonel of engineers and aid-de-camp to Washington. He afterwards headed his countrymen in their resistance to Russian oppression; but his efforts were unavailing. He was wounded and taken prisoner by the Russians, who treated him with great respect, and the Emperor Paul gave him an estate. He died in Switzerland, in 1817.

Klopstock, Frederick Theophilus, a very celebrated German poet, was born in 1724, and died in 1803. His " Messiah," by which his name is chiefly immortalized, was published at Halle in 1751. He was likewise the author of three tragedies, called " The Death of Adam," " Solomon," and " David." His funeral was conducted with extraordinary pomp, being attended by the senate of Hamburg.

Laud, William, archbishop of Canterbury, during the reign of Charles I. From the moment of his attaining power, he acted the part of a furious persecutor of those who differed from him on religious points. He was born in 1573, and was beheaded for high treason in 1645.

Lavater, John Casper, was a Swiss clergyman, born in 1741, and died from a wound given by a French soldier, in 1801. The subject which brought him into notice, is his work on *physiognomy*, or the art of discerning the character of the mind from the features of the face. His

BIOGRAPHICAL SKETCHES.

work on this subject has been published in various languages, but its popularity has declined.

Ledyard, John, a distinguished and adventurous traveler, was a native of Connecticut. He was with Captain Cook in his last voyage, and witnessed his death. After suffering almost incredible hardships in various parts of the world, in the course of his travels, he died at Cairo, in 1789, while preparing for a journey into the interior of Africa.

Linnæus, Charles Von, the most celebrated modern naturalist, was born in Sweden, in 1707. He is considered by many as the father of botany. Even from his infancy, he manifested his fondness for the study of plants, and he almost lived in his father's garden. His sovereign luly noticed his services in the cause of science, and besides other favors, conferred on him the honor of nobility. With an unexampled ardor in the pursuit of knowledge, Linnæus explored the inhospitable deserts of Lapland, and exposed himself, on foot, to every sort of fatigue. Science is indebted to his exertions for the useful and familiar division of plants, animals, &c., into classes.

Locke, one of the greatest of British philosophers and metaphysicians was born in England, in 1632. By the patronage of Lord Shaftsbury, he held a respectable situation under government, and wrote several political tracts. When Shaftsbury was obliged to flee for safety to Holland, Locke accompanied him, and while there he completed his celebrated " Essay on the Human Understanding," in the composition of which he had been engaged nine years. Great as are his merits in other respects, it is principally as the champion of civil and religious liberty, that Locke is entitled to the reverence and gratitude of mankind.

Malte-Brun, Conrad, a poet, political and philosophical writer, and geographer, was born in Jutland, in 1775, and was obliged to quit his native country, in 1796, in consequence of the persecution he received, for having written in favor of the liberty of the press, and the enfranchisement of the peasants. He settled at Paris, and from 1806 to 1826, edited the foreign political department of the Journal of Debates.

Marlborough, John Churchill, duke of, was born in England, in 1650. He was engaged in a great variety of military services on the continent, and his success has placed his name among the most illustrious of generals. He rescued the Low Countries and Germany, and humbled the pride of France. He died in 1722.

Melancthon, Philip, a celebrated German divine and Protestant reformer, was the friend and convert of Luther. To the diffusion of the doctrines of the Reformation he powerfully contributed ; but he displayed a moderate and conciliatory spirit, which was displeasing to the more impetuous spirit of Luther. The Confession of Augsburg was the work of this reformer. He died in Wittenburg, in 1560. Even his ene

BIOGRAPHICAL SKETCHES.

mies respected the virtues, the talents, the learning, and the mild temper of Melancthon.

Milton, John, the greatest of modern poets, was born in London, in 1608. His political and controversial writings are also justly celebrated. He was a firm advocate and defender of liberty, and his views on many subjects were far in advance of the age in which he lived. His *Paradise Lost* is the greatest poem which modern ages have produced. In his life-time justice was not done to his poetry; but posterity has, and will render homage to his genius. He was blind at the time he composed this noble work, and one of his daughters wrote it down as dictated from his mouth. He suffered from the attacks of personal and political enemies, and died comparatively poor and forsaken of the world.

Medicis, Cosmo, the founder of his illustrious family, was born at Florence, in 1389. He was so successful in commerce, that his riches were superior to those of the potentates of his times, and he applied the resources of his great fortune to the patronage of the sciences and of learned men. He collected a most valuable library, which he enriched with rare and curious manuscripts; but while he expected gratitude from his countrymen, he found that his conduct was viewed with jealousy, by the arts of his enemies. Yielding to the ingratitude of his enemies, he retired to Venice, where he was received with the greatest respect. His countrymen, however, recalled him, and placed him at the head of their government, and gave him the title of "Father of his people, and liberator of his country."

Montesquieu, an illustrious French writer, was born in 1689. His great work is the "*Spirit of Laws*." While compiling this work he visited various countries for information. This work acknowledges three sorts of government, the republican, the monarchial, and the despotic; and in examining these divisions, the author displays great depth of thought, vigor of imagination, and solidity of judgment.

Morris, Robert, an eminent merchant in Philadelphia, a member of congress, one of the signers of the Declaration of Independence, and an able financier. He was appointed treasurer of the United States, and during three years of the revolution rendered important services to his country, by his skill as a financier, in sustaining public credit.

Mozart, Wolfgang, one of the greatest of modern composers, was born in Germany, in 1756. He began to display his musical talents when only three years old, and by the time he was six, he was listened to as a prodigy, in various parts of Germany. He visited France, Italy, and England, and was everywhere received with enthusiasm. In his tenth year he applied himself closely to the study of composition. For his musical talents the pope honored him with the order of the golden spur.

BIOGRAPHICAL SKETCHES.

In 1781, he settled in Vienna, and was liberally patronized by the emperor of Germany, and the court. He died at the age of thirty-five.

Murray, Lindley, a grammarian, was born in 1745, near Lancaster, in Pennsylvania. He was a member of the society of Friends; he settled in England, and became known by his school books.

Newton, Sir Isaac, the most illustrious philosopher and mathematician that ever lived, was born in England, in 1642, and died in 1727. At the age of eighteen he entered Trinity college, Cambridge. During his abode here, he made his three great discoveries, of fluxions, the nature of light and colors, and the laws of gravitation. To the latter of these it is said his attention was first turned by seeing an apple fall. His great work, the *Principia*, which unfolded to the world the theory of the universe, was not published till 1687. The character of Newton is represented as being amiable, and adorned with all the virtues of a Christian. The Bible he made his favorite study, and irreverence towards the Deity or the holy scriptures, always drew from him the severest censure.

Nelson, Horatio, the most celebrated of British naval commanders, was born in 1758. He went to sea at the age of twelve, as a midshipman, with his uncle. After various exploits and victories, for which he was highly honored by his countrymen, he lost his life, by a rifle ball, in his celebrated victory over the united French and Spanish squadrons, off *Trafalgar*, in 1805.

Ossian, the son of Fingal, was a Scotch bard, who is supposed to have flourished about the beginning of the third century. According to tradition, he accompanied his father in his wars, and in the latter part of his long life became blind. The poems that go by his name are marked by a simple and sublime wildness, and are the most poetic compositions in the English language. They are represented as having been translated from the Gaelic by Mr. Macpherson, who died in 1797. Much controversy has existed about the authorship of these poems, which is not yet decided; it is believed, however, that their chief merit belongs to Macpherson.

Paine, Thomas, a political writer, was born in England, in 1737, and bred a stay-maker. Coming to America, he published a number of pamphlets, which had a powerful effect in favor of the American cause, particularly that entitled "Common Sense." He went to London, in 1790, and published "The Rights of Man." To avoid a prosecution, he went to France, and was chosen a member of the national assembly. He returned to the United States, where he debased himself by his deistical writings. He died in a miserable manner, in New York, 1809. During the latter period of his life he so devoted himself to intemperate habits, that he was shunned by the respectable part of his associates.

BIOGRAPHICAL SKETCHES.

Paley, William, an eminent English divine, was born in 1745, and educated at Cambridge. In 1785, he at once obtained a high reputation by his Elements of Moral and Political Philosophy. He is also the author of "A new view of the Evidences of Christianity and Natural Theology." Dr. Paley ranks high as an author, and his services to the cause of virtue and Christianity, were honorably rewarded by the patronage of the great. He died in 1805.

Petrarch, Francis, one of the four greatest of the Italian poets, was born in 1304, in Tuscany. He is celebrated as one of the restorers of classical learning, and displayed all the powers of genius, not only in his native language, but in Latin. Having settled at Avignon, he saw the beautiful Laura, whose charms inspired him with a lasting passion, the effusions of which he poured forth in those sonnets and odes which have rendered his name celebrated. His poetry, however, failed of having much effect on the object of his affections. His literary reputation attracted the regard of princes, and Rome, Paris, and Naples, at the same moment, invited him to come and receive the poetic crown.

Pindar, the greatest of lyric poets, was born in Greece, upwards of 500 years before the Christian era. Little is known of his real history. Of his works, which were numerous, and in various kinds of composition, time has spared only four books of Odes; but what it has spared is amply sufficient to vindicate his claim to be ranked among the most illustrious of ancient poets.

Pitt, William, was earl of Chatham, and is commonly known by that name, and was the most able minister that England ever produced. He was born in 1708, and at the age of twenty-seven was elected a member of parliament, and soon distinguished himself by his eloquence. He opposed with great force the measures relating to the American war. In April, 1778, while rising to speak in the house of lords, he fell into a convulsive fit, and expired in a few days. As a statesman and orator, he stands at the head of men of his profession, in modern times. His son, of the same name, was also distinguished as a statesman.

Pope, Alexander, a celebrated poet, was born in London, in 1688. He was somewhat deformed, small in size, and of a delicate constitution. His first regular composition was his Ode on Solitude, written when he was twelve years of age. His Pastorals were written when he was sixteen, and they obtained for him the friendship of many eminent characters. This was followed by his Essay on Criticism, the Messiah, and other poems. The translation of the Iliad, by which he realized a fortune, was completed in 1720. His "Dunciad," a satirical work, and his "Essay on Man," appeared afterwards.

Priestley, Joseph, a distinguished English divine, and experimental philosopher, was born in 1733. He embraced the Unitarian sentiments. This, with his partiality for revolutionary principles, drew upon him

BIOGRAPHICAL SKETCHES.

the rage of political partisans, and his house, library, manuscripts, and apparatus, were committed to the flames by an infuriated mob, and he was exposed to great personal danger. He came to America, in 1784, and took up his abode at Northumberland, in Pennsylvania, where he died, in 1804. His works, on various subjects, extend to upwards of seventy vo.umes.

Raphael, Sanzio, was born in Italy, in 1483. By the general consent of mankind, he is acknowledged to have been the prince of painters, and has received the appellation of divine "Raphael." He also excelled as an architect, and was employed in the building of St. Peter's, at Rome. He came to an untimely grave in consequence of his addiction to licentious vices,—dying at the age of thirty-seven.

Rollin, Charles, an eminent historian, was born in 1661, at Paris. He filled a number of important offices in the literary institutions of France, from which he was removed by the intrigues of the Jesuits. His Ancient History of the Egyptians, Carthaginians, Babylonians, &c., is one of the best compilations of the kind which ever appeared. Rollin was as amiable in private life as he was respected in public : pious, benevolent, and humane, the friend of virtue, morality, and religion. He died in 1741.

Rosseau, John James, one of the most eloquent and singular of writers, was born at Geneva, in 1712. His life was somewhat eventful, and the strangeness and inconsistency of his character subjected him to trouble. His works show that he had the most brilliant genius, combined with eccentricities, licentiousness, and infidelity. By a prize Essay he maintained the superiority of savage nature to the comforts of domestic and social life. This opinion he defended for a long time against all the writers of Europe. His " Confessions," published after his death, in 1778, is one of the most singular productions of the human mind.

Shakspeare, William, "the illustrious poet of nature," was born in 1564, in England, of a respectable family. Being connected with some thoughtless companions in the criminal act of taking deer, was the means of driving him to London. Here he became engaged among the players, and became an actor on the stage. From acting, he passed to the writing of plays ; and by the productions of his pen, and by the management of the play-house, he acquired a competent fortune, with which he returned to his native town, where he lived respected and beloved by his neighbors. He died in 1616, in the 53d year of his age. As an author, Shakspeare excels in originality, sublime conception, force, and delineation, and he has surpassed almost every poet, of every age and country, and is the boast of the English nation. In the midst, however, of his great and incomparable beauties, there are some moral blemishes and defects.

BIOGRAPHICAL SKETCHES.

Sidney, Algernon, an English gentleman, second son of the earl of Leicester, was born about 1620. In the time of the civil wars he joined the parliament's army, and was appointed a lieutenant-general of horse. He was nominated a member of the court to try Charles I.; but he took no part in the proceedings. At the restoration of the monarchy of England, he became a voluntary exile for seventeen years, till his father obtained for him a special pardon. Sidney, however, was a too firm friend of liberty to be tolerated by the ministers of despotism; he was accused of being concerned in a plot, and the most infamous perversion of justice was resorted to, in order to convict him. He met death, by being beheaded on Tower Hill, in 1681, with heroic fortitude. This strong republican was of extraordinary courage, sincere, but of a temper that could not bear contradiction; a Christian in principle, but averse to all public worship, and an enemy to every thing that looked like monarchy. He left behind a meritorious work, entitled Discourses on Government.

Stael, Madame de, a celebrated female writer, the daughter of M. Necker, the French financier, was born at Paris, in 1766. Her talents were so early displayed, that she was said to have never been a child, and the utmost care was taken to cultivate them. In her 20th year she married the Baron de Stael, the Swedish ambassador, and from that period she took an active part in literature and politics. At the commencement of Bonaparte's career she was one of his admirers, but she afterwards became hostile towards him, and in 1901, she was ordered to quit Paris. She died in 1817. Her works form seventeen volumes.

Swift, Jonathan, a celebrated writer, was born in Dublin, in 1667. He was chaplain to Lord Berkeley, and in 1710, became active as a political writer, and went over to the monarchial party, and received for his services the deanry of St. Patrick. On his return from England he became exceedingly unpopular; but he lived to be the idol of the Irish. His "Gulliver's Travels," a satirical romance, and his Tale of a Tub, in which he ridiculed popery and puritanism, were popular works.

Thompson, James, one of the most popular poets, was the son of a Scotch clergyman, born in 1700. He was educated for the church, but this profession he relinquished for that of an author. His most celebrated work is his "*Seasons*," which display animated and interesting descriptions of nature, in language distinguished for dignity, elegance, and simplicity.

Voltaire, one of the most celebrated of French writers, was born at Paris, in 1694. In early life he showed superior powers of mind, especially a sprightly imagination. His fondness for satire directed against the government, caused his imprisonment in the bastile, till he was liberated by the influence of his friends. After this event he devoted himself more entirely to poetry. His principal efforts were directed to-

BIOGRAPHICAL SKETCHES.

wards the drama. For a long period he was a sort of dictator in the republic of letters in Europe. By his free remarks on government and religion, he contributed, perhaps more than any other one, to lay the foundation of that state of things which afterward existed in France, during the time of the revolution. He died in 1778, while on a visit to Paris, and according to some accounts, in great anguish of mind from reflections on the irreligious tendency of his writings. The blasphemous atheist often, indeed, appeared in his works.

Washington, George, the illustrious commander of the American army in the war of the revolution, and the first president of the United States, was the son of Augustine Washington, of Virginia, and born February 22d, 1732. His father died when he was but ten years of age, and the care of his education fell upon his mother. At this period the means of education were scanty, and he had only common instruction in the usual branches of education. At the age of nineteen he was appointed an adjutant-general of Virginia, with the rank of major. He distinguished himself during the French war, particularly at the defeat of Gen. Braddock. When the colonies, in 1775, determined to resist the oppression of Great Britain, Washington, who was a member of the first congress, was unanimously appointed to the chief command of the American army. He accepted the office with diffidence, and for a period of eight years' laborious services, refused any compensation beyond his necessary expenses. After his public life, Washington retired to his estate, and devoted himself to agricultural pursuits. He died on the 14th of December, 1799, of an inflammatory affection of the windpipe, occasioned by exposure to a light rain, while attending, the day previous, to improvements on his estate. The senate of the United States, in their letter, on the occasion of his death, say,—" With patriotic pride we review the life of Washington, and compare him with those of other countries who have been pre-eminent in favor. Ancient and modern names are diminished before him. Greatness and guilt have been too often allied; but *his* fame is whiter than it is brilliant. The destroyers of nations stood abashed at the majesty of his virtues. It reproved the intemperance of their ambition, and darkened the splendor of victory."

Watts, Isaac, a poet and non-conformist divine, was born in England, in 1674. He was a writer of poetry from the age of 15 to 50. His writings are numerous, and his name is celebrated among all denominations of Christians. His lyrical poems, his Psalms and Hymns, and his Divine Songs for children, give him a high rank as a poet and a Christian. It is doubtful whether any other man has done as much good in repressing vice, and implanting the true principles of religion in the minds of his readers, as Dr. Watts.

Young, Edward, an English poet and divine, was born in 1687. His most celebrated work is his "Night Thoughts on Life, Death, and Immortality," a poem which abounds in sublime passages, and is written in a strain of pure morality, though occasionally obscure.

Zimmerman, John George, a physician and miscellaneous writer, was born in Switzerland, in 1728, and died in 1795, a victim to hypochondriac disease. Among his works, a Treatise on Solitude has been highly popular.

www.ingramcontent.com/pod-product-compliance
Lightning Source LLC
Chambersburg PA
CBHW030019240426
43672CB00007B/1014